A Sufi Master Answers:
On the Sufi Message of Hazrat Inayat Khan

A Sufi Master Answers:

On the Sufi Message of Hazrat Inayat Khan

DR. ELISABETH KEESING

MOTILAL BANARSIDASS PUBLISHERS
PRIVATE LIMITED • DELHI

Reprint : Delhi, 2008
First Indian Edition: Delhi, 1997

First Published by
Fine Books Ltd., 115-123 Bayham Street, London NW1 0AL
East West Publication Fonds B.V.
78 Anna Paulownastraat, The Hague.

ISBN: 978-81-208-1433-2 (Cloth)
ISBN: 978-81-208-1434-9 (Paper)

MOTILAL BANARSIDASS
41 U.A. Bungalow Road, Jawahar Nagar, Delhi 110 007
8 Mahalaxmi Chamber, 22 Bhulabhai Desai Road, Mumbai 400 026
203 Royapettah High Road, Mylapore, Chennai 600 004
236, 9th Main III Block, Jayanagar, Bangalore 560 011
Sanas Plaza, 1302 Baji Rao Road, Pune 411 002
8 Camac Street, Kolkata 700 017
Ashok Rajpath, Patna 800 004
Chowk, Varanasi 221 001

PRINTED IN INDIA

BY JAINENDRA PRAKASH JAIN AT SHRI JAINENDRA PRESS,
A-45 NARAINA, PHASE-I, NEW DELHI 110 028
AND PUBLISHED BY NARENDRA PRAKASH JAIN FOR
MOTILAL BANARSIDASS PUBLISHERS PRIVATE LIMITED,
BUNGALOW ROAD, DELHI 110 007

Foreword

This reprint is published by the Indian publisher of *The Message of Hazrat Inayat Khan*. It stays as close to the original text as possible. This implies that there are no references to the three volumes of the new revised version of *The Message*. As at present only three volumes of this latter edition[1] have been published, a second edition of this work will be considered at a later stage. For the time being readers may profit more from the references to the complete series available now.

[1] Hazrat Inayat Khan, A Sufi Message of Spiritual Liberty, Vol. II: The mysticism of sound and music, vol. VIII: Sufi teachings: The art of being, and vol. XIV: Sufi teachings: The smiling forehead. These new volumes VIII and XIV together cover the old vol. VIII to which has been added extensive hitherto unpublished material.

Contents

Preface

When my publisher and several readers suggested that I might write a book on Hazrat Inayat Khan's ideas as a complement to the story of his life, I was at first inclined to say no. Inayat had a rare gift to distribute his knowledge and experience in such parcels and in such a way as those before him needed and could understand. This method of lecturing, and his own strong personality, gave everything he said an extra dimension which a mere exposition of ideas would lack.

Putting this objection into words showed the way to its solution. I should cite Inayat's answers to questions, and these questions I could arrange systematically, thus sketching an outline of his philosophy and aims, at the same time showing as much of his personality and the way he spoke as the written word can convey.

This method presented difficulties of its own. To begin with, there was the amount of source material, even excluding the non-published courses for pupils. As can be deduced from the survey of Hazrat Inayat Khan's work on page 238, out of thousands of pages I had to choose a restricted number of characteristic answers. I have tried to select the essential recurrent themes.

A further difficulty arises from the fact that most of Inayat's recorded answers were given to laymen of the 1910-1920 period: either pupils or a chance audience consisting of dogmatists, occultists, *Schöngeister,* agnostics or dreamers, many of them theosophists or marginal Protestants. These listeners, dedicatedly romantic or content in their rationalism, echoed a different mood than the unsatisfied escapists or critical searchers of today. Out of respect to historical fact I had to leave in some problems typical of those years, but I have concentrated on questions still raised today, especially in the West.

Then as now Europeans and Americans consider the East as the source of mysticism but tend to interpret what they find according to their own cultural context. That is why Inayat, before expanding on a subject, often had to draw attention to preconceived ideas and conventional notions. In consequence, some paragraphs in the present book open with what he called un-learning. To avoid further such biased mental associations, but also with a view to the general reader, I have made sparing use of standard theological or philosophical terms. Similarly, I have refrained from comparisons with other schools of teaching, apart from the few occasions when such a comparison was inherent in the subject.

Most subjects were lectured on more than once by Inayat, very much in the way of the Indian classical composer and poet-musician he originally was: he chose a theme and improvised on it according to inspiration and circumstances. Two lectures under the same title have intrinsically the same contents, but differ in tone, form and elaboration. For this survey either the shortest or most striking quotation has been chosen. After an initial attempt to give nothing but quotations, I saw that some commentary and connecting text were indispensable, but I have endeavoured to keep these as brief as possible.

Of some books and chapters only a short resumé is given, and in several quotations either a few words are omitted (indicated by three dots) or one or more sentences (indicated by four dots), in order to avoid repetitions and elucidations that would take too far from the subject at hand. The omission of interjections or conjunctions is not marked for the sake of legibility. The original source is indicated directly after each quotation. III 75 means: volume three of the collected work *Sufi Message.* The same system is used for some quotations from the reminiscenses of Inayat's pupils and others who met him, as collected by Mrs Smit-Kerbert. SK 3 means *Smit-Kerbert Collection* number three. Other titles are not abbreviated and quotations from other books than Hazrat Inayat's are indicated in footnotes. Of the recently reprinted *Gayan* both the old and new page number is given.

I have added to this survey of ideas a chronological survey of Inayat's works, including the Indian and musical publications. This will give an idea of the extent of Inayat's legacy. Musicians and orientalists will note that the last word has not yet been said; mystics will understand Hazrat Inayat's remark:

'I found that where an Eastern teacher began, that was the end that I was to arrive at in the training of my pupils. So my task, compared with that of the spiritual teachers of the East, was quite different to theirs.' (*Appendix* to *Autobiography*)

One of my principal sources, the twelve volumes *Sufi Message* (1960-1965), has some philological and editorial drawbacks. They are grouped according to subject matter, which is very effective, but in the interest of this classification passages are shifted from one book to another. Texts authorized by Inayat are set side by side with apocryphic scrap-book notes, and many Arab, Persian, Hindustani or Sanskrit expressions, garbled by secretaries, have not been corrected. No mention is made when the wording of a text has been altered, and unfortunately an index is lacking. I have often preferred the original answer and context from the old quarterlies *Sufi* and *Sufism.* All the same, the twelve volumes, by their range and comparative completeness represent an enormous advance for the study of Inayatan Sufism, which at different times has gained popularity in highly disparate circles in the West.

Cataloguing of the two principal archives, the one of the Headquarters of the Sufi Movement in Geneva, and the *Fondation Nekbakht* or *Biographical Department* in Suresnes has just begun. The present book may be regarded as another of today's inventories. As yet there has been scarcely any analytical study of Inayat's work, an *oeuvre* of striking originality and unquestionable fascination.

I should like to end this preface with a word of warm thanks to Penelope Goldschmidt who dedicatedly went through every chapter to correct the English; and to Hazrat Inayat Khan's nephew Shaikh-ul-Mashaikh Mahmood Maheboob Khan and my husband Dr H. W. van Tricht who both read through the manuscript several times as indispensable advisors.

Ellecom, April 1976 ELISABETH DE JONG-KEESING

I Answers and Audience

Inayat's methods of answering

Anyone can, at any time, open a book by Hazrat Inayat Khan and find an answer to his questions, even an answer that had not struck him before. Inayat had a faculty for explaining subtle notions like everlasting change, the necessary movement of all that exists, in exactly those words readily grasped by the audience at hand.

In between his own themes, he might react to personal problems of his listeners, the stumbling blocks of their daily life or the well-defined distinctions of theological argument. Often after a lecture, his pupils would exchange comments as to which remark was meant for this person or that, or they remembered him looking to the one whose problems he was touching upon.

Some people did not appreciate the understanding way in which he adapted his answers to his audience, others thought he did not say enough. Quite often he had to explain why he was brief, seemingly incomplete, or even contradictory:

> For my yes there was a reason and for my no there was a reason. Not for myself but for the person who asked the question. (*Sufism,* Sept. 1921, p. 13)

> All this may not be dealt with by the same words nor all treated in the same manner. (III 237)

> One should consider the place, the space, the number of persons present, the kind of people and their evolution, and speak in accordance with the understanding of others. (II 28)

> There are some questions which can be answered, and others which should wait for an answer until those who ask them are able to understand. (X 50)

The variety of his answers was essential. It was one of his basic philosophical ideas put into practice, i.e. his definition of religion:

There is one religion, the unswerving progress in the right direction towards the ideal, which fulfils the life's purpose of every soul. (I 16)

growth and change essential

What is meant by this ideal will be explained in the next chapters. The other principle of this definition is movement, change and growth. Inayat expressed this point in many ways, sometimes in the form of an aphorism, more often in a personal, ethical, spiritual or even a social context.

Progress is life, standing still is death. (VII 178)

All things are good; but all things are not good for every person, nor right at all times. (*Gayan,* p. 36, n. 60)

The right and wrong of every person is according to his stage of evolution and according to his understanding. (III 250)

All men are not alike; the tendencies of every people differ; their habits are not the same. (VII 26)

What is good for one may be very bad for another. For one it may be very good to be a nun or to sit all day in a church or a mosque, but for another it may be very bad; and yet another may need to go to the cafés and learn the meanings of the experiences gained there. (VIII 21, 22)

But though Inayat's answers were according to each one's evolution and understanding, he had a clear line and purposeful direction in mind.

For everything there is a time; so there comes a time for the unfoldment of the soul; but the period of that development depends upon the speed of the progress man makes through life. (*Gayan,* p. 53, n. 89)

Every object has its particular value to every individual; and as a person evolves through life so the value of things becomes different. (III 260)

Though occasionally Inayat may mention that to a sage many wishes and worries seem childish, there is no trace of the pedant in his words. To encourage his audience he might relate his own experiences, showing that he too had started at the beginning and had gone through change and growth. As told in VI 26 he once composed music to a Persian poem which moved him greatly; but it was not until ten or twelve years later that the real meaning of the verse became clear to him. Speaking of the same discovery in VIII 34 he adds:

> For everything there is an appointed time; and when that time comes it is revealed. That is why, although on one hand we may be eager to attain to a certain revelation, yet on the other hand we must have patience to wait for the moment of its coming. (VIII 35)

balance Another reason for varying his answers is balance. Again Inayat meant balance not only in spiritual growth, but also in daily life, in society and politics, in psychological and in physical things.

> The secret of life is balance, and the absence of balance is life's destruction. (*Gayan,* p. 39, n. 64)
>
> Balance is the keynote of spiritual attainment. (*Vadàn,* p. 84)
>
> The essence of to-day's Message is balance. (*Nirtan,* p. 26)

These fundamental statements are found explained in Inayat's lectures. One of these, VIII 61-67, may be summarized in a few sentences as follows: in the natural rhythm of life and nature—day and night, sleeping and waking—there is balance. 'It is balance which enables a man to stand and walk without falling . . . . the growth of plants and the life of trees all depend upon balance; and when . . . we study the condition of the stars and planets . . . we realize that one heavenly body holds the other.' The difficulty is how to maintain balance. Hyper-activity and exaggeration spoil it. Everyone, including the mystic, tends to exaggerate: a patriot turns chauvinist, a merchant thinks only in terms of trade; to the artist only music matters or poetry is the only thing in the world; and a disciple may be over-enthusiastic and often too hasty.

> If we become very spiritual we lose the world; and if we were not meant to live in this world we would not have been sent here. VIII 61

But balance does not mean equalizing the quantities of two opposites:

> Life is movement and balance is something that controls it; but perfect balance controls movement too much, bringing it to a state of inertia. VIII 65

That is why Inayat advised material-minded man to give some attention to spirituality, and why he warned too ethereal people not to forget daily life. But he did not say that a tradesman should not be a tradesman and that a mystic should not meditate. When Henry Ford asked him, 'If one meditates too much there is not likely to be much work done,' Inayat answered:

> But if one meditates somewhat there will be much work done, and better done, and with it will be happiness and peace. I do not preach the denial of things of the world, nor do I condemn worldly accomplishment. I preach only that with the things we must do here in the material world there must also be real attainment in the world of the spirit. (*Detroit News,* 7-2-1926)

His pupils he reminded of balance with a warning or a joke.

> Those who only evolve spiritually become one-sided. (IV 237)

> A disciple was taught by Muhammad a practice by which he experienced ecstasy. After some days he came . . . thanking the Prophet greatly . . . . 'My prayers, which used to last a few minutes, now last all day.' Muhammad said, 'I am glad that you liked the lesson, but please, from to-day, stop the practice.' (VIII 63)

> A man who is one-sided, however great his power of clairvoyance or clairaudience, whatever be his knowledge, yet is limited; he cannot go very far . . . There must be balance, the balance of the head and the heart, the balance of power and wisdom, the balance of activity and repose . . . . Never imagine for one moment that those who show lack of balance can ever proceed further on the spiritual journey, however greatly in appearance they may

seem to be spiritually inclined. It is only the balanced ones who are capable of experiencing the external life as fully as the inner life; to enjoy thought as much as feeling; to rest as well as to act. (I 66, 67)

A Sufi does not believe in one-sided tendencies. (III 236)

warnings against rigidity

The tendency to one-sidedness is great in all of us. It makes things seem simpler than they really are. But simplification may lead to cut-and-dried ideas. Again and again Inayat warned against rigidity; rigidity in general, in social relationships, in mental and emotional attitudes, and above all in religion.

People build four walls around their ideas, lest their minds escape out of the prison bars. (*Gayan,* p. 32, n. 53)

People in the world want to make everything rigid. (VIII 171)

Those who want one law to govern all have lost sight of the spirit of their own religion. (VII 27)

People have made their belief rigid; and therefore instead of being benefited by their belief they are going backwards. (IV 108)

We keep our teachings free from speculations and dogmas, for we believe in actual work with ourselves. (II 233)

The message would be rigid, like pebbles, if there was no contradiction . . . . The message is nothing but an answer to every question, every need, every demand of the individual and collective life. (IX 151)

When in 1915 Inayat was asked to put down his ideas in brief definitions, the second of these 'teachings' was worded:

Never be enslaved by principles. (*Sufi,* February 1915)

Ten years later Inayat no longer wanted to use the words 'Sufi teachings' but only 'Sufi ideas', in order to avoid dogmatism. He did not prescribe what to do, still less command; he suggested possibilities. He showed ways. In those years he wrote:

> Principles are to guide one's life, not to restrict it. (*Vadan,* p. 81)

Several kinds of rigidity made it difficult for him to be fully understood. There were the orthodox believers and unbelievers, simply opposed to something new or different, and, also, those who wanted confirmation of their own brand of newness or difference.

> Very often I am in a position where I can say very little, especially when a person comes to me with his preconceived ideas and wants to take my direction, my guidance on the spiritual path; yet at the same time his first intention is to see if his thoughts fit in with mine and if my thoughts fit in with his thoughts. (IV 108)

The opposite of those-who-know-already, but just as rigid, were the eager listeners who turned Inayat's guiding words into rules.

> They should not depend upon my words; self-realization is the aim. Belief in doctrines are pills to cure sick people. Actually all things are true up to a certain point, but when compared with the ultimate truth they fail to prove their existence. Things appear different from the various planes from which one looks at them. (VIII 171)

In the Edinburgh interview of 1919 (*Sufi,* June 1919) we find a clear picture of how people asked for a hold, for rules. In his answer, Inayat offers a wide choice of possibilities, prescribing nothing; but his words spring from an undercurrent of strength and purposefulness.

not rules, but guidance

'Some of the new pupils of Inayat Khan came from a great distance to Edinburgh to see him; they asked him if he could give them some advice with regard to their life in the world. Inayat Khan replied that he gave freedom to everybody, and even to his mureeds, to have whatever way in life they considered to be the best. He did not believe in forcing his principles on others, considering that each person must live his life according to his evolution, and the principles of the one are not necessarily suitable for another. They still continued to ask him, saying that they had followed, being won by his teachings, and they would greatly value any words of advice that they might hear from his lips. Inayat Khan then said,'

> As you really desire to hear a few words on the subject, I will tell you how, under certain circumstances, I at least try to act. In all things I see from the point of view of another, as well as from my own, I therefore give freedom of thought to everybody, since I take it myself. I appreciate what is good in another, and overlook what I consider is bad. If any one behaves selfishly to me, I take it naturally, as it is human nature to be selfish, and I am not disappointed by it. But when I appear myself to be selfish, I take myself to task and try to improve. There is not anything that I am not ready to tolerate, and there is nobody whom I would not forgive. Those whom I trust I never doubt; whom I love, I never hate; whom I once raise in my estimation, I never cast down. I wish to make friends with everybody I meet; if I find them difficult, I make an effort to gain their friendship. If I cannot succeed in my effort, then I become indifferent to them. When once I make a friend, I never wish to break the friendship. If anybody causes me harm in anyway, I think that is probably because I deserve it, or that the one who harms me knows no better. I have no enemies, but every soul that raises his head in life gets much opposition from the world . . . . I consider no one is either higher or lower than I am. I see in all sources that suffice my need of life one source, God, the only Source, and in admiring, and in bowing before, and in loving anyone, I consider I am doing it to God. In sorrow I look to God, and in joy I thank Him. I do not bemoan the past, and I do not worry about the future, but try to make the best of to-day. I know not failure, even in fall I see a stepping stone to rise, and yet to me rise and fall in life matters little. I do not repent for what I have done, and I think, say and do what I mean. If I wish to accomplish anything in life, I do not fear consequences; I simply go and do it and hold what will be, will be.
>
> Take from these ideas what seem to you best, and forget the rest. (*Sufi,* June 1914)

II What is Sufism ?

cultural contexts

A definition of Sufism is difficult, even for scholars restricting themselves to a description of historical currents and literature. Their studies mostly pertain to the Middle East, Turkey and Persia. Until recently Indian Sufism was not often studied by Western orientalists, although there are a few specialist works on the classical epoch. But Indian Sufism and its remarkable continuity are worth attention; important centres are in existence still today and the pilgrimage to Ajmer is made as often as it was in Akbar's age. Inayat considered Indian Sufism as a crowning development. (*Sufi,* 1915 overleaf, IX 252, VIII 13, 14).

When Hazrat Inayat came to the West, in 1910, he found several Vedanta centres in America and theosophists everywhere, but the word Sufism was almost unknown. Many felt a vague distrust when they discovered a connection with Islam. In their cultural context Islam meant a foe of a thousand years' standing, foreign, unchristian, uncivilized, and, at the time, still embodied in Turkey. In his *Autobiography* Inayat refers to this wide-spread prejudice with resignation. To him Muslim culture and tradition, from the heat and zeal of Arabia, onward through the gold and blue of Samarkand and Bukhara, their bustle, smell and power; through the art and elegance of Persia to the splendour of Moghul emperors combining swordsmanship and poetry, were familiar and beloved facts of history. But so was India, and he felt himself to be representative of her two cultures, Moghul and Hindu. But he was not a missionary or propagandist of any kind and soon adjusted himself to speaking in such a way as his audience could most readily understand, often using Sanskrit terms because these were more or less familiar to many. For others he alluded to the Bible, and when addressing a Jewish society he used a kabbalistic term like *shekinah.*

Inayat could use 'extraneous' terms not only as a student of religion and mysticism, but because for him the final aim and result of all mysticism were one, whatever the initial differences (see chapter IV). But Sufism cannot be explained in a religious and mystical context only. It is almost impossible to translate the complete sense of the word Sufism from one culture into another.

varied aspects

Besides, Inayat's quiet empathy and adaptability have often been misinterpreted. It is important to bear in mind that he used the word Sufism in a dual sense, 1. in the historic, cultural and technical sense of the mystical schools of Islam, 2. as mysticism in general.

Even the latter view can be regarded as derived by Inayat from an Islamic conception of the term Muslim, designating not only an adherent of Islam, but any monotheistic worshipper. He described this Muslim view on monotheism explicitly.

> In the Semitic races this higher form of worship is known to have been introduced by Abraham, and it is this idea which was called Islam, which sometimes disappeared and sometimes appeared during the time of different prophets mentioned in the Bible, and became materialised more during the time of Muhammad, when a nation was formed and was made the custodian of a religion, the main spirit of which was this idea. (IX 210 and 195, original edition *The Unity of Religious Ideals,* page 233)

In the same passage (IX 209, 210) this 'higher form of worship,' connoting not only monotheism but also a formless God (see next chapter), is connected with the teaching of Shankaracharya, the great Hindu mystic of the eighth century. Thus, the way of thinking has an Islamic base, the conclusion approaches universalism, resting on the universality of mystical experience.

> There have been Sufis at all periods of human history. Though they have lived in different parts of the world, speaking different languages and born in different faiths and beliefs, they have recognized and sympathized with each other, through the oneness of their understanding. (V 16)

> The central idea of Sufism is believed to have existed from the beginning of creation. Traces of Sufism are to be found

> in all periods of history, but mostly during the age of the Hebrew prophets and ecstatics, who themselves were Sufis. Abraham, Moses and Jesus propagated Sufism until the coming of Muhammad, by whom this Brotherhood was formed, while it was advanced by Ali and Siddik. (*Sufi*, 1917 onwards, overleaf notice.)

So much for the historical view and mystical interpretation. Just as complicated is the cultural and technical aspect, since Sufism covers more than one or two fields of life, whereas, in our analytical world, we tend to separate practice and ideas.

During his first years in the West (1910-1914) Inayat usually explained Sufism as 'wisdom', 'religious philosophy', 'divine wisdom', but he soon added, 'not wisdom acquired from without' or 'not philosophy as taught at universities'. He also approached the problem of definitions by answering in contradictions:

> Sufism is a philosophy among the religions and it is a religion among the philosophies. Among the religions it is a philosophy by reason of the Sufi's freedom of thought; among the philosophies it is a religion because of the Sufi's idealization of God, his devotion and his worship. (VIII 23)

Indeed, when they heard the word God, Westerners first thought of religion. But when Inayat's words and deeds did not accord with their concept of churches and dogmas, people asked, again and again, 'Is Sufism a religion, a philosophy, or mysticism?'

> It is all three. It is a religion, if you want to learn religion from it, it is a philosophy, if you want to learn wisdom from it; it is mysticism if you wish to be guided by it in the unfoldment of the soul. And yet it is beyond all these things. It is the light, it is the life which is the sustenance of every soul and which raises a mortal being to immortality. (*Sufism*, December 1923)

> Sufism cannot be called a religion, because of its freedom from principles, distinctions and differences . . . . Neither can it be called a philosophy, because philosophy teaches the study of nature in its qualities and varieties. Sufism on the

contrary teaches unity. Therefore it may be plainly called: '*training of view*'. (*Sufi,* 1915, page 69; IX 256, 257)

Sufism is not a religion, for it is beyond the limitations of faiths and beliefs which make the diversity of religions in the world. Sufism, in short, is a change of *outlook on life.* It is like viewing from an aeroplane a town, the streets of which one has known and walked through, and yet one has never before seen the whole town at a glance. (V 191)

Sufism is not a new religion or community; . . . . It is an *attitude of life.* (VII 179)

These explanations were addressed to a general public. Other listeners, though well aware of the manifold implications of the word Sufism, were puzzled by Inayat's definitions and his attitude towards Hinduism. For modern nationalist Muslims he appeared not Islamic enough, and for Westerners too 'muhammadan'. During and immediately after the First World War certain Western followers pressed Inayat to concentrate wholly on the universalist interpretation and to replace the word Sufism by a 'neutral' English name. This he consistently refused, maintaining that it was only through the particular that one might rise towards the universal.

All through Inayat's work we will see him putting emphasis on basic unity, but never denying differences. To him the most obvious differences requiring mention are some philosophical distinctions between Sufism, Vedantism and Buddhism, and the varying methods of the principal Sufi orders in India.

Sufism, Vedanta and Buddhism

There are three principal schools of philosophical thought in the East: Sufism, Vedantism and Buddhism. The Sufi school of thought was that of the prophets of Beni Israil: Abraham, Moses, David, Jonah and others, Zarathustra, Christ, Muhammad; . . . . Sufism is the ancient school of wisdom . . . and it has been the origin of many cults of a mystical and philosophical culture. Its roots can be traced to the school which existed in Egypt and from which source all the different esoteric schools have come. (VIII 18)

'Beni Israil' is an Indian-Muslim term to denote the three co-related religions based on the Old Testament, New Testament and Quran; it can be compared with the denomination 'Abrahamic religions' as current in some circles in the West. Akhnaton and the mystery schools of Egypt, and Zarathustra's philosophy of light have been regarded as precursors of monotheism.

Of the several philosophical distinctions between these Western religions and the two Eastern ones Inayat considered the latter's doctrine of reincarnation as the most characteristic. (V 121, VIII 163, IX 147) But even when he described such a basic difference he tended to show that in some ways the philosophies concerned are related, for the aim of mystics of all religions is the same. And when he enters into the very different methods of the four great Sufi schools he knew from practice, he ends with the words:

> In the different schools the ideal remained the same, although the methods varied. (VIII 18)

The conception of the same underlying ideal in all religions and mystical schools is essential to Hazrat Inayat's teachings, though I should repeat that he remains well aware of the outer differences.

Inayat's emphasis on underlying unity

As for the history of Sufism—the idea of continuity from the Egypt and Greek esoteric schools is a common speculation, and the connection between neo-platonic, hermetic and gnostic currents with earlier Islamic schools is almost generally accepted by students of mysticism. Some fervent Muslim modernists are apt either to contest any such connections whatever, or, being opposed to all mysticism in principle, to insist on Sufism being wholly of alien origins. Inayat regarded both tendencies as being unduly assertive.

> The tendency to dominate arose, and with it the patriotism of the community and prejudice against others. (VIII 13)

Inayat was sometimes attacked by his own Muslim friends. One of them asked, 'In joining a Sufi community I believed I was associating with Muslims, of my own religious faith. Is the Sufi Order really Muslim—or to put it in the straightest terms, Muhammadan?' (*Sufi,* January 1919, p. 4). It is possible that those friends at first took Inayat for a missionary, and they were probably rather disappointed when they got the same sort of answers as those Westerners who asked whether Sufism was not 'really' the mystic side of Islam.

> Mystics in Islam have been called Sufis, but Sufism, Divine Wisdom, is for all, and not limited to a certain people. It has existed from the first day of creation and will continue to spread and to exist unto the end of the world. (*Sufi,* October 1917, p. 1)

> We do not shut ourselves off from any community, but are ready to unite with all and any, for within we are already united in the Infinite. Our order is composed of truth-seeking people of different faiths and beliefs, who are not in any way obliged to give up the faith or belief they may have nor to accept a certain faith or belief, nor are they, if they have none, compelled to accept one. (*Sufi,* January 1919, p. 4)

> Sufis, who have received spiritual training from all previous prophets and leaders, likewise received training from Muhammad. (V 21)

> Many people claim to know all about Sufism from simply reading about it in books, but what such people know is in reality only the system, the outer garment, not the inner truth. (V 222)

> The idea that Sufism sprang from Islam or from any other religion is not necessarily true; yet it may rightly be called the spirit of Islam, as well as the pure essence of all religions and philosophies. (V 23)

Some people have taken Inayat's universalism for syncretism, which it most certainly is not. He teaches the underlying unity of all faiths and beliefs, he respects the outer differences, but stresses that which all people have in common:

> All that is from God is for all souls. (*Gayan* p. 39, new 65)

> The tendency of the Sufi is rather to unite than to differ. (V 121)

> As soon as thought is restricted, it ceases to be Sufism (I 57)

> What is a Sufi? Strictly speaking, every seeker after the ultimate truth is really a Sufi, whether he calls himself that or not. (I 45)
>
> What is Sufism? It is wisdom. To learn wisdom at every step on the path of life is the only work of the Sufi. (XI 232)
>
> Every person can be called a Sufi either as long as he is seeking to understand life, or as soon as he is willing to believe that every other being will also find and touch the same ideal. (I 45)

There has been some strong opposition against this universalist view and probably there still is, because this opposition is born from and fed by political tendencies. In their struggle for honour and recognition of their identity many Muslims and Muslim states tend to stress differences more than underlying unity. Answering both this opposition and the unhistorical tendencies of followers who wanted to substitute the word Sufism by another name, Hazrat Inayat Khan clearly indicates his view of universal Sufism's place in history: it continues and renews.

Inayat's definition: continuity and renewal

> The Sufi Message which is now being given in the Western world is the child of that mother who has been known for so many years as Sufism. It connects the two lines of the prophetic mission, the Hindu line and that of Beni Israil in order that they may become the medium to unite in God and truth both East and West. It is the same truth, the same religion, the same ideal, which the wise of all ages have held. If there is anything different, it is only a difference of form. The Sufi Message has adopted the form suitable for the age. (IX 148)

This is a very comprehensive answer, covering several points that will be dealt with in later chapters. It is cited here because of the important statement that Inayat wanted to combine the Eastern and Western lines of thought. This aim is best understood from within India, where the Islam and Hindu socio-religious cultures lived in close proximity for centuries. Culturally the Muslim conquerors had a marked impact on the North. As to religious philosophy, there are traces of Vedantic influences on Indian Sufism, as are those of Sufism upon the Bhakti Movement.

Inayat knew both cultures by experience and, though raised in a Muslim family, he learned Hindu tradition and culture at school and through his profession. It is not unusual, in India, for a Muslim artist to sing Hindu songs. Inayat was trained by his grandfather Maula Bakhsh, a Muslim, who had mastered the luxuriant, bel-canto and virtuoso music of the North as well as the Southern, Carnatic style of Hindu-Dravidian tradition with its strong grasp of theory and thematic development. In his very first lectures and concerts, when he was scarcely twenty years old, Inayat always stressed the need of mutual appreciation and of harmonizing India's twin cultures. On his wanderings through India he had experienced the ritual discrimination of the Muslim and observed the social discrimination of the untouchable. And in his last days, after having returned to his homeland, he sadly commented on the rift between Hindu and Muslim. However, his preaching of unity was not based on mere social experience, but on his philosophy of underlying unity. And, in 1907 in Hyderabad, the last blessing his spiritual teacher gave Inayat was accompanied by the words: 'Go out into the world, my child, and harmonize the East and the West with the music of thy soul.' (*Autobiography* and XII 150)

how and why Inayat became a preacher

East and West could mean Hindu and Muslim, the latter being closely related to the Jewish and Christian tradition. But East and West also meant India and Europe. And so, in 1910, Inayat sailed for the West, accompanied by his brother Pyaromir Maheboob Khan and his cousin Mohammad Ali Khan. Later the younger brother Musharaff Moulamia Khan followed. They all devoted their life to their brother and murshid, and his work and ideals.

From 1911 till 1914 Inayat and his companions toured America and Europe, mainly demonstrating and explaining Indian Music. They acquired a certain fame, especially in France and Russia. But in those early years Inayat also initiated some Western disciples, and as soon as his English improved, he gave lectures on his mystical philosophy, always emphasizing his two aims, the awakening of one's real self, our common origin; and through this common unity learning to accept each other, in spite of any outward difference.

One book was published by him in those years, edited with the help of English, French and Russian friends. The brief Preface of this work, *A Sufi Message of Spiritual Liberty* (V 9-36) ends with the words:

> By the request of many European and American friends interested in the Divine knowledge, I have written these few pages as an introduction to Sufism. I hope this may help in establishing goodwill among mankind and friendly understanding between nations. (P. 3 of the 1913 edition, not reprinted in SM V)

During the First World War Inayat lived in London and adjusted the form of his teachings so that western people could grasp and use the essence. There are many, slightly differing, statements of aims in the magazine *Sufi* between 1915 and 1920, but the recurrent theme is the revealing of the inner truth and underlying unity. For instance in September 1915:

Inayat's aims

> What the Sufi order aims at accomplishing in the world is to bring about an understanding between the followers of all different religions by revealing the essential truth which underlies them all.

In all the ensuing definitions of aims some items may be added which are really means (like using certain methods, or 'simplifying mysticism' so that more men in daily life can 'receive glimpses of the Truth of Unity'), but always the spreading of the knowledge of unity is the principal idea, and the result of better understanding between men is always emphasized; later not only better understanding between creeds, or between East and West, but also between Westerners among themselves. In 1918 the objects of the Sufi Movement were drawn up in a definite form that is still used to-day. They are:

> 1. to realize and spread the knowledge of unity,
> 2. to discover the light and power latent in man,
> 3. to help to bring the world's two opposite poles, East and West, closer together. (IX 267/8)

Accordingly, the following chapters will look into the philosophical foundation of Inayat's Sufi universalism, its application for mystical training and its use in daily life. His creation of forms suitable for the West had taken years, among other things because there were all sorts of misunderstandings to cope with. One trend was to regard Sufism as a special sect; another wide-spread tendency, of admirers and sceptics both, was to confuse his esotericism with thrilling occultism.

In 1919, at the annual conference of his order in July, he closed the meeting with a few words to his growing group of co-workers, and towards the end of this printed speech one perceives something of the depth of his feelings and the power of his inspiration.

> It is not our aim by forming a Sufi Order to add to the communities of the world, which are pulling each its own way, dividing humanity into innumerable divisions . . . . Our motive is to serve humanity in general, regardless of their joining us. We do not wish to compete with any movements working on the same lines. On the contrary we are only too glad to watch if there are any other movements succeeding in a similar trend of thought. It is to the result that we look, ... I am glad to say that I have not gained your friendship by exciting your curiosity about superstitions. I have not interested you in stories about ghosts and spirits. If I had done so I should perhaps have attracted twenty thousand followers, whom I could have entertained with fairy tales, and what a joy to find myself amidst twenty thousand fools. And as many times as I had fooled the world, so many times would I have covered my spirit with a thousand covers of stupidity. I have not asked you to pray in a particular house of the Lord. I have not forced upon you any rituals, forms or dogmas. I have not taught you to take up a particular Scripture alone as the sacred book. I have not given you any particular principles, that you should subject your life to them. I have not encouraged in you the desire for seeking after wonders, though I have told you that in the spiritual pursuit, as your sight will be keen, so the whole life will become a wonder. I have not wanted you to revere me, or to consider me

wonderful, good or great, and to raise me so high that some day you may have to throw me down from that height. I desire you to consider me friend, your brother, your comrade, someone in the world you can call in your time of need, someone who rejoices in your joy and sorrows with your sorrow. If there is anything that I ask of you it is this: you only in the world know of the voice that comes to the ears of my heart, for it is the voice which has brought you closer to me, it is the voice which holds you with me. You know Whose voice it is, though it is expressed in my words. I wish this voice to reach to the end of the world, I wish this voice to spread wide, I wish this voice to become audible to the hearers and visible to the readers who may be ready to hear it and to read it.

If I had no means of help and no helpers standing by my side in my strife, and if the whole world were opposed to me, I should do my work nevertheless. And when I see you, my Mureeds, standing by my side in readiness to help, I feel much stronger and I have every hope of furthering our blessed cause by the help of God . . . . Here I find a few sincere friends united with me with all their heart in the Sufi cause, and why should we not be able to remove mountains? . . . . be sure we shall remove them if only we work together with mind and soul, bearing in mind that a good work done for a return is nothing but toil, but work done for the sake of good is as good done to God. (*Sufi*, January 1920, p. 3/4)

What does Inayat mean when he says God? What is the voice which brought him and his pupils together? What is the underlying unity?

III Concepts of God and Belief

And now we come again to the question of God. Because this is the important question we must first make clear in our minds before we take a further step in spiritual progress. Since to analyse God means to dethrone God, the less said on the subject the better; but at the same time, the seekers for truth who want to tread the spiritual path with open eyes and whose intellect is hungering for knowledge, should know something about it. (VI 212)

opposition to the word God

Once, after I had given a series of lectures, a man came up to me and said, 'All your lectures appeal to me very much, I think every word is true; I have always thought on these lines. I would be most happy to follow your guidance, but only on one condition: that you do not mention the name of God. For a man like you, who can touch the depths of life, a man of high principles and lofty ideals, does not need to use that old name which every simpleton uses and believes in. (XII 11)

This kind of objection was but one of the sort Inayat learned to cope with when he came to the West. In former ages mystics often had to demonstrate that they were faithful to the religious dogmas of their country, and they had to disguise their broader outlook. Twentieth century mystics are not in danger of being excommunicated or condemned, they only risk being shrugged at and not listened to. Many modern semi-mystic groups do not call themselves religions but sciences or techniques. Inayat did not go as far as that. He did not disguise his broad outlook, but he could veil it and talk to everybody in the terms they understood. He could weld a lever out of a well-known and accepted idea:

Some call it evolution and others call it God. (*Sufism*, December 1923, p. 12)

This is not a little ironical joke. Inayat was fond of citing (as in VII 39) Rumi's poem depicting the evolution of consciousness from the mineral to the human state and thence onwards to the divine, often also summarizing it in his own aphoristic style: 'God slept in the rock, dreamed in the plant, awoke in the animal, and realized himself in man.' (VI 226). This infers that the scientist and the mystic believe in the same process: that from dense earth the mineral, the vegetable, the animal and the human have gradually developed. (XII 14)

the concept of God as the common source

But the scientist covers only part of the way. For the mystic the development begins earlier and ends later. He sees one eternal source from which all created beings, all souls, originate. Therefore this continuous being is the core of all. During the process of creation the original common being assumes a myriad of different forms. These forms are the scientist's object of study. The mystic picks up where the biologist leaves off. The important point for him is the moment when man starts remembering the source he came from and consciously strives to find it again.

> As there is a gradual process of evolution from the mineral to the human kingdom, so there is also a gradual process from a certain state of human evolution to a state of perfection. (II 187)

Evolving to a state of perfection means finding one's way home to the original source, which comprises all and is perfect.

In outline this conception of a common source, and outgoing and home coming souls is found in the mystical philosophies of almost all developed religions. In the description of details, mystics of the various cultures may widely differ; for instance, the number of stages back to the source range from ninety five to a simple three. More fundamental differences can be sought in the question whether there is an individual soul which survives or not, and whether mystical union is a meeting of two, God being essentially different, or a melting back, a return to Oneness. These subjects will be dealt with below.

The philosophy of manifestation and return was the first theoretical lesson Inayat learned from his own master; this happened after six months of silent practical training. In 1913, in *A Sufi Message of Spiritual Liberty,* Inayat explained the idea in the traditional form with the original terms. The most comprehensive and most personal description is found in *The Soul Whence and Whither* (I 107-185), lectures for his pupils given in the summers of 1922 and 1923. In 1925 he had adapted his terminology to western customs and western tabus in such a way that in *Philosophy, Psychology and Mysticism* (XI 11-223) he scarcely used his original highly technical vocabulary. He also used the name of God with increasing circumspection. But this much abused word is the most current designation for the Source of All. And so the first and basic idea of the ten Sufi thoughts is phrased:

> There is One God, the Eternal, the Only Being; none exists save He. (I 13, IX 267)

This is a clear statement, an abstraction intellectually understandable for the philosophically inclined; opposed by some; and mere words for many. As it was Inayat's purpose to make this conception more than just a theory, one finds him explaining in many ways how realization of unity can be attained gradually. But before he could do that he had first to look into the notions people usually associate with concepts like God and religion. Among his audience were many so-called unbelievers; many enthusiasts with a tendency to run away with one cherished idea; now and then people attached to their own set of ideas who wanted to show they were right. And sometimes there was a void, a collection of modern people with a vague scepsis and no clear concept of spiritual life at all. To such a random group, on board ship to America in 1925 he said:

> . . . all life comes from one source which is the very life of all things, and not only life but intelligence also; that is what religion calls God. Whatever we call it, it is the same. The difference is only in the name. (VI 108)

Causes of unbelief

A remark like 'That is what religion calls God,' shows how well he understood those for whom the idea of God was unfamiliar or even improbable. He never forced his ideas upon unbelievers, but he looked into various causes of their unbelief.

He knew very well what could cause irritation.

> The ignorant believer, by his claim of belief, causes a revolt in an intelligent person, thereby turning him into an unbeliever. (*Gayan,* 53/4, n. 89)

Or he described those who had not learned to believe as children.

> Parents think nowadays that by giving the children the belief that has been held in the family they make them narrow, yet at the same time they have no substitute, no other belief and it is very difficult to believe later on. (IX 56)

There are so many causes for unbelief that Inayat is careful to mention exceptions when he points out some very common and rather childish kinds of unbelief like intellectual snobism, or naive egoism.

> Very often the unbeliever is an unbeliever because of his own vanity, though this is not always so. He says that only simple people believe in God; he sees that there are millions of souls who worship God, and yet this worship does not raise them higher, and so he finds no virtue in the worship of God. Others believe in the God-Ideal so long as they are happy, but when conditions change, when sorrow and trouble come, they begin to doubt whether there really is a God. (IX 71 and 75/6)

> There are others who think that if God knows our needs, and still does not satisfy them, this shows great cruelty on the part of God. Many have given up their belief for this reason. (IX 46)

Of course one finds Inayat considering the wide-spread phenomenon confusing church as an institution with more or less developed God-concepts. For many the association is: God means church, church means authority, authority is wrong.

> Men, revolted by the abuse of religion, have often given up religion itself, and it is this that has made men ignorant of the divine source of the law that rules the world. (IX 32)

Inayat's answers to those who lost their belief because of sorrow, or because of so much injustice in the world, will be cited in the chapter on Sufism in Daily Life. The acknowledgement of doubt as a stage in spiritual development will follow later, in this chapter.

rigid forms of unbelief

There is but one thing that Inayat might hold against unbelievers: rigidity, a kind of reversed dogmatism. Those who cling to atheism or agnosticism or unbelief out of revolt against the Santa Claus concept of God, or against the institutional church, are blind to other possibilities.

> Many . . . with intelligence and reason and understanding of life, rebel against religion, as the child when it grows up throws away his rattle, for it is no longer interested in it. So to-day the condition is that religion remains in the hands of those who have kept to its outer form . . . ; and those who are, so to speak, grown-up in mind and spirit, and who want something better, cannot find anything. Their souls hunger for music, yet when they ask for music they are given a rattle; and then they throw away the rattle and say that they do not care for music. (X 256. Originally *Unity of Religious Ideals,* third chapter)

> Most unbelievers have a very near horizon, like birds in a covered cage which do not know that there is anything beyond. (XI 228)

rigid forms of belief

But narrower, often, was the outlook of those 'who kept to the outer form', especially if they fought other people's ideas, calling them pagan, heretic or idolatrous.

Inayat did not discuss the simplicity of a belief; on the contrary, he often defended simple believers against overzealous and too hasty speculation of some of his own pupils. He considered a simple beginning as a necessity. But it was, again, rigidity that he pointed out.

> First there is a time when a person believes in God and that is a very blessed time; and when he is more evolved in the worldly life then he fights for his Church, that is then his main idea; and when he goes further, then he despises other

> creeds . . . it is this evolution which is called bigotry. (III 38)

> There are many others who are bigoted in regard to their belief. They stand on a certain belief, and instead of keeping it in their head they keep it under their feet . . . Their belief has nailed them to a certain spot, and they cannot progress because of that belief. (IX 54)

Inayat respected any concept of God, as long as this concept had a real meaning for the one who used it.

> One person in praying feels he is fulfilling a certain duty which he considers to be one among the other duties of life. He does not know to whom he is praying; he thinks it is to some God . . . . Praying, to him, is something that he must do . . . in order to fall in with the custom of the family or the community . . he acts like everybody else. His prayer is mechanical, and if it has any effect it is very little. (IX 39-41)

But when a person was happy in a simple belief, it would protect him or her. An old-fashioned lady listened, disapproving and bewildered, to her cousin, a devoted and serious pupil of Inayat. The pupil could not help explaining that God was in everybody and in everything, that all was One. The master sat with the old aunt and said smiling that he was he, that she was she, and that God was in Heaven. So how could all be one? She agreed happily. He did not talk to her about underlying unity—though he showed it by understanding her—, it was of no use at her stage of living and thinking.

rigid fancies of belief

Inayat did not meet many of her kind, in general they remained safely in the old trail and did not seek him out. But among those who did look for new ways in religion and who did have an inkling of a greater life, some might be given to speculation which also ended in rigidity,—the rigidity of the fanciful. Such enthusiasts had either a sensationalist or a rationalizing tendency to tie up creation in neat and well-defined parcels, which were a horror to the rigid believer, and a laughing stock to the dogmatic a-religionist. Inayat quietly warned them:

When a person believes that an old Egyptian comes from the other side to inspire him, or an American Indian comes to lead him on his way, he is building a wall between himself and God. (II 261)

He may believe that on such and such a mountain a fairy descended on a certain night, that beautiful colours appeared and that one should go there and become illuminated; or he may believe that in the heart of Tibet, in remote places, people sit with closed eyes for a hundred years, and that there is a country where there are martyrs' tombs and that that is the best place in which to become illuminated. It is only as he believes; whether higher or lower, it is a belief all the same, and if a person has formed a certain belief in himself he cannot easily change it. (IX 54)

It is clear that the master smiled a bit at those fancies. But for some people they could be steps in their personal evolution.

Belief is like a staircase; it is made in order to go upward, but if one remains on one step then there is no progress. One belief after another comes to a person as he goes further on the path of spiritual progress. (IX 54/5)

That is one of the reasons why Inayat has no use for abstract knowledge, it is too static.

rigidity of abstract under-standing

It is very easy to read in a book that it is the absolute that is God, that it is the abstract. This means no one and nothing, or all and everything. Indeed, there is some truth in it. But the idea of God being the absolute is larger than man's mind . . . . Many intellectual people have lost their way by reading somewhere that God is abstract. It means nothing to them, for they have not yet arrived at that state of evolution where they can assimilate such an idea. Before getting to that stage they have swallowed a pill they can never digest. (XII 17/8)

This passage continues with the description of the only attitude Inayat rejects and about which he is severe.

On top of this come people who say, 'You are God; I am

God'. In this way their insolence becomes greater and greater. (XII 18)

This refers to the solipsists (only-myself-ists). When they hear that God is the only Being, which means that all and everybody is a manifestation of God under the cover of different outer forms, they bluntly proclaim, 'God is in me', or, pitifully comic, 'I am God.'

It is easy to claim, 'I am God!'; but it is bringing the highest ideal of God down to the lowest plane. It is as if the bubble were to say, 'I am the sea.' (IX 110)

limits of abstract under-standing

Apart from the danger of superficiality, Inayat points out certain limits of abstract understanding.

It is no use beginning with the idea that if one analyses God, one will come to believe in Him. (VII 100/1)

We may ask why we should worship God, and whether the theoretical knowledge of His law in nature is not sufficient for the highest realization. The answer is: no. Theoretical knowledge of a subject can never take the place of experience, which is necessary for realization. (V 14/5)

To be sure, abstract understanding serves scholarly purposes, but Inayat's aim was '*expanding* the soul of man', 'to *realize and spread the knowledge of unity*', '*to discover* the light and power latent in man' and 'to *bring people nearer* to each other.' (IX 267/8). Of these active purposes 'realizing the knowledge of unity' is the first and most difficult one. Realizing God is much more than believing.

realization and know-ledge of God differ-ent from belief

Of all the millions of believers in God perhaps only one makes God a reality, and that is because the picture man makes of God is as limited as himself . . . . He cannot raise his imagination above what he is used to, and he cannot reach beyond his imagination to where the being of God is. The secret of God is hidden in the knowledge of unity. (IX 12/3)

This knowledge of God is also different from belief, and is needed before one can start on the work towards realization.

Religious authorities of different times have kept humanity ignorant of the knowledge of God and have only given it a belief in God; and it is lack of this knowledge which has made the man of reason rebel against that which he could not understand. There remained no link between the two, knowledge and belief, and that is how the reign of materialism came to the world, a reign which is still spreading. (VI 260)

That is to say, belief is functional as long as it is not held to rigidly. Starting from simple belief, one may come to fuller understanding and a beginning of realization.

progressive stages of belief

The first stage is the belief of the follower. This belief reminds one of sheep: where one goes, all the others follow, and that is the belief of most people. . . . Whether it is a right or wrong belief, they are only attracted by someone else and they all follow. (IX 55)

The second stage of belief is faith in authority. A person believes because it is written in such and such a book, or said by such and such a person. This is a slightly better belief, because if a man is not sure of himself, he is at any rate sure of some personality, or of a sacred book or scripture. (IX 55)

This kind of belief Inayat considers as one step higher, 'because it is a belief in somebody in whom one has trust.' (VI 210) Trust rates high with him. He who cannot trust himself, is already progressing when he dares trust someone else. Although the belief of the follower and also the belief in authority are only beginners' beliefs they are necessary steps and one should not attempt a next step until one is really ready for it.

The third belief is that of reasoning, which means that everything one believes one reasons out within oneself. This is a still greater belief; but how few there are who reason it out. There are also many who begin to reason before arriving at this third stage, and then they cannot progress as they should because two stages are left out. Some begin to reason in childhood, and if they have no proper guidance reason will lead them astray. (IX 56)

Inayat says a good deal about the usefulness of reasoning and about the dangers of its distortion into rationalizing. But believing and proving one's belief with reason is an important stage, which produces self-confidence and leads to conviction.

> And then again there is a fourth belief. That belief is a belief of conviction, which stands above reason. There is a sense of conviction in man which is not discovered for some time in life; but there comes a time when it is discovered; and that is a blessed day. Then there arises an idea which no reason can break, a feeling which is not a passing feeling but is a conviction. However high the idea may be, one seems to be an eyewitness of that idea; one is as strong, as confident as a person who has seen with his own eyes. (VI 211)

Conviction is used here to translate the Arab word *Iman,* which Inayat also translates as faith. From a corresponding text (IX 57/8) one learns that this faith springs from an inner experience. The one who has this kind of conviction already is on his way as a mystic.

the stage of doubt

In this growing from stage to stage doubt has its place.

> The existing of God is a question which arises in every mind, whether of the believer in God or of the unbeliever. There are moments when even the greatest believer in God questions His existence—whether there really is a God. (IX 83)

Inayat himself had known that moment of doubt as a boy. One evening when it was time for prayers, the thought struck him that he had said these prayers for so long and that he had never received an answer. Why pray to someone invisible? He went to his grandfather and told him that he would not offer any more prayers to Allah until he had seen him. The wise grandfather answered with a verse from the Quran. 'We will show them our signs in the world and in themselves, that the truth may be manifested to them.' And when grandson Inayat was not yet content he added, 'The signs of God are seen in the world, and the world is seen in thyself.'

> These words entered so deeply into my spirit, that from this time every moment of my life has been occupied with the thought of divine immanence. (XII 131)

'God is seen in the world.' 'God is seen in you.' 'You can know him'. These are the ideas hinted at in the description of the fourth stage of belief, when 'one is as a person who has seen with his own eyes.'

> . . . conviction. Where does this belief come from? It comes from the divine element in man known both as love and as intelligence. It is known in these two different aspects but in reality they are one in essence. If there is no intelligence there is no love; if there is no love there is no intelligence. (IX 57)

Both love and intelligence are connected with the widening of one's self, with keener perception and living more deeply. There is a special meaning of the word Intelligence, almost identical with higher spirit, but in this context it is covered by the definition of intelligence as a quality given in I 39: 'intelligence is the grasping faculty of consciousness, which by every means recognizes, distinguishes, perceives, and conceives all that is around it.' This indeed resembles the activity of grown-up and firm love.

why historical and institutional God-concepts were needed

Inayat considered the development of active love as one of the reasons for the many historical God-conceptions, from the most primitive to the most highly evolved ones.

> Whatever diversity may exist among religions, the motive of all has been one: to cultivate and prepare the human heart for divine love. Sometimes the spirit of guidance drew the attention of mankind to see and admire the beauty of God in the firmament, sometimes in trees and rocks, making them sacred trees, holy mountains and purifying streams, sometimes it had guided men's attention to see the immanence of God among the beasts and birds, calling them holy animals, sacred birds. (V 184)

In the last sentence we find another motive for worshipping God in various forms; the idea of underlying unity, of God as the only Being, is difficult to grasp.

> To see life as a whole is beyond the power of the generality of mankind. (III 177)

Of course, as soon as we try to explain this Only Being which comprises all we use limited words for something that in its fullness has no limitation.

> It is impossible to define God in words. It is like trying to put the ocean in a bottle. (VIII 123)

But, says Inayat in another place:

> A cup of water is as interesting as the ocean, or perhaps more so when one is thirsty. (X 14)

Therefore the great ones, the founders of religions, gave their people God-concepts that suited the people's environment, development and age, even though their own insight was further developed.

> To the eyes of the wise in all ages the universe has become one single immanence of the Divine Being; and that which cannot be compared, or which has no comparison has been difficult to explain in the human tongue. Therefore the idea of the wise has always been to allow man to worship God in whatever way he may be capable of picturing him. (IX 207)

> For the ordinary mind it is not sufficient to feel that something exists as an idea. It is too vague. Man wishes to feel its existence with his own hands; then only can he acknowledge something to exist. The wise, therefore, have given different objects to such peoples . . . Some said, 'See God in the sun;' and the people understood this. They were not satisfied with thinking that God was an idea; they were much more pleased to know that God would be seen by them—God who is incomparable even with the sun, who is unattainable . . . . Some said to a simple man who asked to see God, 'Go into the forest and find a certain tree, that tree is God.' The search for that tree gave that man something to do which was essential, and the patience with which he sought for the tree also did something to his soul. There was joy, too, in finding a rare tree, and in the end he found what he was looking for, for God is everywhere. (IX 86/7)

Not only the so-called primitive God-conceptions are considered a means to develop love and other qualities, or symbols for the unapproachable, but the shape and ideas of highly evolved religions too. A summing up of the many attitudes and ideas of religions, and the mystical outlook as well are found in these lines:

forms of worship

> There are three aspects of worship; the worship of God in heaven by those who understand him as a separate being; the worship of God on earth, as a god or goddess, in the form of an idol, or of some being who is considered as an incarnation of God and who is worshipped by the multitudes; and the worship of the God within, the innermost self of our being. It is the aspect of God that is understood by the Sufis, the Vedantists, and the great teachers such as Christ and Muhammad (V 203)

'An incarnation of God' refers to Rama and others of the Hindu pantheon. The worship of God as a separate being is the most usual western idea of God.

father image and underlying unity

This supreme Being is generally understood in a more limited way than the Only Being of the mystic, and often leads to the much discussed and indignantly rejected image of God as a father. Many twentieth-century men consider this concept an example of untenable paternalism and, as they take it for the only meaning of the word God, they throw away all thought of religion and declare that God is dead. Inayat explains this father concept, not only as a means to have an inkling of God as long as one cannot know and realize him, but also as an expression of the Oneness of God. In a book on the education of children he says:

> The way of Christ was to give humanity the ideal of God, God as the heavenly Father. And what was the reason? The reason was that it is conceivable. Even a child can understand that idea. . . . Besides, all the different names that the prophets and teachers have given to God are really not appropriate; it was only to make people understand. Their mind could only conceive these names: the Judge, or the Creator, or the Supreme Being, or the King of the Day of Judgment. They are not the names of God. God cannot be limited to those names; they are too small for God. Yet at the same time it is the best one can do to make the ideal of God as concrete to the mind as possible. (III 41)

In a passage on heredity, elsewhere, he goes into another reason for the concept of God as a father. Man inherits some of his qualities from his earthly parents and ancestors, but there are also the hidden qualities he brings with him from the common source. Underlying unity means that we all are related to the Only Being, from which we come and to which we return.

> That is the meaning of Christ's constantly pointing out to humanity the Fatherhood of God; to see the Father in God, and so inherit the qualities of God. (IV 277)

This is the mystic's way of looking at it. One finds the same view in the many references to 'Be ye perfect even as your Father in heaven', which is interpreted by Inayat—and by Vedantists—as 'remember your godly origin and try to reach it again.' There is always our God-part and our man-part to consider. As a rule we only know our man-part.

> What little man knows about himself is only about his body . . . They limit themselves to that small physical region which is called body, thus making themselves much smaller than they really are. The truth is that man is one individual with two aspects, just like one line with two ends. If you look at the ends it is two; if you look at the line it is one. One end of the line is limited, the other end of the line is unlimited. (II 132)

This 'unlimited side' is the same as 'the light and power latent in man'. It is the spiritual man's aim to discover this unlimited side of one's self. To discover, not to theorize.

from belief to realization

> How are we to conceive of the idea of God the Absolute? We are not meant to conceive of this. As limited beings we are not able to know perfection; only perfection itself can know perfection. We can imagine and make a God of our own, in order to make God intelligible to us and to make it easier for us to advance on the spiritual path. As we advance, the unlimited Being, working through us, makes his own way and realizes His perfection. (IX 101)

By using a form we can love and understand, become

acquainted with, interested in, we forget our limited personality, we expand, we think more of the beloved ideal than of ourselves, and what was only an ideal becomes a reality.

This making of an ideal and thinking of nothing else until the ideal becomes real is beautifully portrayed in Inayat's play *Una* (XII 215-231), and explained IV 287/8. The play is based on a motive found both in the West and in the East: an artist makes a statue and becomes so deeply absorbed in this image, this work of his (her) hands, that the image comes to life.

the ideal as a means

This necessity of making an ideal first is to be found throughout Inayat's work.

> The ideal of God is a bridge connecting the limited life with the unlimited. (VII 33)

> Before one comes to the real conception of God, the first thing is to build Him in one's heart. (VII 218)

These, and many explanations in the same vein, imply that, in addition to the many concepts of God offered by the many religions there are also the personal conceptions of God; and for a mystical purpose those are important.

personal God-conceptions

> Different religions have different conceptions of God; but not only religion, every man has his own conception of God. We cannot think of any being without making a conception in our mind of that being . . . . It is a natural tendency to make a conception according to one's own experience and therefore very near to one's own self . . . . it is not a fault when someone has his own idea of God. But it is a great fault on the part of those who want to take away that idea and wish to give that person another idea . . . . No one can give to another his own conception of God because each one must make it real for himself. The prophets of all ages have given some idea to help man to form a conception of God. It has been said, 'If you have no God, make one.' That is the right way and the easiest way of realizing the unlimited truth. (VI 184/5)

Thus, Inayat's great emphasis on not fighting someone else's religion is not just tolerance; different God-conceptions are needed. Even a simple one is a means to go further. Inayat often protects the simple believer (e.g. V 184, IX 72) but also tells the modern intellectual not to believe more than his intellect allows him to. (I 200, VIII 38) And when someone—it could have been a theologian or priest—expressed doubt about leaving everybody with his own imagination of God, he said:

why God should be imagined as great

> But, one might ask, if we leave everybody with his particular imagination or ideal of God, will he then progress and one day come to the realization of the self which is the highest attainment taught by all great teachers of humanity? the answer is yes. There are three stages on the way to spiritual perfection. . . . The first stage is to make God as great and perfect as your imagination can. . . . We cannot give God pleasure by making him great, but by making God great we ourselves arrive at a certain greatness; our vision widens, our spirit deepens, our ideal reaches higher. We create a greater vision, a wider horizon, for our own expansion. We should, therefore, by way of prayer, by praise, by contemplation, try to make God as great as we can possibly imagine . . . The second stage is the work of the heart. . . . The first lesson that love teaches us, is: 'I am not, thou art.' . . . . As long as we do not arrive at this idea, so long the word love remains only in the dictionary. Many speak about love but very few know it. (VI 213-215)

Inayat illustrates this point with the anecdote of a peasant girl who passed through a field where a pious man was praying. 'And the law was that no one should pass by this place of worship. When the girl returned by the same way, she was seriously rebuked by the pious one: 'You passed by this way! It is a great sin. I was praying, thinking of God!' She said, 'Were you thinking of God? I was going to see my young man. I did not see you; how did you see me when you were thinking of God?' Inayat continues:

> To close the eyes for prayer is one thing, and to produce the love of God is another thing. That is the second stage . . . where in the thought of God one begins to lose oneself, in the same way that the lover loses the thought of

self in the thought of the beloved.

And the third stage is different again. In the third stage the beloved becomes the self, and the self is there no more. For then the self, as we think it to be, no longer remains; the self becomes what it really is. It is that realization which is called self-realization. (VI 215)

duality and unity

The two selves in the last paragraph are the limited self, the created outer form, and the inner Self, the underlying unity, our God-part. These last lines also contain an answer to a possible remark that all those concepts of God and images of God, be they loved, admired or worshipped, are as dualistic as can be, which they are.

Many theologians and students of historical mysticism stress the difference between the concept of God as perfect and therefore different from imperfect man, and God as perfect and therefore including all imperfect beings. For Inayat this is not a difference of philosophy but of development.

The whole manifestation is duality, . . . and behind duality is unity. (II 151)

First believe in the God who is all-exclusive and then realize the God who is all inclusive. (*Vadan,* p. 73)

The limitless God cannot be made intelligible to the limited self unless he is first made limited. This limited ideal becomes like an instrument, a medium of God who is perfect and who is limitless. (XI 242)

The ideal is a means but the breaking of the ideal is the goal. (VI 252)

There are some who believe in God and others who love God; and there are others who are lost in God. Those who believe in God, they are on earth and God is in heaven for them. Those who love God, for them God is before them. And those who are lost in God gained their real self. . . . Spirituality is not a certain knowledge, spirituality is the expansion of consciousness. (IV 186/7)

Inayat's own lyric and warm utterances in his musical work *Minqar-é-Musiqar* and in his later *Gayan* and *Vadan* show much of the dualistic aspect: loving God, looking for God and finding God in all sorts of names and forms. For the dualistic experience is the last stage that can be approximated in words. Mystics all over the world have known that one can 'taste and see God', but not explain him.

What limits God? His name. (*Vadan* p. 72)

IV Concepts of Mysticism and Initiation

popular misconceptions

People say that a mystic is someone who dreams and who lives in the clouds; my answer to this is that the real mystic stands on earth, but his head is in heaven. (X 24)

People think a mystic a dreamer, an unpractical person who has no knowledge of worldly affairs. But such a mystic I would call only half a mystic. (X 13)

The many misconceptions concerning mysticism are partly the same as those concerning God and faith, especially the preconceived ideas of rationalists and of 'those afraid of any experience except that of the senses' (X 139). But most of the answers to be cited here are addressed to people who associate mysticism with occultism, to those who look for something sensational, and to those who have met commercializing and fake mystics.

The Sufi does not dabble in wonder-workings. (X 49)

In this world of commercialism there is a tendency . . . , even for a person who wants to promote the spiritual truth, to cater for the taste of the people . . . . If people seem to be tired of the God-ideal, those who have that tendency want to give them occultism. (VI 207/8)

To-day a man of common sense or a man who is called a practical man is in the habit of laughing at the idea that someone has visions or experiences of ecstasy . . . . But there is nothing to be surprised at, nothing to laugh at. All these things are laughable, however, when done by the undeserving. (IV 118)

People have many misconceptions of what a mystic is. They have called a fortuneteller a mystic, or a medium, a clairvoyant, a visionary. I do not mean that a mystic does not possess all these qualities, but these qualities do not make a mystic. (X 13)

Such qualities may develop with the widening of the heart, but they are not the mystic's purpose. The Sufi's aim is to find his way to the experience of unity, that means to his innermost being, to what he essentially is.

supposed aims of mysticism

> Why do Sufis study esoteric subjects? Is it for the acquisition of spiritual powers of inspiration, to bring about phenomena, or out of curiosity? If this were so it would be wrong. Is it in order to accomplish something material or for worldly success? That is not desirable. Self-realization, to know what we are, should be the Sufi's aim. (X 87)

Hazrat Inayat's definitions

Now mysticism and self-realization are words that, through all sorts of associations, are easily misunderstood and misinterpreted. Mysticism does not mean mysterious and secretive, only hidden. Inayat did not avoid this term, but more often, especially as titles for books and lectures, he used descriptive words like 'Inner Life', 'Spiritual Attainment', 'Tuning of the Heart', 'Expansion of the Soul', 'Awakening of the Soul'. In one of his lucid explanations he says:

> The process of going from limitation to perfection is called mysticism . . . . What is meant by limitation and what by perfection? These are only conditions of the consciousness. When one is conscious of limitation, one is limited; when one is conscious of perfection, one is perfect . . . . To give an example: there was a son of a rich man who had plenty of money put in his name in the bank. But he did not know this; and when he wished to spend some money he found very little in his pocket. This made him limited. In reality his father had put a large sum in the bank, but he was not conscious of it. It is exactly the same with every soul. (IV 120)

A further description of Self-realization is God-realization or God-consciousness.

> The aim is to find God within ourselves, to dive deep into ourselves, so that we may touch the unity of the whole Being. (X 80)

One should bear in mind that the two selves, the small

temporal one—the limited being—and the Great Self—the perfect and all-embracing Being—are mutually inclusive in this philosophy of unity.

> Perfection is not in the unmanifested alone, nor in manifestation alone, but in the union of both. (VIII 26)

Because there are two selves, the created one and the only Being, there are also two aims in life, a small one and a great one.

the small and the great purpose of life

> Every intelligent person comes to a stage in his life, . . . when he begins to question himself as to what purpose there is in life . . . . 'Why am I here? What am I to accomplish in life?' he asks . . . . There are in reality two purposes of life. One is the minor, the other is the major purpose of life. One is the preliminary, and the other is the final purpose. The preliminary purpose of life is just like a stepping-stone to the final one. Therefore one should first consider the preliminary purpose of life. (VI 31 and 34)

The great purpose is to find one's way home to the common origin, and that means expansion of the soul, development of the inner life—in short 'mysticism.'

> The ultimate purpose of life . . . is always one and the same; for every man has in the end to accomplish the same purpose, in whatever way he will. He will come to it either consciously or unconsciously, easily or with difficulty; but he has to accomplish it. (VI 41)

'Is it possible for every soul to attain God-consciousness?' someone asked after a lecture, either doubting his own powers or that of his fellow-men. Inayat answered:

> Every soul is born for it. (*Sufism,* Dec. 1923, p. 13)

But the earthly purpose must be fulfilled first.

> Every soul is here on earth in order to fulfill a certain purpose in the scheme of life. (VI 222)

> The preliminary purpose is what a man will contribute to the world before awakening to spiritual perfection. (VI 36)

> The purpose of our life on earth is to look at all the distinctions and differences without being overwhelmed by them . . . We should go on, rising above them all, and at the same time experiencing them all. (VIII 98)

one-sided inclinations

Often Inayat had to warn people not to rush headlong to the great purpose. In those days it was often thought that spiritual life necessarily entailed rejecting all worldly possession and values. Ascetics or would-be ascetics asked whether they should throw out their position, their rank, and everything they had so far thought worthy of pursuit. (XII 76)

> The answer to this is that if you let the desire go unfulfilled and you lack the patience needed to accomplish the desire, your progress will be arrested. (XII 77)

That is because the unfulfilled earthly desire keeps nagging.

> If a person wishes to collect wealth, his whole mind is absorbed in it. He may be told, 'What is wealth after all? It is unreal, useless. You ought to be devotional, spiritual.' But his mind will not be there. He cannot be spiritual . . . . If one forces upon him spirituality, religion, devotion, prayer, they will not help him . . . . Spirituality comes in its time. (VI 36)

One should not force another, nor oneself. Inayat, a great mystic himself, preferred the greater world he knew, but that does not mean that he told people to deny this one.

> Why are the eyes given if not to appreciate all that is beautiful; why are the ears given if one may not enjoy music: why has one been sent on the earth if one cannot look at the earth for fear of being called materialist. Those who make spirituality out to be something like this make a bogey of God, something frightening. In point of fact spirituality is the fullness of life. (IV 129/30)

the small purpose, a stepping-stone to the great one

The fulfilling of the preliminary purpose even helps, every form of attainment is an exercise.

> One might ask, 'Would the outer purpose lead to the inner purpose of life?' Certainly it would. Everything a person

> does, spiritual or material, is only a stepping-stone for him to arrive at the inner purpose, if he can only take it to be so. (I 190)

> When once you have accomplished one desire, you will have that something which is needed for the accomplishment of something greater . . . . The steps you take towards the goal by accomplishing your desire, your patience in doing this, your perseverance with it, these are what teach you . . . . The mind gets strength and confidence. Then he can take the next step, which is the spiritual step. (XII 77/78)

This spiritual step is the beginning of 'mysticism'. One could call it initiation, again a word that may be used as a flag instead of a fact.

initiation in daily life

In a series of lectures on 'The Path of Initiation and Discipleship' (X 57-114) the master begins by giving the simplest definition possible, which not only refers to mysticism but to growth and evolution in daily life as well.

> Every experience in life is an initiation, even in worldly life one takes a step forward. (II 117)

> In point of fact initiation only means a step forward . . . If I were asked to explain the meaning of initiation in plain words, I would say that it is like the experience of a person who has never learnt how to swim, and he steps into the river or into the sea for the first time, without knowing whether he will be able to float. (X 61)

Then follow everyday examples of the first attempts of a man who wants to learn to ride, and of a businessman beginning an entirely new enterprise, but Inayat adds:

spiritual initiation

> Initiation in the real sense of the word . . . takes place when a person . . . feels that he should take a step in a direction which he does not know. (X 61)

This natural initiation, as Inayat calls it, may come at any time of one's life, to the young as well to those advanced in years. Sometimes it occurs after great illness, pain or suffering (X 72), but it may happen without any conceivable cause. The ways in which it is manifested differ too. 'It may come as a vision, as a dream, as a phenomenon,' (X 72), but also as just wondering.

> It comes in the form of a sudden change of outlook on life; a person feels that he has suddenly awakened to quite another world; although he remains in the same world it has become totally different for him. Things which seemed important become less important. (X 92)

What happens at such a moment is depicted by Inayat in another image. Some of the covers of the soul (see Chapter 'Life before Life') are rent or partially lifted, and one loosens one's thoughtless identification with a limited form.

> Naturally with the next step the horizon of his outlook becomes wider, and the soul reaches further while life becomes more clear. (X 92)

The tragic fact is that, especially in the West, people do not often understand this change.

recognizing natural initiation

> Among a hundred people perhaps only one is really conscious of it. (X 93)

The one who understands what is happening will try to go on. As a rule one looks for a master (X 85) to learn what it is about and to be shown the way. A few specially gifted souls retire into solitude and there may receive direct guidance, but almost every advanced recluse had a master once.

Most of Inayat's disciples in the West were, and are, people who feel that there is something more than meets the eye, but who have to go on living their daily life. For them

> the Sufi Movement has made it possible . . ., by serious study and practice, to obtain glimpses of the truth which the ancient mystics possessed. (II 171)

lay mystics

This simplifying of mysticism and its adjustment to western circumstances had been difficult. Inayat worked at it during the years 1914-1919. Step by step he developed a graded 12-year course for his disciples, which could be read to them in his absence and after his death. A disciple is invited to a next course as he goes along. Everyone is given his strictly personal exercises, adapted to his needs and his evolution; one is supposed not to talk about these with others, not even with fellow-mureeds. (mureed = pupil, disciple). In general, keeping quiet about the inner work, not making a show or fuss about it, is essential.

> The really initiated ones hardly ever mention the word initiation. (X 74)

how to recognize a great mystic

How, then, is one to know that a person is a true mystic? This is a question that Inayat, when he himself was a disciple, put to his own master.

> Once I asked my spiritual teacher how we can recognize the godly man. And my teacher replied, 'It is not what he says and it is not what he seems to be, but it is the atmosphere that his presence creates. That is the proof. For no one can create an atmosphere which does not belong to his spirit.' (IV 133, 156; XI 35)

Of course this refers to the great mystic, the master. These advanced ones are 'God-realized,' and their blending into the Only Being means such a widening, such a progressing far beyond any limitation of visible things and beyond the power of normal words, that radiating something of this experience is almost the only way in which it may be at all communicated.

how to recognize the beginner's progress

The beginner and the lay mystic can know whether they are really progressing by observing their change of outlook which should, also, be recognizable as a widening.

> There is only one way to recognize this process, and that is to see the progress in one's own outlook on life, to ask oneself the question, 'How do I look at life?' This one can do not by judging others . . . ; as long as a person is concerned with the faults of others, . . . he is not yet ready to make his sight clear enough to see if his outlook on life is right. (X 89)

Inayat had often to repeat such simple remarks—maybe admonishments—, because in their first zeal many were hasty and expected to reach the ultimate purpose in a single leap.

They ask for concentration at the tea-table. (IV 173)

Very often people ask, 'How long has one to go on the spiritual path?' There is no limit to the length of this path, and yet if one is ready, it does not need a long time. (I 197)

attitude more important than speed

To be ready is essential. Some are born mystics, and their progress is great. But for most people the goal can only be reached by a laborious process of growth, adjustment and gradual widening. Inayat's answers are mostly to the latter, but he often describes the former.

A mystic is born; it is a temperament, it is a certain outlook on life, it is a certain attitude towards life that makes a man a mystic. His chief characteristic is that he knows the meaning of every action. (X 32)

It is a certain type of mind which is born mystical; but mysticism can also be acquired. A soul who is born a mystic will from his cradle show mystic tendencies; but mysticism which is acquired is a greater achievement, for then one has made a normal progress towards divine wisdom. (XI 151)

The important thing is sincerity.

There are no fixed rules to follow on this path. For every person there is a special rule. But there is one law which applies to everything in life: sincerity, which is the only thing that is asked by a teacher of a pupil, for truth is not the portion of the insincere. (X 74)

when should one become an initiate

In one of the old issues of the periodical *Sufi* the question 'When should one become an initiate?' is posed and answered.

When you feel inclined to know something different from the knowledge that is taught in the world./ When your heart begins to become more sympathetic than ever before./ When from within you feel a seeking for something which you do not know./ When your sense of justice begins to judge yourself before judging others./ When all opposites, such as good and evil, right and wrong, friend and foe, seem to you drawing nearer. (*Sufi,* April 1919, p. 6 and 7)

when not

This list is followed by some warnings concerning those 'who should rather not become an initiate'. One should refrain from it, if one comes 'merely for the sake of curiosity', 'to peep into the secret Order'. Joining was also not appropriate for a rigid character, 'he who advanced himself to a certain extent in some spiritual ideals, and set before himself certain unmovable principles.' Furthermore, one should not change teachers. 'He who belongs to some secret order of a religious or mystical kind,' should not take an initiation in Inayat's order 'for it would be as dangerous as taking a prescription from two doctors at the same time, or travelling in two boats, one leg in one and the other in the other.' But that does not mean that one order is considered better than the other. And of course one should not ask for Inayat's initiation if one 'distinguishes among the great Masters of humanity who were but the embodiment of the divine Spirit, and attaches importance to the differences of the principles of the world's various faiths.'

This corresponds with the ideal of universal Sufism as explained in a previous chapter, but it does not follow that all the different forms are denied. On the contrary, Inayat knew and described various methods and forms and sometimes gave a short summary of the main methods of inner development:

different schools and methods

> The methods of gaining that realization (God-realization) are many, but there are four principal ones: by the heart, by the head, by action, by repose. A person must choose from among these four different methods of developing himself and preparing himself to journey on the way, the only way, which is called mysticism. No religion can call it its own, but it is the way of all religions. (X 28)

Indeed the description of the final result, in as far as it can be described, is the same in schools as far apart as some forms of Japanese Zen and medieval Kabbala; the one a mysticism without a God concept, the other beginning with a personal God distinctly delineated and marked off from mankind; the first exercises of the one may be found in concentrated sword fighting or archery, of the other in concentrated ordering of letters—starting points widely different from those of the virtue-conscious Christian mystic and even from the many-sided Hindu. But all culminate in God-realization, also described as Being or Self-realization. And their descriptions of light, wideness, inexpressible peace all resemble each other. Complete concentration is one means they all have in common.

In the ensuing chapters some of the methods, Inayat's reports of means and results both of the great mystic and of the beginner and lay mystic will be traced. In the last chapter the possibility and effect of a mystical attitude in daily life will be considered. For one of the characteristics of Inayat's universal Sufism is a positive attitude to daily life.

mysticism and daily life

> The inner life is not necessarily in an opposite direction to the worldly life, but the inner life is a fuller life. The worldly life means the limitation of life: the inner life means a complete life. (I 67/8)

> The work of the spiritual man is to forget his false self and to realize the true Self, which is God; and to realize that this true Self is in his brother also. (XI 250)

'In his brother also.' If God is the only Being, he is shared by everyone. Inayat never forgot that. He often defined mysticism as 'serving God and mankind'. (for instance IV 126)

> If we can be of some little use to anybody, we can more easily learn what mysticism is; for the only real mysticism is when a person realizes he pleases God by pleasing mankind. (VII 271)

He was well aware of the fact that some schools of mysticism do turn their back to the world and he regarded this as the one difference with the practice of Sufism. But as he had learned in the first movement of his own 'change of outlook': God is to be found in what He has created. (see p. 31)

> The mystic seeks God both within and without: he recognizes God both in unity and variety. (XI 254)

This means completeness, balance. Mysticism was so natural to Inayat that he once said:

> To be without inner life is like being without an arm or a leg or an eye or an ear. (VI 151)

At the same time he came to realize that many did not

understand what he meant.

> If we say to a person who has never had a headache in his life, 'I have a headache,' he will never understand it; he will not know what it is. Therefore the word mysticism means nothing; it is through the inner experience that one realizes its meaning and fullness. (XI 145)

mysticism not an aim in itself

He also warns that mysticism is not an aim in itself.

> Mysticism is a means to an end. Mysticism is not the goal, but through it one arrives at the goal. (XII 20)

What does a mystic do?

> In man there is a spark somewhere hidden in his heart . . . What does the mystic do? He blows this spark in order to bring it to a flame till it comes to a blaze . . . To become spiritual means that by blowing upon this spark one produces light from it and sees the whole of life in this light, and by bringing the inner light to a blaze one is more able to think, to feel and to act. (IV 147/148)

V Mysticism, Methods and Means

preconceived ideas about techniques

'How is it done?'

This is one of the first questions coming from the audience after a talk on Sufism. It is a twentieth century attitude to expect a handy little push button for everything. Inayat had soon discovered this almost unconscious belief in techniques, but he did not cater for it as many others do. He might warn against it with a tactful joke, even if the occurrence that induced his remark had been painful to him. Once a man posed as an enthusiastic member of his society but really intended to 'steal' his method. This experience had amazed and shocked Inayat, but he merely remarked:

> It is not an engineer's invention that could be stolen. (*Sufi*, 1918, April, p. 7)

drugs

He also commented on drugs, which were not yet as widely used in the West then as in the second half of the century. Once or twice he mentioned the use of drugs by a certain kind of adept in the East, but he noted that it could have no lasting effect.

> There are people who take strong drink, opium, drugs and all such things. Under their influence the troubles of the body are felt less and the thoughts are blurred, the soul feels relieved; but it is a transitory happiness because it is dependent upon matter instead of spirit. (V 86)

theoretical knowledge and occult experiments

There are other things Inayat considered to be outer, ineffective methods, in particular playing and experimenting with so-called occult phenomena. Moreover, an occidental may wonder and even frown at Inayat's frequent criticism of too much reading. What he meant was that theoretical knowledge and talking about mysticism will not, in themselves, lead to an experience of unity.

How many souls are searching for some outer things that

can make them spiritual: dogmas, phenomena, experiments, anything but the exploring of the self! . . . . Man is pleased with something he cannot understand and thinks that it therefore must be mysticism. (XI 203)

To my great surprise, while travelling in the West I saw people looking for books about Yoga, Yogis, spiritual attainment. Many have lost their mind by reading such books. They cannot keep balance. Trying to do what is in the book is just like going into the drugstore to get some Yoga-pills in order to attain spirituality. (IV 174)

Imagine how reading about occult science should entitle one to spirituality! The language of that country is different, and intellectual knowledge is not current there; the learning there consists of unlearning what we have learned here. (VIII 161)

unlearning To unlearn is a keyword and one of the first things to practice. It means getting rid of preconceived ideas and such knowledge as keeps the consciousness limited. There is a lecture on the subject to be found in IV, p. 108, and *Vadan* 72 says:

The real learning is unlearning all that one has learned. (*Vadan* 72)

To begin with, this means taking nothing for granted.

The first step in learning mysticism is just this: to develop our observations. We are always looking at a hundred things around us, and hardly ever study one thing properly at all. To understand and know a thing better we must keep looking at it. (XII 66)

This thorough study of people, of oneself, of reactions, of nature, of anything is so essential a method that it is included in the ten Sufi Thoughts:

There is one Holy Book, the sacred manuscript of nature, the only scripture which can enlighten the reader. (IX 267, I 15) *study of life* Study of life is an old method, a classical one. Inayat loved to tell the story of Shams Tabriz, Rumi's spiritual teacher who threw out his books—Rumi being a scholar—and told him to study life instead (for instance X 137/138). This rejection of bookish knowledge often was the reaction of mystics who followed the 'religion of the heart' as opposed to the orthodox clinging to a book. But in the West, and in the twentieth century, the warning made sense as well. Not only because of too theoretical or dogmatic dependence on theological or other philosophies, but because of a naive belief in the printed word in general. For nature, in the Sufi idea quoted, does not mean trees and birds, though they come into it too, but all that exists. Once, after a lecture, Inayat was asked, 'In the rules[1] of the Sufi Order what is meant by the Book of Nature?' He answered with a single word:

> Life. (*Sufism,* December 1923, p. 13)

Inayat's lectures abound with remarks like 'if one studies life rightly,' 'for the student of life', 'by studying life one finds', etcetera. He used it for all fields, for observation of cosmological facts, for the probing of art and history, but above all for spiritual development.

> Life itself becomes a scripture to the kindled soul, (*Gayan,* p. 22, new 36)
>
> The work of the mystic is to study life. (X 34)
>
> Life is the answer to the mystic's question. (XI 212)

Of course, it has to be a real observing.

> One can see, one can look, and one can observe . . . By observing we understand something about what we see; by seeing we take full notice; by looking we glance at it without necessarily understanding it or taking notice of it. (VIII 39)

Inayat's disciples were often amazed to notice how well and how much their murshid used to observe. Sometimes they themselves were given an exercise to observe unknown persons

[1] The word 'rules' marks the speaker. Inayat did not set rules, for rules may breed rigidity. (See page 8)

and to conclude whether these might be spiritually gifted or not. Most pupils could not do it, such observation was quite new to them. All the same, study of life is a method that can be applied for outer as well as for inner knowledge.

> The seekers after the truth of life, the students of life, are of two opposite kinds. The one wishes to learn from outward appearance; the other wishes to find out the secret that is hidden behind it. The one who learns from the external, gets the knowledge from the external, which we call science; the one who finds out from within, from what is hidden in this manifestation, is the mystic. The knowledge he gains is mysticism. (II 121).

The mystic can combine the two kinds of knowledge, letting the inner knowledge complete the outer one. (IV 266) But for his spiritual development proper he has to begin with studying human nature.

> The definition of spiritual attainment can be found in the study of human nature. (VI 17)

> No book can give the joy and the pleasure that human nature itself can give. The wise, the foolish, the good, the weak, whom we meet every day with their tendencies and their attitudes, are all the greatest material for study. Besides, there is so much to study in success and failure, in sorrows and pleasures, and in all things in life, whether unfavourable or favourable. All that we do right, all that we do wrong, everything is a lesson, everything is a study if we take it as such. But the important thing is this: that the one who is life's student, the one who is really initiated, studies himself before studying others. (X 89/90)

The study of human nature comprises both outer actions, reactions and facts, and the inner truth. The aim is to discover 'the universe in man' (XII 47-51). Therefore study of human nature can be specified more closely as study of one's own nature, by talking with oneself.

study of self

> To explain in simple words what the spiritual path is, I would say that it begins by living in communication with

oneself. (X 48)

Inayat means a real and simple questioning and answering. It is important not to be vague but to find accurate and unbiased answers to one's wondering and probing.

> The first training is analysis, and the second training is synthesis. The analytical striving is to analyse one's own consciousness, in other words one's conscience; . . . . One should speak to one's conscience as a man going to the priest . . . 'Look what I have done. Maybe it is wrong, maybe it is right; but you know it. . . . If you are happy, only then I can be happy . . . how can I do it?' (IV 233/234)

There are many examples of such self-conversation in the lectures, but the most interesting thing is that we can trace how he did it himself. In his book on Indian music, dance and poetry, *Minqar-é-Musiqar,* p. 2, there are a few poems written by Inayat himself in the years of his own discipleship (1903-1907). It is touching to hear him address himself: 'O Inayat! Where are you? Just walk cautiously. It is a place of respect. Control yourself, control yourself.' Or, still more severe with himself, 'O Inayat, be through with it. You and this high talk. How dare you shout aloud about Truth.' (p. 8). How many beginners will be critical of their love for a beautiful word?

Words are a help and a danger. Inayat's study of western life had taught him that his words often met with a wrong association and he was careful to state that self-analysis and communication with self did not mean worrying or egocentric gloom.

> Now the question is, how does man communicate with his self? By self-analysis. No doubt there is a danger in self-analysis. When a person is always wondering how wrong he is, how bad he is, how wicked he is, or how stupid he is, he will never stop worrying and troubling himself . . . The mystic delves deeper in himself in order to discover what it is in him that lives and what it is that dies, what it is in his being that is limited and what it is that is beyond limitation. (XI 151)

In a chapter on 'Self-Knowledge' (XI 196-200) a survey of the stages of self-discovery is given. First there is the body, in its physical appearance and also as an instrument 'more perfect than a radio-receiver'. Through the body one finds the power of breath; then follow one's possibilities of developing mind and feeling; until one comes to the underlying unity of being.

The beginner should look into himself to examine his motives, his attitude and qualities. One may start from sheer curiosity, but to proceed one needs more solid qualities.

One of these qualities is courage, for the adept has to go into an unknown world (X 61) and his family and surroundings may be opposed to his choice or laugh at it. (X 78/79 and 92) He needs patience, for the beginning is as tedious as every beginning. (VI 261, X 79) But the two most imperative qualities are openness (love) and trust.

trust

Trust includes faith, confidence and self-confidence. In a chapter on 'Faith' (VII 87-97) Inayat states that—'when we study life minutely'—we find that every soul is born with trust, but in most lives the original gift of trust becomes diminished, broken, buried or almost lost.

> The course of human life involves so many disappointments, so many failures, so many heart-aches, that no one can avoid doubting. There is a peasant saying, 'He who has once burned his tongue with hot milk tries to cool even buttermilk by blowing on it.' When a man has been deceived by one person, he distrusts ten people. . . . Ater failing in one thing he suspects he will fail in a thousand things. (VII 88)

misgivings about trust

After Inayat's lectures many people put questions which showed that they looked for rigid and absolute standards such as 'should one trust everybody?' Or they cherished sly sceptic objections like 'is it wise to trust?' But confidence and trust do not mean blind faith. Inayat warned the gullible not to believe sheer nonsense or deluding promises (VII 90) and to the sad sceptic he said:

> You need not trust the one whom you do not know, so long as you do not distrust him. (*Vadan* p. 70)

> Confidence is assured, not by blind belief but by careful insight into the life which surrounds us. (VII 91)

The first answer is typical for Inayat's way of meeting daily problems, uncertainties and evil. The second refers to the study of life. One should observe things—and trust one's own observation. Self-confidence is the base to build on.

> A person who does not believe in himself cannot believe in anybody else, and is really an unbeliever. Faith must begin within. Belief in oneself should be so strong that even if a thousand people say 'no', one will say 'yes'. To look to others for every opinion, not trusting oneself to say whether it is day or night, is to end by not only distrusting others but by developing a kind of insanity. (VII 90)

In our days, wherein people readily profess opinions unhampered by knowledge of facts, it is perhaps wise to repeat: a conviction should be based on observation and inference, which implies a rational use of reason.

> Reason is the master of the unbeliever and the servant of the believer. (*Gayan,* p. 48, n. 81)

Inayat's examples of the wrong combination of trust and reason and the right one mostly concern an achievement in everyday life, like failure or success in one's work (int.al. VII 95). For spiritual growth the re-establishment of trust and confidence needs discernment and self-knowledge and most of all unbiased attitude of mind.

re-development of trust

There is a difference between ready mistrust, ready trust and offered trust. To offer trust, to begin with an open attitude has psychological results.

> A person may think, 'is it right to trust everybody? There are many people who are not worthy of trust; shall we then trust everybody in order to develop our trust?' The answer is, yes. (VII 95)

To learn skating one has to skate, never mind falls. To learn trusting one has to trust, never mind disappointments. To go on mistrusting will feed mistrust in oneself as well as in the one who is mistrusted.

> Perhaps we will have a few failures, but we will only trust another person when we trust ourselves. . . . To have faith in another is to have faith in ourselves. It does not matter if once or twice we are disappointed; but if we are afraid of being disappointed . . . there will never come a time when we will be able to trust anybody, even ourselves. There are many things that can develop our trust. Sometimes an unworthy person can become worthy of trust. (VII 95/96)

The last remark goes with Inayat's philosophy of movement and growth, which also applies to ethics. But to accept failure without giving up is a spiritual exercise indeed.

> Failure in life does not matter; the greatest misfortune is standing still. (*Gayan,* p. 29, n. 47)
>
> To fall down does not break or discourage me; it only enables me to rise to a still higher sphere of life. (*Gayan,* p. 65, n. 104)

Inayat's trust

Inayat's own life is a true example of success through trust. In his work, both as a musician and as a teaching mystic, he had to recommence several times. Often because he had left a place where he was well-known for a new site where he was a stranger; several times because outer circumstances shattered the foundation he had been laying for his work. But in the end he did attain everything he had ever wished to attain. His own spiritual teacher had shown him from the first the importance of trust for an adept. Amused, Inayat used to recall how amazed he was when his murshid (master, guru) blessed him with the words 'may your faith be strengthened.' (VI 211, XI 84)

looking for a master

His pupils needed to be reminded of the importance of trust and self-confidence. Even in his *Autobiography* Inayat mentions that some of the difficulties they had were caused by their lack of confidence, especially self-confidence. One should not seek a master—which is the second stage in one's spiritual growth, not the first—unless one can trust and is worthy of trust.

Initiation by a spiritual teacher means both a trust given by the teacher to the pupil, and a trust given by the pupil to the teacher. (X 72)

fear of authoritarian masters

The words 'master' and 'full trust in the master' gave rise to much misunderstanding. It is a common presumption that a 'master' is 'authoritarian' and wants to boss or use his pupils for his own purposes. Indeed in everyday life there is no lack of men in leading positions who tend to abuse their position; which generally means they are basically uncertain and afraid, or that they love power for power's sake. A real spiritual teacher is not afraid and he is not interested in power. But many of those who protest against authorities and masters are themselves prone to bossing others around. Of these Inayat said, with sad irony:

> Man does not like to be a pupil, he likes to be a teacher. (II 150)
>
> Today the prevailing thought is that no man should guide his fellow-men and that there is no virtue in such guidance. This thought is so widespread that it is preventing people from seeking guidance from someone who is facing the same struggles, the same troubles, who has the same experiences as everyone else. (X 96)

These last words imply that a master has gone through struggles similar to those faced by the pupil, and that a disciple will some day outgrow another person's guidance.

> In reality there is no such thing as a teacher; God alone is Teacher, we all are disciples. (X 103)

Initiation means initation on the part of the disciple and on the part of the teacher, a step forward on the path of both. (X 77)

> The satisfaction of the teacher lies in the advancement of the pupil. (X 74)
>
> The teacher does not hold the pupil indefinitely. (X 97)
>
> It is the desire to learn continually that makes one a teacher, and not the desire to become a teacher. (X 109)

There are many answers in this vein for those afraid of being *expecting perfection*

mastered and subjected. The reverse was needed just as often, maybe still more. Very many people came for shelter, for help and support from the master. This kind of follower expected a rigid perfection and became critical when he did not fit their fancy.

> However great, however deep, however spiritual a person is, with all his goodness, with all his inspiration and power, he remains limited. His thought, speech, word, and action are all limited. A man cannot make himself as his pupil imagines him. (X 67)

> If man wants to find perfection in a limited being, he will always end by being disappointed in whoever he meets, whether it is an angel or a human being. (X 105)

many kinds of masters

Then what is a master, if he is neither an authoritarian tyrant nor a day dream's image of perfection come true?

There are many kinds of masters. Given the word *guru*, many Westerners think of the holy recluse in the Himalayas. Those retired saints do exist, but there may well be many other enlightened souls who hide their powers from others, except from these few who are open and trustful enough to recognize a master. Among those *gurus* who present themselves to the world as such there may be several kinds of fraud, like the hypocrite, the money-hunter, the vain one greedy for servility, and the trickster, catering to the taste for occult phenomena. (XII 147, X 63) One can discern the true masters, because they spread quiet and healing. A layman will have some difficulty in discovering the hidden mystics; and he may be puzzled because they differ in talents, in power and attainment. Great saints are few, simple teachers of different grades of evolution are everywhere. They will do.

> It is the devotion of the initiated which supplies all that is lacking in the initiator, and it is the trust of the initiator which supplies all that is lacking in the initiated. (X 85)

Then what is the work of the master, if the pupil has to contribute so much himself?

ways of teaching

> The work of the mystical teacher is not to teach but to tune. (X 73)

> What the murshid does in the life of the mureed is to show him how he can clear his path towards the light within him by his own self. (I 47)

> The murshid is only a medium and as high as the response of the mureed reaches, so strongly does it attract the message of God. (X 109)

This means that, in the first place, the master does not theorise nor supervise exercises, but he gives a chance to join in his own experience of underlying unity. Inayat himself had been inspired in that way by his own master. 'The chain of murshids'; and 'the unity of illuminated souls' are essential conceptions in Sufism. Eastern adepts are taught an exercise in which all the names of a chain of murshids are repeated; thus one may share the light of guidance.

> The chain of murshids, . . . means the passing on of divine knowledge from one soul to another, and from that soul to another yet again. (IV 281)

> We see how one person is illuminated by another, how one learns from another. Whatever the name of the teacher, there is still the one stem of life and light. (VII 225)

That is why there is so much teaching in silence. The master gives his most important 'lessons' by being, by his attitude, by radiating. And when he does speak it is often in symbols. Quite often his words are not understood immediately; and his silence still less so.

> The teacher does not always teach in plain words. The spiritual teacher has a thousand ways. It may be that by his prayers he can guide his disciple; it may be by his thought, his feeling, or his sympathy, so that even at a distance he may guide him. And therefore when a disciple thinks he can be taught only by words or teachings, by practices or exercises, it is a great mistake. (X 106)

> People often ask me questions which I cannot very well answer in words; and it makes me sad to think they are unable to hear the voice of my silence. (*Nirtan* p. 22)

Of the many who expected an interesting discussion on metaphysical ideas, Inayat said:

> Such a person may be called a student, but not yet a disciple. (X 104)

help in personal difficulties

There was another western attitude that surprised the master. Most people came to him for support, not for spiritual attainment. He did not reject them,—nor did he reject the talkative lovers of metaphysics—he did give support but as much as possible, he showed the clinging ones how they could become stronger. The reminiscenses of his disciples abound in examples of his help and of the tactful ways in which he bent their weak or self-pitying attitude to something stronger. 'If we came to him with difficulties, he let us find the answer ourselves, in one split second.' (SK 32, similar notes 33, 35, 37, 44, 67, 78)

However, a seeker of spiritual progress also needs his master's help to outgrow his personal difficulties.

> The first thing the teacher does is to find out what is the pressing need of his disciple, whether the disciple speaks of it or not. And the teacher's effort is directed towards removing that first difficulty, because he knows it to be an obstacle in the disciple's way . . . . Thus a desire can be fulfilled, it can be conquered, or it can be removed. If it is fulfilled so much the better. If it is not right to fulfil it then it should be conquered or removed in order to clear the way. The teacher never thinks that he is concerned with his disciple only in his spiritual progress, for if there is something blocking the way of his disciple it will not be easy for the teacher to help him. (X 106/107)

paying one's debts

Apart from desires one wants to fulfill because of one's earthly purpose of life, there are the debts to consider. Especially for those who hope to travel all the way, it is important that they have no 'debts' to their family: that there is nobody dependent on them. It is well-known that in the East a Hindu family man may retire for spiritual life, after fulfilling his task, his duty to his family and his community. For the lay mystic to pay his debts may mean that he has found the right attitude to the people in his surroundings.

> The first thing that is necessary is to see that there is no debt to be paid. Every soul has a certain debt to pay in his life; it may be to his mother or father, his brother or sister, to his husband or wife or friend, or to his children, his race, or to humanity; and if he has not paid what is due, then there are cords with which he is inwardly tied, and they pull him back . . . . Man must also consider, before starting on his journey, whether he has learned all he desired to learn from this world . . . . Every desire, every ambition, every aspiration that he has had in life must be gratified. Not only this . . . . there must be no grudge against anybody, and no complaining of anyone having done him harm, for all these things . . . would become a burden on the spiritual path. (I 65/66)

> There are many other debts, to our neighbours, to strangers, to those who depend upon us or who expect from us some help, some counsel, a word of advice, some service. They are all debts we have to pay . . . . There is a condition that must be fulfilled, and that condition is our consideration for every soul. (VI 162/163)

many kinds of disciples

Apart from the difference between the full mystic and the lay mystic there are all sorts of differences in character and disposition, and a great many ways one can choose. Some types one finds described I 102-106. Anyhow one should choose the way most suited to one's character and never force oneself.

> There is no end to the variety of the outward appearance of spiritual souls in life; but at the same time there is no better way of living in this world and yet living the inner life than being *oneself,* outwardly and inwardly. (I 105/106)

beginner's difficulties

One finds lectures and chapters about discipleship in more than one volume. (for instance IX 125-144, X 57-114, XII 106-117) Some of these talks describe the evolution of full mystics and great sages; Inayat's audiences loved to hear about them and he himself loved to tell about them. But his own pupils were laymen mostly and very often he had to speak about their specific difficulties. Most Westerners when attempting to meditate, are disturbed by straying thoughts, struggle with their first exercises and often drop them. Inayat's centre conductors in America, who had to work alone most of the time, asked him what they should do in such cases. The master answered:

> This is not a serious matter. If the mureed has good feeling, a desire for progress, is respecting his Teacher, has sympathy with the others, wish for spreading the Message, and because of pressure of work or some other reasons he cannot do the practices, it does not matter. The Initiator must not be troubled by it. Yet he must continually bring to the ears of the mureed that the practices are the most valuable thing in the world. Do not command that they *must* be done. The very command will spoil the thing. Bring before him the benefit of it. It is this which will rouse them. I have seen . . . . a day came when they were awakened to it. It is never too late. (*Instruction Interview,* Detroit, 1926)

In this instruction-interview Inayat stresses another point: the mureeds should not talk about their exercises, not even with their co-mureeds or with husband or wife. For beginners this is imperative.

> When the husband or wife is advanced in the Order then they might if they may help each other. If they are only beginning both have different practices; by discussing them with one another they spoil the benefit. (*Instruction Interview*)

One finds a similar remark in I 51. There is a variety of masters, a variety of disciples and a great variety of exercises at the start.

> The murshid is also like a physician. He prescribes to each mureed medicine suited to his needs. The same medicine could not be given to all. (V 222)

variety of exercises and lessons

So one cannot give a survey of all exercises. Some pupils were given little symbolical acts to perform. Many were helped by a vow; they themselves could choose the vow and then tell it to Murshid; telling him made it almost impossible not to fulfill the vow; and having fulfilled one little thing, they could proceed with something more difficult. Now and then a pupil was taught the physical hatha yoga exercises, a rather unusual thing in the first quarter of the century. The earliest pupils were still given musical and poetical exercises, as is usual in the Chishti training. But the Persian poems were unfamiliar to most pupils, only some students of oriental classics profited by them. A much used and well remembered means were the symbolical tales illustrating unconditional love and perfect concentration. On the other hand Inayat might give very realistic and down-to-earth lessons. In a course for centre-conductors the candidates were led in group discussion; they should answer each other's questions; these questions were not to touch on metaphysical subjects, but on problems of daily life and psychology only. 'If we could not answer each other's questions, or sometimes when an answer had been given, Murshid said a few words and opened for us the depth of the questions and problems that were touched upon.' (SK 37) The reminiscenses of disciples have one remark in common: the printed words of his inheritance are nothing compared to his presence. His presence answered questions, his presence lifted his pupils above their daily level, he inspired and consoled.

The only thing those living later can do is to approach his recorded words with the open attitude of the disciple; and some of the warmth and power of the way they were spoken will echo. One may start reading intellectually, even put down the book, but one sentence will stick, one cannot forget it and will turn it around in one's mind. That is exactly what a pupil should do:

> receiving the knowledge, meditating upon it patiently, assimilating all the outcome of it intelligently. (X 66)

This way of study from listening to assimilating through thinking about the subject, will do for secular courses too. However, the student of mysticism does not only learn facts, but above all actions, non-actions and attitudes. To assimilate the so-called esoteric exercises one needs conscious concentration, and this concentration has to be learned. The disciple who has reached assimilation and is practising the teacher's lessons in life, can go further without a master. (X 66)

In the early stage, the receptive one, there are some experiences every adept has to go through. One of these are the tests.

tests

> The path of initiation is also a path of tests: tests from the initiatior, tests from God, tests from the self, and tests from the world; and to go through these tests is the sign of real progress in the mureed. (X 81)

Maybe to counterbalance some disciples' trend to invest things spiritual with dark solemnity, Inayat often calls these tests amusing. He loved to tell the story of a Sufi-master of old, a good Muslim, who went to pray in the temple of the Hindu goddess Kali. Only one of his disciples had faith enough to follow him there. When asked why he did, he too gave the right answer: 'None exists but God'. (X 64-66)

One may conclude that this act of the master tried the disciples on two points. It was a test of trust and a test of assimilation; did they trust their master unreservedly, and was the underlying unity only a word for them or a reality.

Other proofs serve to test imperturbability and self-confidence. Again Inayat illustrates his subject with a light touch:

> It is like looping the loop; sometimes the teacher gives the pupil such tests that he does not know where he is, or whether a thing is true or false. (X 64)

But essentially the test is deep and probing.

> If you wish to probe the depths of a man's character test him with that which is his life's greatest need. (*Gayan* 30, n. 49)

Furthermore, a test may be needed as a spur against rigidity. A real adept is supple, always growing. Sometimes Inayat compares the work of the teacher with that of a gardener, or with a goldsmith 'who has to melt the gold first in order to make an ornament of it'. (X 97) *the pupil as a test for the master*

In some respects the pupil becomes a test for the initiator. Inayat's American centre leaders put their problems before him in June 1926 and some of his answers to them are answers to other people's questions too. Therefore I quote from this interview not only two bits about the initiator's difficulties but also one about another subject that goes with tests: self-discipline and the many wrong conceptions about it.

> The wrong attitude of a mureed is the one time when the initiator is most tested . . . the power of the initiator must work all the time, must turn a pebble into a diamond, slowly and in time, he must maintain the hope of helping this person. But to maintain a hope and to persevere with a person is one thing, to trust a person who is still unripe with practices is another. The first attitude is strength, the second is weakness. It is the work of the initiator to go on with patience, it does not matter how long.
>
> . . . . Then about self-discipline. Some mureeds think it good to fast all day long. Others think it good to fast three or four days; they prescribe for themselves. But the mureedship is not for that. . . . Fasting is good but not always a virtue. Sometimes it is a great disadvantage without having taken the advice of the initiator. There are many things they prescribe for themselves, for self-discipline. That proves he is neglecting the existence of the initiator.

preconceptions about self-discipline

There are already warnings against the overrating of fasting and the like in the 1913-book. (V 9-36) But there were others who connected discipline (trust of the master) and self-discipline with being ordered about, with unnaturalness, and repression of spontaneity. Nothing was more foreign to Inayat's nature than forced virtues and maxims on naturalness and spontaneity are found in *Gayan* and *Vadan* and in the lectures; they are both a condition to begin and a result of one's spiritual growth. Those who mistrust the idea of discipline confuse the moralism of suppressing desires and the art of acknowledging and handling desires. Thus on the one hand Inayat had to calm down the demonstrative lovers of fasting and self-torture, on the other hand he had to explain to the lovers of freedom that discipline and self-discipline need not rob one of one's freedom but make it stronger and more real.

> What counts most in the path of truth is self-discipline, for without this our studies and practices cannot produce great results. . . . No doubt it frightens people living in the world, accustomed to a life of comfort, even to think of self-discipline; and when they do think of it they imagine it only in its extreme forms. (VIII 45)

> People come with preconceived ideas. They are willing to learn, but they do not want discipline. (IV 195)

> Self-discipline, however difficult and tyrannical it might seem to us in the beginning, yet is that which in the end makes the soul the master of self. (II 239)

what self-discipline is

> Once one is master of self one is master of life . . . we become its master in proportion to the degree in which we have attained self-mastery. (XII 108)

> Self-discipline is to be able to say: I can. (VI 199)

To develop self-discipline there is one thing that should not be applied and that is force, constraint. 'Spiritual attainment has to be reached little by little (IV 151), forced virtues are of no use (see page nos. 186 and 198), will-power can develop naturally. (IV 169)

The opposite of forcing is needed: relaxation. To relax one's muscles one has to use them first. The same goes for mind and feeling.

> How does one relax the mind? The method for relaxation of the mind is first to make the mind tired. . . . Relaxation of feeling is achieved by feeling deeply. (IV 166)

mastery through relaxation

These words are the gist of a chapter on 'Mystic Relaxation'. (IV 162-174) Sometimes the question was asked whether 'relaxation' or 'stillness of the mind' would lead to laziness. Of course not. (VII 124)

That is one of the strange preconceived ideas of people who seek to escape in over-activity; or of those who escape from life in over-passivity and want to give laziness a nicer name. But the greatest difficulty for Hazrat Inayat Khan was to show Westerners that mind and body are not opposite and basically different forces but that they are closely connected.

body and mind interdependent

> The first step to the relaxation of the mind is the relaxation of the body. (IV 112).
>
> The mind cannot be mastered until man is master of the body. (VII 158)

preconceptions about the body

In such lectures as deal with 'The Control of the Body' (IV 126-132) and 'Physical Control' (VIII 49-53) Inayat had to reckon with centuries old western mistrust of the body. Mastering the body does not mean to deplore its existence and to try to forget it, but to understand, know and rule it.

> Many people think that the physical has little to do with the spiritual. Why not, they ask, cast the idea of the physical aside in order to be entirely spiritual? If without the physical aspect of our being the purpose of life could be accomplished, the soul would not have taken a physical body and the spirit would not have produced the physical world. (IV 126)
>
> The conception that the physical body is made of sin, and that this is the lowest aspect of being, will very often prove to be a mistake, for it is through this physical body that the highest and greatest purpose of life is to be achieved. (IV 127)
>
> The body is equipped with the instrument, with the means, by which to experience both the life outside and the life within. (IV 130)

preconceptions about self-denial

Preconceived ideas about the body also meant preconceived ideas about self-denial, renunciation and asceticism. Therefore much un-learning and explanation was needed as soon as one of these three words was introduced. The important principle is self-denial, if only rightly understood as outgrowing the limited self. But if one is not accustomed to the thought of underlying unity and the concept of the greater Self, the mention of self-denial is rather alarming. To those in whom memories of sombre religious teaching were stirred, Inayat said:

One might ask whether the spiritual path is a tyranny over oneself. No, for it is by treading it that one moulds one's character. (VI 95)

But more often there were among the listeners persons who considered self-denial a virtue in itself. Some did because this conception belonged to their cultural inheritance, others because it seemed to give their weakness a shine of goodness, but neither self-denial, nor ascetism, is a virtue in itself; and many times Inayat had to show the difference between selflessness from strength and selfish selflessness born out of weakness.

false and real self-denial

Self-denial which comes as a result of helplessness and culminates in dissatisfaction cannot be a virtue. (XI 241)

True renunciation is that which a person makes who has risen above something that he once valued . . . . But the other renunciation is one which a person is compelled to make when circumstances prevent his achieving what he wished to achieve or from getting back what he lost helplessly . . . that renunciation is a loss; and instead of leading towards perfection it drags man down toward imperfection. (III 259)

There are two people who become tired of life in this world: the one who has risen above the world, and the one who has fallen beneath it. The former has attained his object, but the latter, even if he left the world, would not be satisfied by another life. His renunciation of worldly things means nothing. It only means impotence. (VI 201/202)

Forced renunciation, whether forced by morality, religion, law, convention, or formality, is not necessarily renunciation. The real spirit of renunciation is willingness; and willing renunciation comes when one has risen above the thing one renounces. The value of each thing in life, wealth power, position, possession, is according to the evolution of man . . . . there is a time in life when he values a cottage, and there is a time when he gives up a palace . . . The Sufi makes no restrictions and has no principles of renunciation. He believes that to sacrifice anything in life which one does not wish to sacrifice is of no use, but that renunciation is a natural thing that grows in one with one's evolution. A child which cries for its toy at one stage of its childhood, comes to an age when it is quite willing to give away the toy it once cried for. (III 254/255)

In this connection there is another and very essential point to consider. One cannot deny one's self unless one has a proper self, a personality. A weak unformed character who has not fulfilled his small purpose of life cannot start self-denying for he has nothing to offer.

no self-denial unless small purpose of life is fulfilled

A man should first of all be a person; then only should he be spiritual. If he is not a person then what is the use of being spiritual? Man is born to fulfil the purpose of life. (XII 36)

Very often when I speak of the development of personality, people ask me 'What about annihilation?' But it depends on what form of annihilation they mean. One can only be a spendthrift if one has wealth; one cannot annihilate what one does not possess. (VI 56)

Words like these are addressed to those who have learned to consider renunciation and self-denial as a virtue in itself, or to those who want to take a shortcut to realization and forget the purpose of life. More often one finds the opposite weakness, when people are too much attached to what they have achieved or gained.

not to be a slave of one's gains

But there is another weakness, and that is holding what has been gained, and indulging in what has been attained. That limits man to his gain, deprives him of a greater gain, and even prevents him in the course of time from holding the gain he already has. (III 259)

It is not by any means selfish or avaricious to want to succeed in life. But often by success man closes his eyes to what lies beyond on his path; he stands still; and that standing still is like death. (VI 202)

What the inner life requires is freedom to proceed . . . . although seeking freedom man is anything from free because he is caught in the trap of his own self. This is the greatest captivity there is. (VI 155) *purpose of self-denial*

This is the heart of the matter. Freedom of the soul is the aim of the mystic. That means freedom from limitation, freedom from the small or false self. This freedom inspired Inayat from the very moment he went out into the world as a mystic, after the death of his own murshid. His first talk with a Brahmin master culminated in their agreement of freedom, moksha, as the final purpose of the mystics of all denominations. His first Western book (1913) was called *A Sufi Message of Spiritual Liberty*, and in later years he often returned to the subject.

> The highest perception of freedom comes when a person has freed himself from the false ego. (VII 192)

In summary: self-denial and renunciation are not virtues to be praised nor masochistic vexations to be feared, but a means to the end of reaching a greater reality than our daily limited reality.

The conception of losing one's limited self in order to find the greater Self is known all over the world. In King Arthur's Court, according to the Celtic legends, there was a chair on which most knights did not dare sit, because the one who did would 'lose himself'. The Freemasons use this self-losing chair in one of their ceremonies, mostly as a symbol. But to Galahad who sat in the self-losing chair it was not a symbol, nor is it for a truly progressing adept.

merging of the limited ego into the unlimited

> The progress of mystical development is in the annihilation of the false ego in the real ego. (XI 201)

Again this is so essential that it is expressed in the Ten Sufi Thoughts:

> There is one path, the annihilation of the false ego in the real, which raises the mortal to immortality and in which resides all perfection. (IX 267, I 21)

The concept of a false ego—sometimes called the 'small ego' and often 'our limited self'—can only be understood, once one is familiar with the philosophy of underlying unity of being. The real (great) ego or unlimited Self is the Whole, our common origin. The mystic does not stop at abstract understanding, he strives to experience this unity; it must become as well-known to his consciousness as are his body and earthly experiences. We all have a limited consciousness, our knowledge of the daily world around us and of our body, thoughts and feelings; but this consciousness can be enlarged and directed to another knowledge.

man is or has what he is conscious of

We all are that of which we are conscious. A man in prison is conscious of the prison . . . . We only have that of which we are conscious. Therefore our greatness or our smallness depends upon our consciousness. Even to become an illuminated soul is only a difference of consciousness. (IV 186)

Spiritual attainment is making the spirit alive, becoming conscious. When a man is not conscious of soul and spirit, but only of his material being, he is dense; he is far removed from spirit. (II 147)

Man develops in himself a false idea, and that false idea is identification with something he calls himself. He says, 'I am a professor, a lawyer, a barrister, a doctor,' or 'I am a king, a lord or something.' But whatever he claims, he is not that. His claim may be humble or proud, but in reality he is not that. (X 19)

Spiritual knowledge does not lie in learning something, but in discovering something; in breaking the fetters of the false consciousness and in allowing the soul to unfold itself with light and power . . . . spiritual means spirit-conscious. When a person is conscious (only conscious) of his body, he cannot be spiritual. It is like a king who does not know his kingship . . . This is told in many symbolical stories. (VI 196)

Expand my heart, Lord, to the width of the sky, that the whole cosmos be reflected in my soul. (*Vadan* p. 10)

means to widen the consciousness

This last quotation is a phrase, a short prayer, that could be used as a means to outgrow one's limitation by constant repetition. All so-called esoteric exercises are means to achieve this widening of consciousness.

The mystic on the spiritual path perseveres in wiping out this false ego as much as he can, by meditation, by concentration, by prayer, by study, by everything he does. His one aim is to wipe out so much, that one day reality, which is always buried under the false ego, may manifest. And by calling the name of God, in the form of prayer, or in Zikar[1] or in any other form, what the mystic does is to awaken the spirit of the real ego in order that it may manifest. It is just like a spring which rises out of the rock and which, as soon as the water has gained power and strength, breaks even through stone and becomes a stream. So it is with the divine spark in man. (X 19)

In this passage asceticism as a means is not mentioned, probably because of the many misunderstandings and wrong applications in this regard. For often when Inayat touches on the subject of asceticism, he adds warnings as to what asceticism should not be.

when and how asceticism can be used and when not

The ascetic shuts himself up in order to have an opportunity of taking another direction. But very often it happens that the one who lives an ascetic life is himself unaware of what he is doing and what it is intended for. . . . His loss is greater than his gain. For asceticism is not happiness; it is only self-discipline. (I 207)

Inayat once told of a holy man in the East who, accompanied by his disciples visited a village where the inhabitants offered him the best meal they could produce. The holy man ate of the food, although he was in a period of fasting. At first his disciples were shocked, until they understood that for their master to eat was a greater asceticism than not to eat. He sacrificed the spiritual benefit of his fasting, in order not to hurt the feelings of the poor by refusing their offering. A similar tale is told in the West of a medieval Christian saint who interrupted her fast because a poor man brought her a meal. For the man who offered the food, it was happiness to do so. Both holy ones renounced their own wish of fasting out of consideration for another soul.

The Bible speaks of self-denial; but this is often

[1] Zikar is the Indian version of dhikr.

misinterpreted. Self-denial according to general belief means denying oneself all that is good and beautiful, all that is worth attaining; but in reality self-denial does not mean denying oneself all that is good and beautiful, it means denying the self; and that is the last thing one wishes to deny. And the automatic action of this denial is to open the door to the inner life. (VI 155/156)

Many . . . interpret self-denial in the form of asceticism, to deny oneself all pleasures which are momentary . . . . the creation is not intended to be renounced. . . . (I 207)

If we deny ourselves the divine beauty which surrounds us, then the beauty which is within will not unfold itself. (I 222)

For some people it must have taken time to unlearn their ideas about fasting and the like. Inayat himself might fast occasionally, for a definite purpose, but the forms of discipline most stressed in the chapters on control of the body, are to keep silence and to control one's movements.

control of the body through postures

There are four principal ways in which self-discpline can be practised. One way is the physical way, the practice of remaining in the same position, of sitting in the same posture for a certain time. . . . Mystics have practised various postures for many, many years; and they have discovered ways of sitting while doing certain breathing exercises. . . . These postures make it easier for man to learn the science of direction . . . Then there is another aspect of self-discipline which is connected with eating or drinking: one avoids certain things . . . and makes a practice of being able to live without them, especially things that one feels one cannot live without. This is one of the reasons, apart from psychological and physical ones, that some adepts live on a diet of fruit and vegetables . . . Fasting is also one of the ways by which the denseness of the body can be diminished. . . . But in point of fact, I am myself the last person to prescribe fasting. I hardly ever do so; I only give some advice to my pupils if they themselves will fast. (VIII 46)

Nowadays the hatha yoga postures and breathing exercises are fairly well known in the West. Half a century ago Inayat often had to answer questions like 'Why is it that your adepts in the East practise acrobatics?' (IV 128) and he explained that it was not a pastime, but a way to increase the sensitiveness of the body. Today many Westerners use yoga for health, and of course that makes sense too, but the essential purpose is to make the body a fit instrument for spiritual attainment.

celibacy and marriage

Both sexual abstinence and normal marriage, normal physical love, can be a means to progress. To denounce all sexuality and advocate abstinence only is a Christian conception. In the East, from India to China and Japan, the containment of sexual forces is considered a great help, as they can be transformed into spiritual forces. The western psychologist may be critical of the idea that sperm and vaginal fluid in itself are forces, but he does know the so-called artist's impotence, which means that in a period of mental and emotional creation the artist does not practise physical love. In the Jewish tradition marriage is so great a moral duty and a sacred mystery that 'at no time was sexual ascetism accorded the dignity of a religious value', although chastity, like Joseph's, is one of the highest moral values.[1] For a Muslim too marriage is a sacred duty, and most saints married, be it after a 'Basharat' (prophetic dream) in which they were told to do so.[2]

Thus Inayat had to counterbalance conventional ideas about celibacy as a virtue for its own sake; and he had to explain that abstinence may be useful, but that love—which means widening oneself—is the greatest 'means' for expansion of consciousness; and that it is no good to disdain half of the creation by looking down upon women.[3]

[1] G. G. Scholem, *Major Trends in Jewish Mysticism,* p. 235.

[2] W. D. Begg, *The Holy Biography of Hazrat Khwaja Muinuddin Chishti of Ajmer,* p. 69.

[3] A note for some Western feminists who protest against 'religion', because God is 'always' considered male. This applies only for the three Western religions, and Roman Catholicism made up for it with the Virgin Mary and the female saints. But the larger part of the world, and the older Western civilisations too, know, or knew, a pantheon full of active and important goddesses. To Ramakrishna, one of the greatest mystics in India in recent times, the strongest inspiration came through the mother-goddess. Apart from these personifications, mystic philosophy everywhere describes the balance of male and female of creation.

A mystic never restricts himself to a certain rule, for instance to the rule of celibacy, although for certain experiences celibacy is of great importance. But if it is necessary for him to fast, practise celibacy, live on a vegetarian diet, or stay in a remote place in seclusion, or any other such thing, he can prescribe it for himsèlf and benefit by it. But one cannot say that a mystic *must* do this or that, or that he must live a certain life. . . . He may be rich or poor, in the midst of the world or away from everything, he is a mystic just the same. (X 18/19)

sexual abstinence not a virtue in itself

In *Rasa Shastra,* III 165, there is a chapter on celibacy, expounding why abstinence may be useful, but warning 'that man's life can never be complete without women, and this is the error that lies at the root of the ideal of celibacy'. Inayat points to the help of women in the lives of Christ, Abraham and 'the prophets of the Semitic races down through the ages', and to the great 'Hindu teachers, glorified together with their consorts'.

Religious man . . . has nevertheless been prone to look at contact with woman with the thought of there being something unholy in the passionate love of woman. Indeed it is a question whether the libertine has actually debased woman as much as religious man, who believes that to hold himself aloof from any woman with contempt, will be for his own spiritual benefit. And is it possible to debase woman and the position of woman in the scheme of life without debasing man and the whole of life? In the evolution of the ego there is undoubtedly a development towards celibacy, but at the same time this carries an increasing regard for woman, and the whole plan of life. (III 166)

Apart from an exercise in self-discipline and, in the eastern conception, a method of retaining and converting vital forces, the principal goal of abstinence is to become free of the limited ego and its wants. This widening process can only produce love and consideration. The one who looks down on the other sex increases his limited ego instead of outgrowing it.

There are many methods to outgrow the limited ego and to

methods of outgrowing the limited ego

break through a narrow earthly consciousness. Self-discipline is a means to become strong enough for concentration. Another means is word-repetition; some of these exercises are used to develop certain qualities, but the essential aim is that of overcoming ego-awareness.

> Let me forget myself, Lord, that I may become conscious of Thy Being. (*Vadan* 15)

zikar (dhikr)

One of the best-known, direct methods of outgrowing limited consciousness and limited ego is *zikar* (*dhikr*), an exercise that can be done in several ways. The Muslim chanting 'there is no God but God' is repeating a *zikar* (*dhikr*). Curiously enough, this rather well-known form is not the beginner's simple phrase. For the new adept there is a more descriptive form to repeat and to ponder on until the idea becomes a reality for him. In this descriptive form the physical aspect is alluded to first, but at the same time denied to a certain degree; then one is reminded of God dwelling in us, which makes the body an abode of God. (VII 197) Another form of *zikar* are the words 'None exists but God.' One cannot very well say this, until the consciousness has already outgrown some of the small ego's limitation.

A person can do these exercises alone, but some repetitions can be chanted and practised in groups.

> Sufis engage in *Halqa,* a circle of Sufis sitting and practising Zikar and Fikar so that the power of the one helps the other. (X 86)

other ways of ego-shrinking

Different people need different ways of outgrowing or denying ('crushing') the limited ego. For persons of exalted worldly position actions may be needed to wipe out the identification with their social role. XII 95-99 one finds anecdotes of kings who had to learn to beg or to do the meanest menial work, and of a mystic's son who learned to bow to the humblest creature. All this to unlearn the unconscious consciousness of an 'important' earthly ego. In VII 14 and 175 Inayat mentions Christ washing the feet of his disciples as a symbol of such egolessness. And in the beatitudes the master saw 'the essence of all that can teach man to bring out the good in the soul of man'. (IX 188) In this context 'poor in spirit' means 'free of the limited ego'.

> What does poor in spirit mean? It means the ego that is effaced. (VIII 103)

These ego-shrinking exercises cannot be done always and not by everybody. They should not be done in case of sickness, when the body is weak (including the days of menstruation), and certainly not when the mind is weak.

> The nervous system must be in proper condition. . . . What is called self-denial is really this: that one controls one's thoughts and wishes and desires and passions. But that does not mean retirement from life in the world; it only means taking oneself in hand. (VI 100)

life in the wilderness not for every seeker

Things may be different for a great sage to whom life in the wilderness may meet a real need and will imply the giving up of earthly honours and possessions.

> One might ask, 'Then what about these ascetics who lived the life of a hermit in solitude, who did not eat proper food, who kept themselves away from all the comfort and beauty of life?' These are not for every one to follow. At the same time it is a mistake to criticize them. Such people are the ones who make experiments of life by the sacrifice of all the joy and pleasure the earth can give. . . . And these ascetics who left everything in the world attained a certain knowledge which they gave us. It is not a principle for everyone to follow, for spirituality does not depend upon such things. (IV 129)

In conclusion: renunciation, self-denial and self-discipline do not call for the spurning and denial of earthly life and the physical body. But the mystic is not their slave, he can direct body and mind 'as a circus man directs his horses.' (IV 256, VI 14) Earthly life must be known and experienced, and the instruments providing the technical support for the attainment of the underlying unity by the consciousness, are to be found in the body. These instruments are the breath, and the inner senses, usually named with a Sanskrit word *chakras*. The interaction between the soul and the physical body is important. One cannot expect results from concentration, contemplation and meditation, unless one has learnt concentrated control of the body.

bodily concentration

> The mystics . . . by sitting or standing in different postures have gained control over their muscles and nervous system, and this has an effect on the mind. . . . And when one knows the secret of posture, and draws from the unseen world the energy and power and inspiration, one gets the power of sustaining one's thought, one's word, one's pleasure, one's joy. . . . . Furthermore, in order to gain physical control one needs thought-power as well as both posture and breath. (VIII 51/52)
>
> In conclusion, physical control makes a foundation for the character and the personality, a foundation upon which to build spiritual attainment. (VIII 53)

Thus the body should not be neglected, but taken care of, even though mysticism means, in the long run, 'how to be able to live independently of the physical body', if only for five minutes a day. (X 40)

> First there is the improvement of bodily health. Very often weakness or ill-health of the body is the cause of the poor condition of the mind and soul. (VIII 298)

the inner senses

> Self-knowledge can be divided in four kinds, of which the first is knowledge of this physical vehicle which we call our body; . . . . Knowledge of the physical body does not end with the knowledge of anatomy; in this body there are also centres which are the organs of intuition. In so far as science recognizes them they are nervous centres, but what a mystic sees in them is a subtle power of perception. And therefore to the mystic the human body is a more perfect instrument than a wireless receiver, . . . the body is a living wireless receiver if it is prepared for that purpose.

breath

These inner senses can be reached by that other great instrument the body provides: breath.

> There are faculties of the soul which express themselves through a certain centre in the body of man; and as there are parts of land that have never become fertile soil because water never reaches them, so it is with these centres when the breath never reaches them . . . . they have never been awakened, for man has breathed only in those parts of his body by which he lives and eats and performs actions. . . . It may be compared to living in a great town and not knowing that there are many beautiful things that one has never seen. (II 158)

Breath may be considered as the most important 'means' to spirituality, as it connects the physical with the unseen.

> The next aspect of man's being is the breathing system, which in reality is not physical. (XI 197)

> This breath, which we breathe from morning till evening, we hardly consider what mystery is behind it. This one subject is of such great importance that if we really studied this science we would be able to understand the whole being . . . there is something in the breath which connects the body with the soul. (XII 50)

In all chapters on breath (IV 188, VII 102-109, 142-144) Hazrat Inayat Khan underlines its importance. Breath unites body, mind and soul like a current pervading all. Breathing is not only inhaling oxygen and exhaling carbon dioxide (IV 100, II 163), but something more subtle and more essential as well. One might—as in the case of the small self and the great Self—speak of the small and the great Breath. Sometimes breath is compared with a bridge 'whereby to pass from the world of mortality to the world of immortality' (VII 106/107), sometimes with a cord: 'the breath is also a cord that runs through human beings, connecting them in one life.' (IV 74) Once with a lift that connects life before life and life after life with life on earth (I 123). But the comparison used most frequently is 'the breath is a current' (I 121) and always it is stressed that 'breath is the power at the back of every action.' (I 133)

> The perceptible breath which the nostrils can feel as air drawn in and air going out, is only an effect of breathing. For the mystic breath is that current which carries the air out and brings the air in . . . . ; a current which runs through the body, mind, and soul, touching the innermost part of life and also coming back. (IV 189)

> The action of the soul is the same as the action of breath. It goes out fully and it is drawn in fully. . . . . Every breath that a person takes touches the very depth of his spirit; and it would not be possible for any one to live if the breath did not touch the depth of life . . . . it is really the life of God, which we take in at every moment with each breath. IV 274

> The mystic knows that the breath which we perceive by exhaling and inhaling through the nostrils is not the essential breath, but only the result of a current which runs not only through the body, but also through all the planes of man's existence. . . . Were it not so we could not explain how the mind . . . can possibly exert an effect on the body and the body on the mind. (VII 103/104)

The actual breathing exercises are many. The first ones are like a musician's finger exercises, just to learn control and a proper rhythm. The advanced mystic learns innumerable intricate details of direction, intensity, duration, speed, wave length, number and combinations. (II 142, 125, II 111, IV 189).

> The whole culture of spiritual development is based upon the science of breath. (II 125)

Apart from the beginner's exercises mentioned before, almost every disciple will be given a simple breathing exercise to do and it is quite an effort to perform this exercise regularly, without tension and with concentration. Most forms of *zikar* (*dhikr*) are based on breath, rhythm and vibration. Only an advanced mystic will have mastered the more complicated breathing exercises, as used for healing, wordless communication and the like. In general one should not do any exercises without an experienced well-qualified and responsible helper.

vibrations and sound waves

Singers, actors, and people suffering from speech difficulties, learn physical breathing exercises, and they, too, learn to produce sound in such a way that they feel and hear a resonance both inside the head and outside in the room. The vibration of breath and sound should be made as wide as possible. This control of vibration is a mystic exercise too; in this case the purpose is to awaken vibration in the inner centres of perception and to produce vibrations of a frequency one does not usually perceive.

> The Yogis regulated the rhythm of the circulation, of the heart, and of every action of the breath, by the help of the vibration of music, of both tone and rhythm. This brought them from the audible vibrations to the inward vibrations. (II 92)

Again a basic conception, this effect of vibration, sound waves and light waves. Inayat was fond of drawing a comparison with radio and electricity to explain what he meant.

> Scientists have discovered how radio messages can reach through space without any intermediary means, but one day they will discover the truth which has been known to the mystics for thousands of years: that man himself is the instrument, the receiver and the sender of that message which is above all other kinds of radio. Radio can explain to us many of the possibilities which otherwise are difficult to comprehend. (II 182)

> The knowledge of vibrations is metaphysics. (II 59)

> The secret behind the whole manifestation is vibration. (I 209)

But the mystic does not stop at observation of vibrations in their different appearances, he puts them to use.

> Vibrations can be changed by understanding the vibrations of one's own life, which means one's own self. In the first place one can study the vibrations of the physical body, and the chief way in which they can be understood and controlled is through the study and understanding of

breathing, for the pulsation of the heart, head and body, upon which circulation depends, is based upon the rhythm of breath. The next step is to understand the rhythm of the mind. (XI 31)

wazifa and fikar

Rhythm of body and mind can be achieved, eventually altered, by exercises based on breathing, rhythm and sound, like *wazifa* and *fikar*. The *fikar* is a subtle exercise for which knowledge of direction and numeral proportion is needed. The *wazifa* may be given to a beginner. It is a word denoting a certain divine name or attribute that should be repeated a prescribed number of times, with a good vibration and a good concentration. The beginner's *wazifa* can be used to develop a certain quality in the pupil. It is not given to everybody, 'only to those who have a feeling and respect for a sacred word'. (*Instruction interview*) In his lectures Inayat only gives a general description of these matters.

> The great teachers have made a science of words, so that by the repetition of certain words a definite result can be produced in one's character, in one's circumstances, or even that a person can help another by the use of a certain word. Man's character can be changed by the repetition of certain words, entirely changed. Thus suggestion often proves the secret of a miracle. (XII 38/39)

suggestion

Suggestion can be used in a desirable and in an undesirable way. The first thing needed is to recognize suggestion. XI 75-98 Inayat devotes some chapters to this subject. He points to the fact that everybody is continually exposed to suggestion in daily life; then he shows how, by studying life, one can learn to recognize it and how to defend oneself against undesirable influences (see page 91). Control of suggestion implies directing the consciousness. To direct one's consciousness towards the inner, or fuller life, one needs exercises. There is suggestion in symbolical actions, but repetition and concentration are the great means. Rhythm, sometimes music and sometimes movement may strengthen this suggestive repetition.

Not all Sufi schools use music and dance. For some Muslims these are controversial subjects, though chanting the suras and rhythmic praying are common practice. Inayat considered a rigid rejection of music as 'misinterpreting the Prophet's teaching, which prohibited the abuse of music, not music in the real sense of the word'. (II 60) He often pointed to unhappy results of misused music, but he was a Chishti by initiation and a musician by tradition. To him music and mysticism were inseparably linked together, both in practice and principle. Often he described the help an adept may receive from rhythm and music, and many times he mentions the mantras of the yogis, which also use the medium of sound, rhythm and music; or he refers to the singers and bards of old who were the keepers of holy legends and knowledge of the gods, handing these down with their music.

> Music is the most wonderful way to spiritual realization; there is no quicker and no surer way of attaining spiritual perfection than through music. (X 227)

rhythm

> Music is the shortest, the most direct way to God; but one must know what music and how to use it. (II 109)

> What secret is there in music which attracts all those who listen to it? It is the rhythm which is being created. It is the tone of that music which tunes a soul and raises it above the depression and despair of everyday life in the world. And if one knew what rhythm was needed for a particular individual in his trouble and despair, what tone was needed, and to what pitch that person's soul should be raised, one would then be able to heal him with music. (II 143)

> Sufis, in order to awaken in man that part of his emotional nature which is generally asleep, have a rhythmic practice which sets the whole mechanism of body and mind in rhythm. (II 46)

Rhythm is connected with balance. There are chapters on rhythm and music in II 44-61, 73-152, IV 73-74, XI 44-48 and passim. The swaying in prayer or in reciting a holy text is an expression of rhythm without much application of music. In other cases suggestive rhythm may lead to ecstatic dancing. But in the West, single word or phrase repetition on a certain tone and in a certain rhythm is more widely used.

sound, word The word itself is a form of sound that can be used as a power. One of Hazrat Inayat's books is titled *The Power of the Word* (II 157-195). This power of sound in words and names is known in other religions too.

> By the help of sound the wise have prepared themselves . . . they have worked with the power of sound. As Zeb-un-Nisa says, 'Say continually that sacred name which will make thee sacred.' The Hindus have called it Mantra Yoga; the Sufis have termed it Wazifa. It is the power of the word which works upon each atom of the body, making it sonorous, making it a medium of communication between the external life and the inner life. (II 133)

> Mantra Yoga means a science of words, words which were sacred and helpful in one's spiritual evolution. The Yogis have worked on this principle for many thousand years, and have discovered a great mystery in the power of words. Sufis of all ages have followed this principle of making words which are suggestive of a certain sense, a sense which one wishes to bring out and make a reality in one's life. No doubt it is necessary to know the meaning of the sacred words one repeats; this gives a thousandfold greater effect. And the spoken word has a greater power than silent concentration, provided there is power of concentration and sincere feeling at the back of the word. (XI 91)

phrase For western Sufis a simple way of using words—with concentration and sincerity!—is the use of a phrase from *Gayan* or *Vadan*. Especially in the chapters headed *Alankara* one finds maxims or wishes or words spoken to one's own self which can serve as an exercise. The pupil may choose the lines or his initiator may offer him a phrase. Once the words are chosen, the pupil will repeat them daily, will ponder on their meaning not only during the quarter of an hour devoted to his exercises, but whenever they come to mind again. At last the contents of the phrase will become part of the pupil's being. This may take years, one does not change a phrase too soon. Inayat tells us that his grandfather did one exercise during all his life, and the results were tremendous. (X 88)

A phrase can be chosen, like the *wazifa* to develop an aspect of one's character, but also, to attain unity.

> The great saints of the East have repeated one phrase, for instance, 'God is one', perhaps a million times in their lives. Should we believe that they were so foolish as not to be able to understand the meaning of it by saying it once? Why then do they repeat it a million times? The reason is that it is never enough. We live in the midst of illusion from morning till evening. (X 26)

prayer Not only the expressly 'mystical' methods like word repetitions should be done with complete concentration and sincerity, but also such a well-known way of communication with God and self as prayer. Almost all mureeds of Inayat's universal Sufism are given some of the prayers one finds in the *Gayan.*

> The Sufi prayers such as Saum and Salat are not man-made prayers. They have descended from above, just as in every period of spiritual reconstruction prayers were given. And there is every power and blessing in them, especially for those who believe. (IX 272/273)

These prayers are classified as Gayatri and one should bear in mind that the Christian connotation of prayer is different from Muslim *nimaz* or Hindu *puja.* A Christian prayer is based on an already existing relationship to a higher being. The oriental worshipper through a prayer of homage and praise, is evoking such a relationship. Inayat's prayers are, in fact, a complicated exercise, based on creating and experiencing the underlying unity of being. One needs some knowledge of Inayat's philosophy concerning the Spirit of Guidance, God in everything, the basic unity of Creator and Creation and the acceptance of different God conceptions. As soon as one begins to contemplate the meaning of every word, Saum and Salat become an important, effective exercise. They should always be said together, for the sake of balance.

There are other prayers in *Gayan* and *Vadan,* some more simple, and most of them easier to grasp than Saum and Salat, but simple things too are only effective if done with full attention.

questions about prayer

Most questions concerned Western ideas of prayer, its general use, abuse, and the enquirer's doubts of prayer. One of these doubts was: 'is it allowed to ask for something one wants', and another: 'why should one pray for one's wants, if God knows everything?'

> Man often thinks that, as God is the knower of the heart, there can be no need of any recital or gesture in prayer; but that it would surely be sufficient if he were to sit in the silence and think of God. But this is not so; it is according to the extent of a man's consciousness of prayer that his prayer reaches God. (*Sufism,* March 1922, p. 4, 5)

> Man asks another question as to why God, who knows already what he wants and what is the need of his life, should require to be asked at all. For answer to this we have the words of Christ: 'Ask and ye shall receive; knock and it shall be opened unto you.' In other words, this means that though God knows your need it has to become clear and definite to yourself by prayer. (*Sufism,* March 1922, p. 5)

Sometimes Inayat adds that, to be sure of one's needs, one should begin with study of life and study of self; but there is nothing against praying for the fulfilment of an earthly wish, if one is sure it makes sense. Only the prayer of the great surpasses the stage of asking and becomes a meditation.

Another common question is whether God has time for so many prayers (IX 36) and why one should praise God (*Sufism,* March 1922, p. 5, IX 57)

> The question whether God has time to give attention to our prayer is answered by the mystic, who says that it is through the medium of man himself that God hears his prayer. (IX 36)

> If one asks why God should create beings in order that they should sing His own praise, the answer is that God does not wish to receive praise; the praise of God is a prescription for man, in order that by this prescription man can come to that understanding which brings him nearer to God. (IX 37/38)

> What does praise of God, praise of His creation, praise of

> His nature, develop in man? It develops in him such an art that nothing can compare with it . . . . He begins to see how natures are attracted to one another, and how they harmonize; he sees how inharmonies are produced. The causes of all such things become clear to him, when once he begins to see into nature, to admire the beauty of its construction, its life, its growth; when he begins to study nature and its causes. (IX 48/49)

Prayer and praise done actively are not a conventional duty, and still less the well-known hesitant 'maybe it helps, maybe it is only wasting time.' Conscious and active praying is creative.

> Then there is a third person . . . who not only prays to God, but he prays before God, in the presence of God. Once imagination has helped a man to bring the presence of God before him, God is awakened in his own heart. (IX 40)

Praying goes with the stages of creating a God-ideal to enlarge the consciousness as discussed in Chapter III.

> The best means of raising the consciousness is by the God-ideal. (XI 158.)

stages of prayer

In a later stage one does not need this personalized form. In many prayers, and also in Inayat's prayers, one can trace the expression of different stages of advancement: wrestling with the limited ego, and thankfulness; wrestling with a sense of sin, and forgiving; the expression of the difficulties of life, and a sense of great joy. (IX 34-39) An advanced stage of prayer is that of the mystic who has attained God-knowledge.

> When he is praying in a room, he is not alone, he is there with God; then to him God is not in the highest heaven, but close to him, before him, in him . . . all names and forms disappear before Him. Then every word of prayer he utters is a living word. (IX 40)

However:

> Advancement on this spiritual path is gradual. One cannot use this way without first having practised the other kinds of prayer. (IX 50)

This practising in earlier stages, also, requires complete attention; therefore it is better to pray aloud, if possible with symbolical or rhythmic movements, and sometimes in groups.

> The singing of a prayer is more powerful than only reciting the prayer in thought. It is the same difference as there is between thinking a song and singing it. (IX 33)

> If your body is still and only your mind is working, it means that part of your being is in prayer and part not; for man has both mind and body, so that the complete being must be praying. (*Sufism,* March 1922, p. 5)

> Then also you should unite in prayer, for the blessing which can be received through prayer becomes a thousandfold greater when received even by a few who are united in the same desire and are praying together. As Christ said, 'Where two or three are together, there will I be in the midst of them.' (*Sufism,* March 1922, p. 6)

concentration

This dedication of one's entire being to prayer means concentration and is a condition for the success of any spiritual exercise. Whatever the differences in preparatory practices, in all mystic schools of all religions everywhere in the world, concentration in the main method of reaching God-realization. All the same there are some misunderstandings as to its meaning.

> Concentration does not mean closing the eyes and sitting in church on Sunday. Many know how to close their eyes and sit there, yet their minds wander about, especially when they have closed their eyes. Concentration means that every atom of the body and the mind is centred on the spot. (X 26/27)

> Concentration is activity of the mind in the direction desired. (VII 129)

As a rule a mureed doing his first exercises discovers that he cannot hold a thought nor direct it, even if he is able to concentrate on his work in daily life. Inayat distinguishes between spontaneous and conscious concentration.

automatic and conscious concentration

> Automatic concentration is found in many people who do not know that they concentrate and yet they do. They concentrate automatically, some to their disadvantage. Those who concentrate to their advantage are the ones whose mind is fixed on their business, on their art, on any occupation they have. They are the ones who because of their concentration can work more successfully. Sometimes concentration works to a disadvantage. There are some people who always think they are unlucky, that everything will go wrong, who think that everybody dislikes them, that everybody hates them . . . . Some by concentration cherish illness, always think of it. (IV 153/154)

Conscious concentration can be used to overcome the undesired effects of automatic concentration on illness and unhappiness, and to counteract the impression of undesirable suggestions. (XI 77) In general, conscious concentration is a method to control and govern the mind (VII 63, 125) and to free oneself of the impression that man is identical with his body only. (VII 42, XI 200) Well-directed, spiritual concentration is creative. To develop this essential power one should start with small things.

> There are things which are within one's reach and there are things which are beyond it. One must first prove to one's own self one's capability of attaining what is within one's reach. This gives one sufficient self-confidence to attain that what seems beyond one's reach. (VI 203)

At first nothing seems more beyond our reach than the realization of that inner knowledge that is said to be formless. How can one grasp and understand the formless? By first concentrating on forms and gradually, when concentration becomes a power, on less concrete things.

By concentration one reaches the knowledge within, which means one is able to see concretely and to be conscious of something which is apart from one's physical body. A person may be conscious of a poem, a word, a picture, an idea of something, and if he can lose the consciousness of

> his limited body for a moment, that is the first step . . . . When a person begins to do it, no sooner does he close his eyes in order to concentrate than a thousand things come before him. Also his physical body becomes restive . . . . Then a kind of nervous action arises in the body. It feels like moving, turning, scratching . . . . The second stage is that instead of being conscious of a thought, one is conscious of a feeling . . . feeling has no form, therefore to fix one's mind on a feeling . . . is not an easy thing. If once a person has done it and has not given in to restiveness of mind, then he certainly feels uplifted. (IV 122)

One cannot very well learn concentration without a teacher. (VII 129), among other reasons as not every subject is suitable for concentration.

> One should not concentrate upon any object that comes along, for what one concentrates upon has an effect upon one. (IV 154)

The problem is to find something that is of interest to the pupil and will help him too proceed as well.

how to overcome difficulties

> The best remedy for a wandering mind is natural concentration; that means not forcing the mind. One should at first let the mind work naturally, thinking of things it is inclined to think about. Why should the mind think of something towards which it has no inclination? It is unnatural; it is like eating something one does not like; it will not be assimilated nor give good results. One should think about anything one loves, then one can learn to concentrate. (IV 169)

> Concentration, which is the secret of every attainment in life . . . is a natural thing in love. (V 149)

stages of concentration

Inayat mentions three aids to an undisturbed concentration. Action, that is certain movements; sound, that is word repetitions; and memory, that is looking at a thing and then closing the eyes and remembering the object, retaining the form without seeing it. At a further stage one can reconstruct a thing in one's imagination, hearing a sound and seeing a thing that is not actually there. (IV 154, 138) This may seem stranger than it is; everybody can mentally reconstruct a landscape or a face or a melody that has struck him. The main thing is that the subject of concentration is of interest to the student.

> How are meditative souls awakened, how do they experience the inner life? In the first place the adept values his object of attaining the inner life more than anything else in life. As long as he does not really value it, so long he remains unable to attain it . . . . It does not mean that in this world he should not pursue the things he needs; it means he should value most something which is really worthwhile. (VI 157)

> Concentration is an act of the will during which the mind actually sees, during which the seeing faculty of the mind acts as well as the hearing faculty. (XII 61)

Surely, one cannot call the action of the mind real concentration, unless a person is full of the object of concentration and always thinking of it.

> One can never think too often or too much of the wish one has. One should dream about it, imagine it, think about it, keep it continually in mind, and do everything possible towards its fulfilment; but one should do this with tranquillity, with ease, and not by thinking hard about it. (VIII 85)

> When a desire becomes a steady thought, its success is assured. (*Gayan* 48, n. 81)

contemplation

If a pupil has advanced to a stage at which his spiritual aim and exercises are in his mind all the time, then contemplation begins.

> It is concentration which brings success, and it is concentration which is the mystery of accomplishment in all things. And when one goes a little further . . . one finds that there is contemplation, which means the retaining of the same thought or thought-picture. The distinction

between concentration and contemplation is that the former is the composition of a form, and the latter the retaining of this impression, this form. (XII 24/25)

As to contemplation, it is only when a person is advanced enough that he can contemplate; because contemplation is not on an object, it is on an idea. (IV 155)

If contemplation does not develop in such a form that everything in life becomes a contemplation, then the contemplation does not do a person any good. (X 78)

And then, at last, follows meditation, and that means much more than the vague associations this lightly used word has for many today.

meditation

Concentration means that every atom of the body and of the mind is centred in one spot. The next step is contemplation; that is to be able to retain an idea which raises one's consciousness from the dense world. The third step is meditation and that is to purify[1] oneself, to free oneself, and to open oneself to the light of truth, in order that it may abide in one's spirit. (X 27)

And when we proceed still further we come to the aspect we call meditation, an experience which is brought about by a perfect control of the mind and by rising above the action of the mind, an experience by which the inner side of life begins to reveal itself. (XII 25)

An adept who has come this far will soon be open for Self-realisation, the highest aim he set out for. But on his way he finds many more results, small and great ones, as will be described in the next chapter. Perhaps all these exercises, studies of life and of self, all this control and concentration sounds difficult, as does so much unfamiliar work. But it is a fascinating voyage of discovery.

The joy of life is the joy of the journey. If one could close one's eyes and be put immediately on top of the Himalayas,

[1] pure means 'not mixed with other things' (XII 29).

one would not enjoy it as much as the one who climbs and goes from one peak to another, and sees the different scenery and meets the different people on the way. The whole joy is in the journey. (V 108)

VI Mysticism, First Results

questions about occultism and miracles

> What experience does a mystic have? Does he see colours, does he communicate with spirits, does he wander in the higher worlds, does he read thoughts, does he recognize objects by psychometry, does he perform wonders? To a mystic all these things are elementary, and those who do them are half-mystics, quarter-mystics. (XI 147)

> There are stories of the wonder-workings and phenomena which occur in the East; many of these stories no doubt are of the jugglers who can perform wonders by sleight of hand or by some hypnotic influence. But there are others who are genuine. Wonders are performed during their lives, and people see them performed. But the genuine ones never say that they can perform wonders, neither do they seek such powers; these powers come naturally. (IV 181)

Inayat was often harrassed with questions about wonder-working. A scientist in New York asked him whether it was possible to lift a pen from a table through spiritual means. (VII 231, XI 221) Inayat answered that such a feat of levitation was quite possible, but would be a mere waste of energy:

> Would a mystic not sooner raise a soul higher, bringing him to another sphere, raising his ideals, his aspirations, instead of trying to raise this little pen lying on the table? (XI 221/222)

examples of and warning against tricks

And then he told his questioner of a juggler he himself, as a boy, had seen in the streets of Baroda, his birth-place. This juggler made paper animals move, walk and run, but such a trick, even if based on occult power, may not be called mysticism.

> Only the non-mystic boasts of his power and shows it off to people, whereas the mystic neither speaks about it nor does he exhibit his powers before others. (XI 221)

When occult feats are not tricks, they spring from

concentration and from control of breath, pulsation, vibration and the like. In connection with these subjects Inayat might mention some remarkable performances he had witnessed in India, always adding that one should not seek these things and that a true mystic hides his power. In connection with the New York scientist's question Inayat proceeds:

> A mystic can know the thought of another even better than can that person who is thinking, and he can feel the feeling of another more deeply than he. (XI 221)

telepathy Telepathy was a very normal and simple achievement to him.

> To some, telepathy is a mysterious phenomenon; but to those who understand it, it is as easy and natural as ordinary conversation. (XII 60)

Inayat's pupils and others who met him remember many instances of his wordless understanding. One of them writes, 'It was wonderful, one did not need say a word and yet one was understood completely.' (SK 12)

The way in which Inayat answered his pupils' needs was a tactful one. Once he unexpectedly asked someone who never did secretarial work to take down a lesson. In that lesson this pupil, a physician, found his own question answered as a general proposal. (SK 79) Often Inayat inserted a tale in a lecture which threw light on the problem of just one listener. (SK 1, 3, 15, 18, 22, 25, 27, 30, 33, 79) When asked point-blank whether he had meant to draw their attention to something he answered, 'that does not matter', or even excused himself because he had seen a man's thoughts and memories. (SK 1, 55 and *Forty Years of Sufism,* p. 15, 16) This contact (in fact more than merely telepathic, see next chapter on Communication) was not with mureeds only. A casual host, who never joined the movement but was interested in things Indian, remembered that Inayat suddenly sang for him the song he loved most, without there having been any talk about it. (SK 23) The most amusing and practical use of Inayat's penetrating 'seeing' (see below, p. 105) occurred at a station. A prospective host came to meet Inayat at the train; they had not met previously, but he expected to discover an Indian in a western crowd without difficulty. Suddenly he felt a hand on his sleeve; it was Inayat who had found him, not by looking at faces, but by receiving a thought. (SK 20)

Among western scholars writing about Sufism R. A. Nicholson recognized how normal telepathy is to Sufi masters communicating with each other.[1] Many later authors who possessed much more material and data than Mr Nicholson had in 1913, scarcely mention the fact. Inayat did not avoid the subject in public lectures and the book *Mind-World* (IV 239-288; separately reprinted as *House of Mirrors*) explains how it works.

uncon-scious tele-pathy

The mystic's telepathy is conscious and well-controlled, but there is, also, much unconscious and accidental thought-transfer. Best known, probably, are the messages of dying persons that reach their far-off friends. There is a reason for this sudden receiving power in an untrained person:

> When one thinks about occult powers, such as knowing the condition of other people's minds, their pleasure and displeasure, also the joy and pain of another's heart, knowing what is going on at a distance, receiving news from far away in the world, we find that all this can be gained without study, just through the power of love. . . . The real lover will know such things without special meditation or concentration, for what can exert a greater concentration than love? (VII 78)

The point is that real love is always a widening. It means to open one's heart and direct one's attention to another, so that one's own limited ego is forgotten. Almost all results described in this chapter are based on this widening of consciousness, and the ego-lessness and concentrated calm that go with it. The further one proceeds the more the unity of all creation is experienced as a reality. It is simply a process of removing bars, outdistancing limitedness. Between those who love each other bars fall away naturally.

Nothing can separate two minds that are focused on one

[1] R. A. Nicholson, *The Mystics of Islam*, London 1914, p. 120

another . . . distance is never a bar to this phenomenon. Have we not seen in the recent war the womenfolk of the soldiers, their mothers, their wives, their children, linked with their dear ones fighting at the front and feeling their conditions and knowing when a soldier was wounded or killed? . . . . One thought, one particular design, one particular picture becomes reflected, and because it is so mirrored upon him, the other person feels it in an instant. (IV 246, also VIII 132)

reflection

Reflection and mirroring are classic Sufi terms, often used by Inayat to explain the working of telepathy. Once, his own master had explained the same to him.

Speaking about the science of telepathy, my Murshid once said, 'it is reflection. If your heart is clear, then you must only know how to focus it, and you need not do anything else. It is a mirror, and all that is before it will be reflected in it'. (IV 264)

The mind-world, in the terms of the Sufi poets, is called 'Aina Khanah', which means the Palace of Mirrors. (IV 241)

The different minds in the world may be likened to various mirrors, capable of projecting reflections, and reflecting all that falls upon them. No one, however great in wisdom and power, can claim to be free from influences. It is like the mirror claiming, 'I do not reflect all that falls upon me.' Only the difference between the wise and the foolish is that the wise man turns his back to what he must not reflect; the foolish not only reflects undesirable thought, but most proudly owns it. (I 159)

unconscious reflection in daily life

This means that reflection on the mind does not only manifest itself in telepathy, but in all sorts of mental influences of people upon each other (IV 247, 262) and on themselves. First, there is the influence of a strong personality on his environment. But there is a counterpart of the mystic's repeating words; many cause a constant mirroring of an influence in their mind, by unconscious repetition of either depressing or helping thoughts:

> Apart from the mystical process, one sees people in one's everyday life who have perhaps repeated in their minds the thought of pain, of hatred, of longing, of a disappointment, of admiration, of love, unconscious of the work it has done within themselves; and yet a deep impression of it has been produced in the depths of their heart, and that becomes projected upon every person they meet. (IV 251)

Thus mirroring, also, accounts for the fact that some persons are felt (reflected) as repulsive and others as attractive. Even 'like attracts like' is explained as a 'phenomenon of mirror-land'.

> There is another most interesting aspect in studying the nature of mind: that every mind attracts and reflects thoughts of its own kind . . . . If a robber or thief goes to Paris, he will certainly meet with a thief. He will easily find out where the thief lives; he will see him at once because his mind has become a receptacle of the same kind of thoughts. As soon as their glances meet there is a communication established; the thoughts are alike. (II 227/228)

conscious reflection

In the case of a stranger who looks for his colleagues or co-patriots in a new city, there is also an element of conscious seeking; but this is helped on by the faculty of reflection. This conscious seeking is different from the mystic's conscious control of mirroring. He can learn to close himself against undesirable or unnecessary influences, he will open his mind to receive what he wants to receive, and as a further step he may learn to direct his thoughts, 'the pictures in his mind' to others. The instruments for this kind of wireless communication are concentration, widening, focusing, tuning and direction.

One method to rid oneself of an unwanted influence would be to concentrate in a different direction.

exclusion of unwanted influences

> How can one wipe out all the innumerable pictures which hinder one? The whole process of the Sufi method is this: to make the photographic plate of the mind clear. This can be done by the practice of concentration . . . . This teaches you to create a thought, and to expel every thought that you do not wish to have . . . . It is the mechanical part of one's

being which is subject to conditions, environments, and which is helpless; and it is the creative part of one's being . . . which produces phenomena. (IV 256/257)

conscious openness to reflection However, for conscious telepathic receiving a passive concentration is needed. A receiver of thoughts—and in a further stage the receiver of God-consciousness—has to empty himself, wiping the inner mirror for clear reflection. That means forgetting all limited knowledge, erasing thoughts, most of all the thought of one's limited self.

> When a person is looking in a mirror, his reflection covers the mirror and in that mirror nothing else can be reflected. (IV 123)

tuning Widening and tuning are interrelated. Both go with ego-shrinking. Inayat gave several lectures on tuning (VIII 271–287, XI 205-209) and considered it as a characteristic of spirituality (VIII 279). The adept can tune himself to the external and to the inner being, and the advanced mystic tunes himself to the essence of all things. (II 83)

Telepathy is a beginner's attainment. All development should be gradual (VIII 282) and the first steps will be, of necessity, as simple as possible.

> Real mysticism or esotericism begins simply with the first step, with looking outside. (XI 205)

This remark is taken from the chapter on 'Tuning of the Spirit;' the art of tuning needs its own study of life. It is already a proof of advancement if one can 'speak to people in their own language'.

> With a child one must have childish talk, with the young one suitable words should be spoken, with the old one should speak in accordance with their understanding. (II 29)

focusing Such attention and consideration for others increases widening and leads to focusing.

> It is not every one who knows to focus his heart to receive a certain reflection. (IV 286)

Here again it is expounded that focusing is done by concentration, at first on simple objects. In the last stage 'one is able to focus mind and heart on God'. (IV 286)

conscious sending

It is quite possible for the lay mystic to train himself in those arts that are needed for a conscious reception of thoughts and feelings. But the conscious and active sending requires the strength, experience and clarity of purpose of the advanced mystic, although the means are almost the same.

> If we wish to retain thought, or to transmit thought, we must learn the process of 'throwing the ball' to hit a certain goal. We must direct our aim right, and we must put enough force in it to enable it to reach the goal. It is the force of will that sends the thought to reach another person, and the aiming, whereby one focuses one's mental eye upon the other in telepathy, is concentration. (XII 62/63)

> The person whose thought becomes reflected in the heart of another may have a concrete form in his thought, may be able to hold it as one design or a picture. In that case the reflection falls in the heart of another man clearly; but if the mind is so weak that it cannot hold a thought properly, then the thought is moving and it cannot reflect in the mind of another properly . . . . If a person's mind is not clear, if it is upset or too active, then that mind cannot convey the reflection fully. (IV 245/246)

> Only some people can hold a thought as a picture. (IV 250)

Inayat does not often speak of conscious sending, and if he does, he adds that it is difficult and that it should be done on a base of sympathy and voluntary communication. This point should give pause to the Intelligence Services of some of the larger countries nowadays said to be interested in telepathy for their own purposes. In fact, sympathy and communication go with widening and belong to the advanced mystic naturally. As there is always a bond of sympathy between teacher and pupil, much esoteric teaching is given without words.

reflection from murshid upon pupil

> The teaching which reaches from a teacher to a pupil does so in the form of reflection. (IV 278)

A reflection from murshid upon mureed may be so complete that, in some cases, the mureed gives answers he did not know he could give. Inayat himself told the story of a well-known mystic of old, who had the humblest of his followers, an obscure servant, answer the questions of an audience.

> He had never done a thing like that in his whole life; it was only because he was asked that he stood up without thinking whether he would be able to give the answer or not. But the answer he gave to every question was as if given by Shankaracharya himself . . . . It is this which is recognized by Sufis as reflection. It was not the pupil, it was the teacher himself who was speaking there. (IV 279/280)

Some of Inayat's disciples experienced the same thing. As a rule they dreaded talking in public, but when they had to, they suddenly could. One of his secretaries was unexpectedly asked to give a talk on the Sufi Movement, in a language not his own. He had not prepared anything and in some desperation he looked at Inayat, who had just finished a lecture. Inayat nodded at him, smiling, and suddenly the young man felt confident, and he even consciously tuned his mind to Inayat's. He spoke for twenty minutes, with ease.[1]

A remarkable testimony is given by a Frenchman, not a disciple, who translated a lecture for Hazrat Inayat Khan in Paris. He, too, felt that the master was helping him through, so that he lost his usual shyness and achieved more than he could have done alone. But this person resented the invisible help, or feared it. He felt an influence 'which no doubt was sympathetic,' but he wished 'to remain completely himself.' (SK 86) Unconsciously this outsider expressed the resistance of the limited ego against widening. He felt safer within his own bounds.

Some of Inayat's pupils knew a kindred fear. At first they felt happy in his engulfing presence, but they could not bear such boundlessness for too long. When in a private interview Inayat felt—mirrored—this reaction of fear he immediately shuttered the impact of his stature. There is a detailed

[1] S. van Stolk, *Memories of a Sufi sage, Hazrat Inayat Khan,* East-West Publications, 1967, p. 58/59

description of this by a mother who assisted him in the healing of her dying baby. (SK 15) There are many records of Inayat's healing (SK1, 8, 37, 39, 41, 62 and[1]), but an especially touching and interesting feature of the healing of this child is that Inayat let the mother herself hold her week old child and reached it through her.

healing Inayat was a great healer. Most mystics are.

> The mystic is a healer by nature. (IV 43)

Inayat's cousin Muhammad Ali Khan had established a reputation as a 'spiritual healer' even well beyond Sufi circles. The first mystic the present author ever met was a healer. It was, in fact, an instance of his healing I happened to witness that removed my doubts about the genuineness of meta-material phenomena. This unassuming man, a normal European engineer, whose master had been a Sikh, possessed all the achievements described in this and next chapter, including silence. (see page 130) His healing power was but one consequence, but it is a power that is conspicuous. Some of Inayat's pupils specialize in healing, mostly the simple methods of magnetism and concentration.

Certainly, Inayat's powers exceed those of most lay mystics. He could even heal from a distance (SK 13, 19, 29, 41, 48, 54 and[1]) and in his book *Health* (IV 11-94) he simply remarks that this can be done by a certain breathing practice and by keeping the thought of the patient before one, but he adds that it is only possible at a certain stage of inner evolution.

> There is no doubt that spiritual evolution is the first thing necessary; without this the mind power of a healer, however strong, is too feeble for the purpose. By spiritual development is meant God-consciousness . . . . It is the belief and realization that 'I do not exist but God,' which give power to the healer to heal from a distance; also it is this realization that gives him the belief that his thought can reach to any distance, because the knowledge of the all-pervading God gives him the realization that the Absolute is life itself. (IV 87)

[1] S. van Stolk, *Memories of a Sufi Sage,* p. 57-60; *Forty Years of Sufism,* p. 18; *Memories of Hazrat Inayat Khan,* by a Disciple (S. Santsbury Green) 19-20

> Grasping this assumes familiarity with the conception of underlying unity and God as the only Being. From those not acquainted with these ideas, Inayat often received astonished and disbelieving questions. In one of his answers to such doubts Inayat remarks that the success of conventional medicine is greater when the patient has trust in his medicine; belief helps the cure. Disbelief can hinder the effect, of pills as well as of spiritual help.
>
> The secret of healing is to rise by the power of belief above the limitations of this world of variety, that one may touch by the power of intelligence the oneness of the whole Being. It is there that one becomes charged with the almighty power, and it is by the power of that attainment that one is able to help oneself and others in their pain and suffering. (IV 41/42)

So here again we find as 'means': control of breath and thoughts, tuning, and above all widening, experiencing unity not as an abstract concept but as a reality, so that being in sympathy, in communication with one's fellow-man follows as a natural result.

> The real healing is when man is in sympathy with another's trouble and gives him a helping hand . . . There cannot be a more beautiful process of healing than this among all the different methods by which people have endeavoured to heal. (VII 17)

Pupils recount numerous and various healings—through touch, through his glance, by some exercise or prescription, healing from a distânce and healing by his presence. All these, and many more, are dealt with in the collected lectures of a course on Health and Healing. Inayat did not reject conventional medicine, and often pointed to psychosomatic causes of ill-health. There is one point in the book *Health* which has special significance here, because it illustrates the mystic's way of observation and perception. He can recognize symptoms in the usual, outer manner, but he knows more from seeing and intuition—two achievements that mean a further inner growth than passive telepathy.

> There are some signs a seer sees, outward signs which explain the fundamental principles of health. (IV 44)

In 'a seer sees' the verb includes more than just to observe with the eyes, it means above all to see with the inner senses.

> It is seeing even without eyes and hearing even without ears. The English word 'seer' means someone who can see equally well with or without eyes. (XII 20)

misconceptions about clairvoyance and clairaudience

Clairvoyance? Clairaudience? Yes and no.

> By seeing, I do not mean seeing with the eyes, but penetrating. It is the penetrating quality of seeing that makes a seer, and which is the real meaning of the word clairvoyance. Nowadays people have misused this word so much that one does not like to use it any more. By hearing, I do not mean listening. I mean responding; responding to heaven or to earth; responding to every influence that helps to unfold the soul. (II 177/178)

> Sometimes people think that a seer is a clairvoyant or a spiritualist, but that is a different kind of person and not a seer. The seer need not see the unseen world; there is so much to be seen here in the visible world. There is so much that man could see in this objective world, but which is hidden from his eyes, that if he were to concentrate all his life upon seeing all that is to be seen he would find more than enough to think about it. (VIII 40/41)

The latter quotation contains one of Inayat's patiently repeated warnings against occultist excitement and also is another way of saying that to see means to penetrate, to understand, to tune. The subject seeing is always connected with insight, sometimes he lectured on it under that heading (IV 215-229), or else the lecture might be called the 'Vision of the Mystic' (XI 210-214) or just 'Mysticism' (XII 20-22). If an audience could follow Inayat past the dangerous rocks of preconceived ideas such lectures ended on a key of unmistakable warmth and enthusiasm. When he could show the meaning and use of seeing, Inayat at last reached his real subject, the experience of the mystic which he loved to share.

For though telepathy may seem a 'phenomenon', in fact one cannot help 'mirroring', but the adept enters into a new state of consciousness as soon as he begins to see and to hear beyond the obvious.

the first great step

> A person whose soul has awakened becomes awake to everything he sees and hears. Compared with that person, everyone else seems to have open eyes and yet not to see, to have open ears and yet not to hear. (VIII 302)

> The mystic side of Sufism may be recognized as seeing and hearing. To see further than one sees, to hear more keenly than one hears; in other words to see that which the eyes cannot see, to hear that which the ears cannot hear. This experience brings us to realization. (XII 20)

Apart from explaining what is meant by 'to see what the eyes cannot see', this passage enters into the question why not everybody strives after this, for surely it seems attractive, 'like having wings to fly'. The reasons are that, firstly, not everyone believes it and, secondly, that even those who do often lack the patience to train themselves sufficiently. 'This is as it should be'. Like all spiritual attainment, greater seeing and hearing asks for strength and control, consideration for others, and the art of silence. It would be no good to know too much for those 'given to criticizing their fellow-men', nor for their counterparts, 'the tender-hearted ones afraid of any harm touching those dear to them'. Even Inayat, to whose wide and controlled consciousness seeing was a natural outcome, uttered in a striking prayer:

> What I may not see, let me not see;
> What I may not hear, let me not hear;
> What I may not know, I ask not to know. (*Vadan* 47)

A prayer like this is apt to come to a person who has arrived at complete seeing, as described by Inayat elsewhere:

> Every soul stands before me as a world, and the light of my spirit falling upon it brings clearly to view all it contains. (*Gayan* 66, n. 106)

The beginnings seem simple. Seeing is an outcome of a

consequent 'study of life', it is a keener power of perception. One learns to see with the mind.

> The mind is listening when it is aware of things without people telling us. We notice when a person is displeased. A person may say 'Thank you', and yet the mind perceives that he is not really thankful but is using these words as a formality, or even out of sarcasm. . . . The more developed the mind is, the more it can listen even without the help of the ears; it listens to another person's thought without the utterance of a sound. (XII 61)

intuition

One may remark that anybody with some intuition is able to spot an insincere word of thanks. That is just the point. Inayat's 'penetrating seeing' is related to intuition. As with telepathy, one can discern between natural and consciously developed intuition.

> There are some persons, also some people, who are naturally intuitive. . . . A person with a fine mind and with a still mind generally has intuition; someone with a gross mind and a restless mind lacks it. Intuition is a supersense; it may be called a sixth sense; it is the essence of all senses. (II 254)

Note the emphasis and enthusiasm accompanying these words. Here at last Inayat is on his own ground. A consciously developed and controlled intuition he rates as a real accomplishment, a step into the greater worlds. Just as concentration on a thought or feeling is more difficult than concentration on a visible object, so intuition is a greater result than telepathy or seeing and hearing.

> Intuition is a greater and higher thing than spirit-communication or thought reading. . . . In this we do not depend upon a spirit, or upon another person sending a thought to us. In this we are perfectly independent; we receive the knowledge from within, which is far superior, greater, and higher. (VII 83)

conscious intuition

Within is the spark of God, the real Self, hidden in everyone and discovered by the mystic.

What comes from without is not intuition; intuition is something which rises from one's own heart and brings a sense of satisfaction, of ease, and of happiness. (XI 229)

Inayat knew that inner world intimately and felt safer trusting his intuition than following another's rational advice.

So long as I act upon my own intuition I succeed; but when I follow another's advice I go astray. (*Gayan* 67, n. 106)

But he did not forget that for the beginner following one's intuition is not that simple. One should learn to separate intuition from thought, be it one's own reasoning or someone else's influence.

how to discern the right intuition

To catch an intuition is the most difficult thing. For in a moment's time both are working, intuition on the one hand and mind on the other; as if two ends of one stick which is placed in the centre upon another stick were to move up and down, and one did not notice which end rose first and which after. And therefore one needs to take very keen notice of the action of the mind, which is gained by the thorough practice of concentration . . . While looking at it one must be able to shut oneself off from all other sides, fixing one's mind solely upon one's inner being. (II 255)

It is not easy to recognize an intuition. The thought waves are just like voice waves. It is quite possible for the thought of another person to float into that field of which one is conscious, and one may hear it and think it is one's intuition. (VII 235)

If one makes a habit of catching the first intuition and saving it from being destroyed by reason, then intuition is stronger and one can benefit by it. (IV 223)

Reason does not necessarily destroy intuition, but, used rightly, it can be a help. Nor is intuition antagonistic to intellectual or other worldly pursuits. It is common knowledge that great achievements are likely to commence with intuition, or even with inspiration. Inayat, too, frequently refers to the inspiration of scientists and artists, for instance in IV 255 and

266, and VI 128. Inspiration is an essential further development of intuition.

> The next step is inspiration. Inspiration is not only the coming of a single thought, a single idea, but a flow of ideas. (VII 85)

inspiration

> Inspiration is a higher form of intuition, for it comes as an idea, as a complete theme with its improvisation, as a phrase creative of a poem. Inspiration is a stream . . . For the really inspired person . . . , whatever be his work, when once he has received an inspiration he has found satisfaction, not with himself, but with what has come to him. It gives his soul relief. (II 259)

The successive stages of intuition are often mentioned, not only in the chapters headed 'Intuition' or 'Inspiration' (II 254-262, V 29, VII 82-86 and 229-237, XI 220-224). The first stage is an impulse or impression 'like a straw floating upon the water' (VII 236). The ultimate stage is called revelation. Revelation is a word with several connotations, which do not all come within the scope of this book. As an attainment of the great mystics it will be touched upon in the next chapter. The lay mystic will be kept busy enough trying to grasp and hold the dancing straw of his first intuitive impression.

Once one can handle one's intuition—that means to discern and grasp the right impression, and then to trust it—one can develop an inner compass. When that is established there follows a form of understanding that in itself is a demonstration of the unity of all beings. First one finds the answer for one's own problems, later one may be able to perceive the right answer for others too.

under-standing

> After having intuition about individuals in their relation to ourselves, the next step is the intuition which occurs when another person is telling us of his projects. We have an impression as to whether they will be successful or not. (VII 83/84)

> There is a stage in the evolution of a man's life when every question is answered by the life around him. (VIII 130)

> One is in at-one-ment with all living beings, and it gives one as much insight into another as the other person has into himself. One knows as much as he knows, even more. This is the simplest phenomenon of this consciousness; not to work wonders. (IV 123)

This understanding of oneself and others is the result of using one's inner senses and the widened consciousness. This perceptive wideness, or 'communication with life' (see next chapter) in all its forms, leads to a still deeper and more rare understanding: insight into causes and reasons.

> A seeker takes his first step in the path of truth when he is able to understand his fellow-men fully and find the solution to every problem connected with them. The next step is to have insight into the nature of things and beings, to understand cause and effect. (VIII 220)

> A mystic does not look at reasons as everybody else does, because he sees the first reason that comes to his mind is only a cover over another reason which is hidden behind it . . . . Then again he sees that this reason which was hidden behind the first reason is more powerful, but that there is still greater reason behind it. And as he goes further, penetrating the several veils of reason, he reaches the essence of reason. (X 22)

> One begins to see from two points of view. One begins to see the right of the wrong and the wrong of the right . . . . One begins to see that everything is reflected in its opposite . . . . One sees the dark in the bright and the light in the dark, death in birth and birth in death. It is a kind of double view of things . . . . The third aspect is that in failure one will not feel such disappointment, and in success not such great joy. In adverse conditions one will not be so dejected. (VII 196)

This deepened understanding and insight are followed by one of the most characteristic qualities of the mystic. It strikes one in any real sage one may meet: his imperturbable calm that is never cold.

> The lesson we learn from the developing of our insight is not to become excited by any influence that tries to bring us out of rythm under all conditions of life; to keep our equilibrium, our tranquillity under all circumstances . . . . because it is difficult it is a great attainment. (IV 219)

loving detachment

As a permanent attitude this tranquillity belongs to the great mystics. But even the lay mystic who begins to see more than meets the outer eye, discovers himself reacting in a new way: at the same time quietly and more deeply. (VII 196/197) One perceives limitedness as limitedness indeed; the opening up of inner possibilities sets all things in a different light.

> Ordinary life will seem to be a life in a narrow small world. It is just like living one's life in the ocean instead of in a small well. (XI 160)

> Spirit is joy, spirit is life . . . As the sun takes away all darkness, so spiritual light removes all worries, anxieties, and doubts . . . . Certainly, the things a person once valued and considered important become less important . . . It is just like seeing the stage in daylight: all the palaces and other scenery on the stage suddenly mean nothing. But it puts an end to the slavery to which everyone is subjected, for the awakened man becomes master of the things of this world. (VIII 306)

> An adept was sitting in a ship with an ordinary person. And this person said, 'Oh, how terrible this noise is, continually going on. It breaks my nerves to pieces. Terrible, terrible . . . . It almost drives me mad.' The adept said, 'I did not hear it until you reminded me of it. I hear it when I want to hear it; I do not hear it when I do not want to hear it.' That is the idea. Both had the sense of hearing, but one had the power to close and open it. (IV 283)

It is clear that this power is reached by concentration and all the other main exercises described in the previous chapter. It is an essential stage of development, but, like all other things, one should not force nor hasten it.

He who arrives at the state of indifference without experiencing interest in life is incomplete, and apt to be tempted by interest at any moment; but he who arrives at the state of indifference by going through interest, really attains the blessed state. (V 27)

Sometimes interest is required, sometimes indifference is profitable. (VI 175)

The question arises, how can one learn indifference? By learning interest. If in our life we do not learn interest, we cannot learn indifference. (VI 179)

Indifference is scarcely the right word. Sometimes Inayat calls it detachment or independence, or he uses the Sanskrit term *vairagya,* 'no other language having a word which can render this particular meaning so adequately.' (I 99/100 and X 94) But the word *vairagya* may be applied to complete mortification as well as to the modest detachment of the lay mystic. The greatest difficulty lies in the association with cold aloofness. Maybe the best way to characterize this 'indifference' is to add the word 'loving'. There is no coldness in the evolving adept, he cannot 'widen his heart' and be cold.

Breadth of heart is what is needed for all this . . . . The great heart does not think about how troublesome a person is and why he should be bothered like this . . . The heart becomes wide by forgetting the self. (XII 93)

The work of the inner life is to make God a reality . . . and when this happens, then all relationships, however near and dear, become less binding. But at the same time, a person does not thus become cold; he becomes more loving. (I 70)

One can love one's friends and serve them, and yet be detached. (III 261)

fascination of greater worlds

It may happen that the fascination of greater worlds is so powerful, that the advancing adept must remind himself of his task in the limited world.

Indifference, my most intimate friend, I am sorry I have always to act against thee as thy opponent. (*Gayan* 4, n. 5)

> In order to arrive at spiritual attainment two gulfs must be crossed, the sea of attachment and the ocean of detachment. (*Vadan* 101)

This is mostly a problem for the advanced and great mystics, whose attainments, happiness and difficulties will be looked into the next chapter. The lay mystic may have some difficulties in the beginning, but soon, if he is really evolving, the benefits are great and his life problems become solved.

> To some extent life becomes easy for a mystic to deal with. For he knows every heart, every nature, whereas those who are untouched by the mystic's secret suffer from their difficulties. (X 33)

> The teacher shows us the only path that frees us from all the pain of which this life is full. (X 105/106)

But—contrary to many standard religious doctrines—Inayat emphasizes that great happiness can be found in this world, during this life.

> There is nothing which cannot be obtained in this world; everything is there, all things good and beautiful, all things precious and worth while; they are all there, if only one knows their nature, their character, and how to obtain them. (X 34)

Inayat means, chiefly, spiritual attainment, and for him, a great mystic, that was the most desirable good in life. But the lay mystic can say:

> 'Though there are many things in life which I need for the moment and for which I shall certainly work, yet there is only that one thing, around which life centers, that will satisfy me: the spiritual attainment, or, as one may even call it, the attainment of God.' Such a one has found the key to all happiness. (VII 45)

doubts of progress

If the lay mystic and the beginner find difficulties or unhappiness in their way, these are mostly of their own making, and they may hinder their own progress. Some people are ambitious and want to do too much, or they are nervous and self-conscious about their progress.

> There is a natural tendency in the seeker on the spiritual path to wonder if he is really progressing. And very often he begins to wonder from the day he sets foot on the path. It is like asking, 'Shall I be able to digest?' while one is eating. The spiritual path leads to selflessness. The more we worry about ourselves, the less progress we make. (X 110)

It is different if, for some time, an adept doubts his progress because he has become more critical of himself. (VI 96, VIII 282/283. X 107) But one should avoid all agitation.

attitudes that hinder progress

> Agitation is not allowed on this path; agitation disturbs our rhythm and paralyses us. (X 112)

Inayat warns and reassures, and is careful in his description of progressive stages.

> There are no milestones to count; one cannot say, 'I have gone so many miles and there are so many still before me.' This does not belong to a spiritual journey. (X 111)

He points to modern haste and ambition that most of us take for granted.

> It is a journey we have to make on foot. This at once changes the character of the journey and makes it different from the journeys we are accustomed to. There is no modern equipment, and we have forgotten how one journeyed in the past. To go through the wilderness, over mountains, to swim rivers in order to get to the other side, to risk all sorts of dangers on the way, that is the kind of journey we have to make in spiritual attainment. The outer journeys are made easy today, but the inner journey has kept its difficulties. (VI 161)

> One should not be ambitious to do other exercises before having had a result from the first one. . . . We distinguish stages, although in reality it is impossible to do so. It is a spontaneous development . . . What is spiritual progress? What is it like? Spiritual progress is the changing of the point of view. (X 88/89)

Much talk about spiritually and progress bars this progress, just like arrogance and its complement, self-centred worry.

> It will not come by talking about it, by discussing and arguing. (VIII 331) (see next chapter on 'Word and Silence')

> Where there is spirituality there is no proud claim. (XI 243)

Along with too much talk and pride, there is another attitude which, though it has its good side also, will stand in the way of real success.

> Enthusiasm is a great thing in life. It is creative, but too much of it spoils things. (XI 240)

> There are many in this world who from enthusiasm push along the object of their attainment like a football. They mean to grasp it, but unintentionally they push it on . . . One should remember that in the path of attainment one must first feel strong enough to bear the burden of what one wishes to attain. (VI 203)

Of course the rigid one stays stuck, but the one who does not know his mind fares no better. The adept needs a clear mind and clearness of purpose.

> Those who are confused, who are constantly hurried, who are changeable in their nature, who are afraid of death, of disease, of their own actions, of their enemies, of their surroundings; those who have constant doubt . . . and so on—it is all these who have less possibility of intuition. (VII 82)

Further it is no good and no use to look upon spiritual powers as a means to get other things, that would be 'like spending pearls to buy pebbles'. (VII 231) This is not a moral but a logical condition: interest in possession adds to the limited ego instead of diminishing it. (VI 196) Even happiness is not an aim but an additional consequence.

> One does not take initiation for the sake of attaining happiness. It is true that one cannot attain wisdom without deriving a certain advantage from it . . . But it is not for this that the journey is entered upon. (I 49)

gains of progress

All the same, the gains are great, once progress has begun.

> Progress means ease, relief, peace, happiness, less strife, less struggle; that is progress. (VII 246)

> With spiritual attainment, the first thing one begins to see in oneself is that thoughts such as 'I cannot' or 'it is impossible', or 'I am helpless' or 'it cannot be done' cease to exist. A soul naturally becomes positive and will say, 'If it is difficult today, tomorrow it will be easy; if it cannot be done just now it can be done later. (VII 229)

> Spiritual attainment is success itself; all things come to the spiritual person. (VII 232)

> A person who has spiritual attainment need not cultivate sympathy morally, for sympathy comes as a matter of course without his cultivating it. (VII 232)

The reverse is true as well.

> The one who has learned friendship has attained spiritual knowledge. (VI 186)

> A man who professed to have no religion profoundly once said, 'I am happy, I have no fear.' He was spiritual, though he did not know it. (XI 165)

But the one who seeks consciously, knows that spiritual achievement will lead to fearlessness, freedom and happiness.

> As man grows through the inner life, so he feels a freedom of thought, speech and action, which comes as a natural course through his spiritual journey. (I 82)

> Every step forward gives a certain amount of freedom of action, and as one goes further and further on the path of truth the freedom becomes greater at every step. (XI 230)

> God is happiness, the soul is happiness, and spirituality is happiness. (XI 244)

As often as Inayat is not confronted with the necessity to clear away, patiently and tactfully, always with great understanding, the many erroneous notions, and whenever he can speak about his actual subject, God-realization, then the happiness shines through, even through the printed words.

> Once I was with a man who was in the habit of meditating, and while we were sitting near the fire and talking about things he went into silence, and I had to sit quiet until he opened his eyes. I asked him, 'It is beautiful, is it not?' and he said, 'It is never enough.' Those who experience the joy of meditation, for them there is nothing in the world which is more interesting and enjoyable. They experience the inner peace and the joy that cannot be explained in words; they touch perfection, or the spirit of light, of life and love, all is there. (I 97)

This joy and peace is always within reach of the great mystic. But the lay mystic, too, may experience glimpses and moments of this freedom.

> When a man has reached this stage, he at first begins to realize God only at certain moments; then as he develops he does it for a longer time; and those who develop still further pass most of their time in that realization. (VIII 148)

Even they have to work for it constantly, as the next chapter will show. But there are many signs of progress, even if they are not that conspicuous. We can find a survey of results in chapters like 'Mastery', (IV 119), 'Sublime Knowledge' (VII 229-232), and often Inayaṭ encourages his mureeds; small failures are unavoidable and can be overcome (IV 105, X 111).

> There are innumerable outer signs of one's progress, but one need not think in the absence of these signs that one is not progressing. What are these signs of progress? the first is that one feels inspiration, and that things which one could not understand yesterday are easy today. Yet if there are things which one is not ready to understand one should have patience till tomorrow. . . . The next sign of progress is that one begins to feel power. To some extent it may manifest physically and also mentally; and later the power may manifest in one's affairs in life. . . . The third sign of progress is that one begins to feel a joy, a happiness. But in spite of this feeling it is possible that clouds of depression and despair may come from without, and one might think at that moment that all the happiness and joy which one had

gained spiritually was snatched away. But that is not so. If spiritual joy could be snatched away it would not be spiritual joy. . . . There is another sign of progress, and that is that one becomes fearless. Whatever the situation in life, nothing seems to frighten one any more, even death. . . .

Still another sign of progress is that at times one begins to feel peaceful. This may increase so much that a restful feeling comes in the heart. . . . One may make the excuse that one's surroundings are worrying one, that one's friends are troublesome or that one's enemies are horrible; but nothing can withstand that peace which is awakened in the heart. All must calm down, all must settle down like dust after water has been sprinkled on it.

But if this power does not come immediately to a mureed, let him not be disappointed. Can one expect this whole journey to be made in a week? I would not be surprised if many mureeds do expect this, but it is a lifelong journey and those who have really accomplished it are the ones who have never doubted that they would progress. . . . . They only know that they must reach the goal, that they will reach it. (X 112/113/114)

VII Mysticism, the Great Ones and the Great Attainments

spiritual and human

> To be religious, to be orthodox, or to be pious does not necessarily mean to be spiritual. (VI 160)
>
> Mysticism is deeper than religion; in other words mysticism is the soul of religion. A person who follows a religion follows its form; the one who touches mysticism touches the spirit of religion . . . . The great teachers and inspirers of humanity in all ages were mystics. One only has to study their lives. (XI 223)

Sometimes people said to Inayat that they regarded social improvements as the way to salvation of humanity. Then the master answered that all ways were needed in life to attain perfection. (SK 67) Inayat regarded those whose aim was to help mankind as religious, even if they considered themselves as a-religious or anti-religious. But only spiritual depth, he added, will make their efforts really fruitful in the long run.

One of the answers to many questions concerned with religion as opposed to social concern or life in the world may be found in 'Five Different Kinds of Spiritual Souls.' (I 102-105) The first kind is the religious character, whose religious consciousness has deepened into spirituality. Outwardly he acts like any one who keeps to the religious forms of his community, but

spiritual souls in different guises

> While others are doing all their religious actions outwardly he realizes them in his life in reality. Every religious action to him is a symbolical revelation; prayer to him is a meditation; the scripture to him is his reminder, for the holy book refers him to that which he reads in life and nature. (I 102)

A second character is that of the philosophical mind with

deep understanding, and the third one the social worker.

> He may seem to be quite a man of the world in business, or in the affairs of the wordly life. He takes all things smoothly, he tolerates all things, he endures all things. He takes life easily with his understanding . . . .
>
> The third form of a spiritual being is that of a server, one who does good to others . . . . Their philosophy and religion are in their action . . . . They consider everyone who comes near them as their brother and sister, as their child; they take an interest in the joy and the sorrow of all people . . . . In whatever form he may appear, the chief thing in his life is the service of mankind. (I 103)

The two characters described next are recognizable mystics. I 104 and 105 present a comprehensive portrait of the mystic in general. To quote a few traits only:

some traits of a mystic

> People are always at a loss when dealing with him. His 'yes' is not the same 'yes' that everybody says; his 'no' has not the same meaning as that which everybody understands. In almost every phrase he says there is some symbolical meaning . . . . You may see the mystic twenty times a day and twenty times he will have a different expression . . . . and yet his outward mood may not at all be his inner mood. (I 104/105)

the hidden mystic

The fifth type often features in Inayat's anecdotes: the *madzub,* who may be a very advanced mystic but who hides his power behind a mask of eccentric innocence. The *madzub* may, also, be described as the very great soul who can protect his entire environment, even his country. (I 105) In summing up the different spiritual types Inayat remarks that there is no end to the variety of the outward appearance of spiritual souls and reverts to those who have to fulfill their mission in outer life, at the same time living their inner realization. (I 106)

In other passages the various kinds of mystics are described in more detail. The *madzub* with his funny ways, and the recluse in his silence are considered enviably free as compared with the great personalities of the prophets, the messengers, who cannot hide, and have to bear the brunt of life in the world.

the prophets

> The seers and saints, who live a life of seclusion, are happy when compared with the prophet, whose life's work is in the midst of the crowd. When he is known to be a prophet, jealousy and prejudice arise; if he is not known, he can do but little . . . . The mystic is free to speak and act; what does he care what people think of him? The prophet, however, must be careful what they think, not for himself, but for those who follow him. (IX 145)

Those prophets, their aims, their lives, their difficulties and happiness, their similarities and differences, their openness and God-connectedness are one of Inayat's great subjects. The great one's and mystics following in their footsteps do not seek their own salvation, they use their widened consciousness, their spirituality, to help others.

the great ones do not seek their individual salvation

> It is not spirituality alone; there have been many madzubs who were very spiritual. They were united with God, but they have gone and no one remembers them. It is not piety: there are many pious people sitting in the mosques and churches telling their rosaries. Their piety is for themselves; they cannot move the world. So if it is not spirituality and not piety, what is it then? It is the development of humanity in us. (VIII 235)

> What is the use of samadhi (touching the presence of God) if we are not first human? (X 87)

These words may have had a special significance for a listener who tended to float instead of to rise. But to be human, to develop personality and to help others are intrinsic elements of Inayat's teachings.

> Among all the different schools of esotericism and mysticism the Sufi school has concerned itself most with the development of personality . . . . Such a personality spreads harmony, peace, thoughtfulness, and consideration. (XI 139, 140)

helpers of men

The great mystics are helpers of men and the work or teachings of great personalities live long after their bodily death. This is said of messengers like Buddha and Christ (X 143, VIII 235), but also of great artists. On the pages IV 226 and X 218 attention is drawn to the power behind the words of eastern and western classics, of Rumi, of Kalidasa, of Dante and especially Shakespeare. Inayat's art of personality will be considered in Chapter IX of the present book; personality is needed in daily life as well as for spiritual advancement.

The prophet, the messenger of God, must of necessity be a great personality, which does not imply that his full stature will be recognized during his lifetime. He sees, knows, feels, understands and experiences more than the average man, but he does not make a show of his attainments.

> The further such souls go, the more humble they become; the greater the mystery they have realized, the less they speak about it. (I 75/76)

> The greatest lesson of mysticism is to know all, attain all and be silent. (II 161)

In the beginning a young adept may be proud:

> Those who begin to see the difference between the laws they set before themselves and the laws that are observed by mankind, at first sometimes condemn and then disregard the common laws. They criticize them; and ask, 'What is it all for?' But those who come to the fuller realization of the inner laws, show respect even for the laws of children. (I 83/84)

It is characteristic of the great mystic that, though daily worries appear as childish to him (VI 83, X 23), he never advertises his detachment. In his dealings with others the great one will join in their games, as a parent joins in his children's games. He will not criticize, though he sees through one's weakness and lies.

> I have seen a mystic walking in a religious procession with the peasants, singing hymns with them before an idol of stone. He himself was greater than the god in the procession

and yet he was singing with the same reverence as everybody else. He never had any desire to show that his belief, his realization, was higher or greater than the realization of others. (X 15)

They have never been willing to point out the fault in another, and to hurt the faulty one. It was in their regard for the dignity of humanity, in their modesty and service, that lay the beauty and greatness of their great lives. (III 190/191)

They know if somebody is telling a lie; but do they accuse that person? Do they say, 'You are telling a lie'? They are above it. They know all the plays of the world, and they look at them all passively; they rise above things of this world which makes no impression on them. They take people quite simply. (I 68)

ego-less but powerful

This ego-lessness and adjustment to others do not mean that the advanced mystic is weak, though this is a common misinterpretation.

Very often people are deluded by the great compassion, by the graciousness, fineness, saintliness of spiritual souls. They perhaps see in their negativeness a lack of power; but it is not really so. On the contrary, behind the refinement, behind the saintliness and compassionate attitude, a great power is hidden, a power of resistance, a power of accomplishment. (VI 230)

Besides, the great one may hide his understanding as well as his loving detachment. There are circumstances wherein even a holy man should show 'ego enough not to be trampled upon.' (VIII 122) If necessary, he may play at ego or at anger.

When once the Nafs (ego) is crushed you will never find it necessary to be angry any more, though you can act the part of one who is angry and pretend to be angry. So if it is necessary to show anger this does not mean the fire of hell for you as it would be for others, for you are only using an instrument, and that instrument is not your master (XII 90/91) *differences of evolution and differences of character*

As Inayat says 'you can' one may assume that this degree of loving detachment is within the reach of any serious adept, just as is a certain degree of God-realization. But there are differences in attainment, which do not depend upon grades of development, but are due to basic temperaments. Once, Inayat narrates, two pupils of the same teacher went out into the world. When they met again, after many years, they exchanged experiences. The one had learned 'how to conciliate another' and he could do this very well. The other excelled in mastering life, all that happened happened by his will. They went to their murshid and this master explained:

> Both of you are right. In the case of the first it was self-denial, in the right sense of the word, which enabled him to conciliate others, in the case of the second there was no longer any of his will left; if there was any, it was the will of God. (VI 53)

In both the ego had diminished and spirituality had grown, in the one on the soil of a passive nature, in the other on that of an active character. Though in reality there are 'millions of qualities' (VI 53), for a general description Inayat usually refers to these basic types, the active and struggling one, the Master, and the more passive, resigned, unobtrusive one, the Saint. A third one, the Prophet, combines these two tendencies; whereas the greatest of all 'becomes what others pursue'. (VIII 21-31, IV 184, 186, VI 222, IX 132-135) Sometimes Inayat uses the Sufi terms indicating different types of holy men (for instance IX 128, 132/133, XII 113), sometimes their Yogi names (VIII 28-31, IV 184), often both (I 98, IX 130). He may allude to differences of emphasis in several religious cultures (XII 106), but he respects them all. As to which attitude is superior, the active or the passive:

> If you were to ask me which of the two is superior I would say that there is neither superior nor inferior. If you work according to your temperament that is the natural work for you. (XII 106)

increasing openness

For the prophets and great mystics too, one may discern

stages of increasing responsiveness. There are several Sufi terms for these shades of evolution. (I 29, IX 128, 132/133) The names used most often by Inayat are Pir, Nabi and Rasul. In *Vadan* three songs or prayers are dedicated to them, of which I cite a few lines, which are more suggestive of their essence than an abstract description. The Pir song begins with these words:

> Inspirer of my mind, consoler of my heart, healer of my spirit,
> Thy presence lifteth me from earth to Heaven. (*Vadan* p.109)

The first lines addressed to the Nabi are:

> A torch in the darkness, a staff during my weakness,
> A rock in the weariness of life,
> Thou, my Master makest earth a Paradise. (*Vadan* p. 110)

In the last lines the Nabi is called the Prophet of God, for he is the guide of a community. (I 29) But the greatest messenger is the Rasul, whose song begins as follows:

> Warner of coming dangers,
> Wakener of the world from sleep,
> Deliverer of the Message of God,
> Thou art our Saviour. (*Vadan* p. 110, 111)

the inner unity of prophets and messengers

The Rasuls are the greatest of all, the founders of world religions. (IX 130/131, 144-151, 158-203) The book *The Unity of Religious Ideals* is written to demonstrate that all great teachers of humanity have intrinsically the same vision and experiences, however outward circumstances and external types may differ. The chapters I 30-38 and VII 221-228 cover the same subject, and one comes upon it throughout the whole work. This inner unity of the greatest masters is one of Inayat's essential teachings. After stating that 'There is one God, the only Being' (see p. 24) the second of the ten basic teachings says:

> There is One Master, the Guiding Sprit of all Souls, Who constantly leads His followers towards the light. (I 14, IX 267)

Guiding Spirit or Spirit of Guidance (originally Light of Guidance) is the important word, and the one-ness and constant presence are its essence.

> The Spirit of Guidance may be pictured as one thread; and all the great masters of humanity are like the beads on that thread. One spirit and many individualities. (IX 142)

> If the masters were not the same in their mortal garb, yet in spirit they were one. (I 31)

This aspect of one-ness in the masters is the core of the prayer Salat, and expounded XI 166/167, because many wonder about the following lines, when confronted with them for the first time:

> Allow us to recognize Thee in all Thy holy names and forms; as Rama, as Krishna, as Shiva, as Buddha. Let us know Thee as Abraham, as Solomon, as Zarathustra, as Moses, as Jesus, as Muhammad, and in many other names and forms, known and unknown to the world. (*Gayan* p. 71/72, n. 113)

Inayat's pupils understood, learning from his example. Often they recall that Christ seemed most dear to him, when he spoke about Christ: when he spoke about Buddha all was Buddha to him; and Muhammad when it was Muhammad. (SK 3, 8, 9, 11, 27)

But in the West as well as in the East there were many expecting a designated saviour to solve all problems and redeem the world, at least the world of those who had created his image. These hopes of salvation might combine political and religious elements as in the Islamic Mahdism or combine Hindu and Christian concepts as did the theosophists. There were many theosophists among Inayat's audiences; and he himself was well acquainted with the religious and political dreams and expectations in the Muslim world. Of the many answers to questions regarding a saviour soon to come, the following has the widest bearing.

> What is the Sufi's belief regarding the coming of a World Teacher, or, as some speak of it, the 'second coming of Christ'? The Sufi is free from beliefs and disbeliefs, and yet

gives every liberty to people to have their own opinion. There is no doubt that if an individual or a multitude believe that a teacher or a reformer will come, he will surely come to them. Similarly, in the case of these who do not believe that any teacher or reformer will come, to them he will not come. To those who expect the teacher to be a woman, a woman must deliver it. To those who call on God, God comes. To those who knock at the door of Satan, Satan answers. There is an answer to every call. To a Sufi the Teacher is never absent, whether he comes in one form or in a thousand forms. (I 45/46)

the teacher is always present

The teacher is always present. Christ said it to his disciples as Krishna did to his (VII 265). Inayat repeats:

> To the real devotees of Christ, Christ is near, as near as they are to themselves to their own selves. In times of trouble, in difficulties, he is always there. (X 67)

> The mystic understands that illuminated souls, guiding souls, are on earth today too. They were not only in the past; they are here now also. Were there none on the earth now how could illumination be continued? (VII 226)

> The Spirit which is called Alpha and Omega is always present and is always doing its work, recognized and unrecognized. (IX 30/31)

One of the causes that a teacher is not recognized may be found in the blindness or the erratic expectations of those he comes to help. But there are also the truly great ones who make no attempt to draw public attention.

> The great ones are initiated by God Himself, and they prove their initiations not by their claims, but in their works. (XI 237)

In our days a religious leader would not make claims to reform society, but, as said above, this was part of his task in former days. Furthermore, a teacher working in modesty and silence, more like a brother than an authority (I 31) is in tune with the spirit of our age. Above all, working in silence, unencumbered by words, can be much more effective.

Nowadays, Inayat says, humanity is mature enough and does not need a personality called a prophet or healer or god-incarnation.

> Now the world can recognize, sooner or later, what is right and what is wrong. The warner, the master, the messenger of today will not claim; he will only work. He will leave his work to prove for itself whether it is true or false. (VII 228)

This silent method diminishes, to a certain extent, the great difficulty all great helpers met with: the misunderstanding and misinterpretation caused by the limitation of words.

> For the task of the prophet is a most difficult one; it is trying to present to the world the whole ocean in a bottle. No one has ever been able to do it; yet they have all tried, for that has been their destiny. People have taken these bottles when given to them, and have said, 'See, here is the ocean; I have the ocean in my pocket!' (IX 150)

> When the prophets and seers of all ages have given to humanity a certain message and law, it was only the giving of a drop from the ocean which they received in their hearts. And this is also a great difficulty, for even this drop is not intelligible. Does every Christian understand the Bible? Does every Muslim know the Qur'an, or every Hindu the Vedanta? No, they may know the words of the verses, but not always the inner meaning. (I 86)

The image of the ocean in a bottle is a recurrent theme in Inayat's lectures. One cannot express the unlimited in limited words. Many things are best expressed in silence. This is true of all subtle feelings and experiences, and for the unlimited it is a necessity.

words and silence

> God apart, can one explain anything fine and subtle in words? (XII 13)

> Man cannot say how much he loves his beloved. (I 77)

> He (the mystic) cannot fully express himself. How difficult it is to translate fully the poetry of one language into the poetry of another. Yet it is only interpreting the ideas of one

part of the earth to the people of another part of the same earth. How much more difficult, then, it must be to translate or to interpret the ideas of the divine world to the human world. In what words can they be given? What phrases can be used for them? And after being given even in words and phrases, who would understand them? It is the language of a different world. (I 86)

Chapters on silence, its attainment and power are found II 13-16, IV 204-209, VII 38-45, 125-131, X 47-51. It is a great art to be able to enjoy silence and to work through silence. Beginning mureeds are taught the importance of not spending energy in talking and fussing; in the great ones the power of silence becomes manifest. One of the first great sages Inayat met as a boy was a *muni,* a saint who never spoke, sitting perfectly still in the woods. Around him there reigned absolute silence; even the trees and plants did not stir and seemed to be listening, 'as if the everblowing wind had lost its power in this perfect silence which came from the peace of his soul'. (unpublished *Biography* by Mehr Baksh)

silence as an attainment

Very remarkable are those places where Inayat, who was born a Muslim, describes how even an 'idol of stone'[1] can be impressive by its very stillness, and bring rest to the restive human before it.

> A person might wonder about the old custom of Brahmins and Buddhists, who . . . sat before an idol which neither spoke to them or took notice of them. He might think, 'What could they gain? . . . .' This human form sitting before them, silent and quiet and not speaking, or hearing, or thinking, absolutely quitet; just think what it means. (VII 41/42)

It means, to Inayat, a symbol of concentration, contemplation and meditation, as said explicitly in a similar

[1] In the recent edition of *The Unity of Religious Ideals* (IX 11-279) the chapter on 'Idolatry' is rather maimed. On the pages IX 204-210, concerning the evolution from idol (a visible form) to ideal, the original subtitles 'An advanced form of idolatry' and 'The higher form of Idolatry' are left out, and the historical development of monotheism from Abraham to Muhammad is cut of in the middle, part of it being transferred to IX 195. Compare the original edition (London/Geneva 1928), pages 230, 232-233, 229.

passage. (VII 129) But the quoted chapter on 'Silent Life' goes on to evoke the wonderful silence and stillness Inayat remembered and always longed for, while going about his own task in the nervous cities of the West.

> What was it in the wilderness that gave peace and joy? What was it that came to us in the forest, the solitude? In either case it was nothing else but the depth of our own life, which is silent like the depths of the great sea, so silent and still. It is the surface of the sea that makes waves and roaring breakers; the depth is silent. So the depth of our own being is silent also.
> And this all-pervading, unbroken, inseparable, unlimited, ever-present, omnipotent silence unites with our silence like the meeting of flames. (VII 42/43)

silence as a means and as a method

Silence is an attainment, a happiness, and silence is used as a method by the pupil, as a means by the teacher. Sound and words are used for inner development, but the use of silence is a greater power.

> The mystic realizes the power of the word and the splendour of silence. (XI 212)

> There are different ways of receiving inspiration, but the best is silence. (VIII 209)

> Where did the great power attained by yogis and faqirs come from? It was gained by having learned and practised the art of silence. (IV 205)

> When man closes his lips God begins to speak. (*Gayan* 88, n. 143)

> Furthermore they (the Sufis) practise Tawajjoh, a method of receiving knowledge and power from the teacher in silence. This way is considered by Sufis to be the most essential and desirable. (X 86)

words limited, misinterpreted and misused

This is not only desirable, but often a necessity, for there is much that causes words and language to fail in transmitting the essence.

> I have often noticed that philosophy when explained plainly

> has been understood quite differently from what it meant. (VIII 61)

> What the prophet says is much less than what he really hears, and the sense of what he says is much deeper than what his outer words mean. (IX 150)

These are two of the many remarks—like the ocean-in-a-bottle simile—wherein Inayat refers to the limitedness of language and the difficulty of making the mystic's experience known. Much is lost and more is misinterpreted.

> People think that many words express things better. They do not know that most often all the words spoken are so many veils wrapped about the idea. (XI 240)

> The words of the mystic may be simple and at the same time full of depth. His every expression is symbolical. (XI 217)

Besides, words breed argument and, in the case of superficial and hasty thinking, language is often misused.

> Sufism avoids words, from which differences and distinctions arise. Words can never express truth fully. Words promote argument. (VI 197)

> Sometimes these (names of movements) are big names with little meaning to them, but much is made of them by those who want to commercialize finer things. (VIII 287)

We already saw (p. 116) that too much talking mars one's progress. But one cannot do without words, certainly not in the initial stage. Because only a few understood silence and because he himself knew clearly what he had to say and how much he could convey in different circumstances, Inayat chose to speak; in simple language and in simple images taken from daily life.

> Subtle ideas are best expressed simply. (*Vadan* 82)

Inayat's simple naturalness was not superficial, nor abbreviatory. And never an easy panacaea as some people wanted. Quite often those unable to understand his tactful gentleness nor his symbols nor the depth of his subject, asked for a quick and ready explanation.

> Very often people ask, 'But what is the truth? Can you explain it?' Words cannot explain it. Often I thought it would be a good thing to write the word TRUTH on a brick, and give it into the hands of such a person, and say, 'Hold it fast, there is the truth!' (VI 193, compare III 202)

Truth and fact

Here the difficulty is not only in a difference of attitude, but first of all in the meaning of the word. For most people truth, a truth, means an established and circumscribed fact. Whereas for the mystic, as Pilate may have sensed and Christ knew, Truth means the highest knowledge. It is in this sense that it has been described among the Ten Sufi Thoughts.

> There is one Truth, the true knowledge of our being within and without, which is the essence of all wisdom. (I 20, IX 267)

To reach this knowledge is one of the highest attainments.

> It is in reality the dissolving of the false self in the knowledge of the true self, which is divine, eternal and all-pervading. (I 21)

To one not acquainted with this concept of truth, many maxims of Inayat in *Gayan* and *Vadan* may appear vague or incomprehensible. Very often Inayat stressed the difference between facts, the limited truths of ordinary life, and the mystic's unfathomable knowledge of God, the Only Being.

> There is a great difference between fact and truth. Fact is a shadow of truth. Fact is intelligible; but truth is unlimited. Truth knows itself, and nothing else can explain it. What little explanation can be given lies in the idea of expansion. (VI 193)

> There are many facts, but only one truth. Facts can be put into words, but not the truth. (XI 254)

> Absorbed in the world of variety we are apt to forget truth, for we are always engrossed in facts. (VIII 133)

> The fact is a shadow which for the moment represents

something which has a certain meaning attached to it, which we can witness, but which at the same time will not continue to be real for ever. (VI 266)

Facts cannot explain Truth, but Truth can explain facts.

Truth is the light which illuminates the whole of life; in its light all things become clear, their true meaning manifests to view. (*Gayan* 54, n. 90)

Sometimes Truth seems almost identical with God. In a way it is. But the word God is used to denote both the Only Being and the more simple God-concepts, whereas Truth is only applied to the highest concept.

One ought to reach truth through God. (IV 136)

Make God a reality, and God will make you the truth. (*Gayan* 1, n. 2.)

So much in words about things beyond words. The best way is to give and to receive in silence. But how many can use that way?

Can a meditative person not explain in words the knowledge that he receives, so that others can read such a book and thus acquire this knowledge? But I should like to say that if a man who had travelled to Venice gave an account of what he had seen, it would entertain you for a moment, but it would not give you the same joy as you would experience by travelling to Venice yourself. (XII 28)

Nevertheless, the travel accounts are written, if only to evoke the journey for others. The image of a journey also serves to remind one of the necessity to go through all stages of development.

It is not always desirable to live on the top of the mountain, because the ground is also made for man . . . . A person who can observe life from all angles, will have a different experience from each angle; and every side he looks at will give him new knowledge, a different knowledge from that which he had before. (VIII 42)

This brings us back to what has been touched upon in chapters III and V (pp. 33-39 and 88, 89)

> The limitless God cannot be made more intelligible to our limited self unless He is first made limited. (IX 150)

words in poetry

Because one must not pass over any necessary stage of development, one needs a tentative God concept and one needs words. Words can be like auxiliary lines in geometry. Words in poetry are different. A truly inspired poet ranks with prophets.

> Inspiration begins in poetry and culminates in prophecy. (X 120)

But this is another subject, for which I refer to Inayat's lecture 'The Poet and the Prophet' (X 119-122) and his lectures on Sufi poetry in general (X 123-154, X 207-221).

> The soul enjoys expressing itself in verse . . . . Even those who do not wholly understand them (= the poems of Hafiz) are won by their rhythm, charm and beauty of expression. (X 148)

mechanical use of words

Even when misunderstood a poem stands in its own right. Though many only give it a superficial glance, it springs to life again to the eye and ear of a congenial reader. 'Beautiful' words in social intercourse fare differently. Words are just signs which do not evoke much more than a convential reaction. This mechanical superficiality is useful in daily life for routine actions, but it makes us forgetful of the many meanings and connotations a word may have. A word used in a new or unusual sense is scarcely noticed. Probably there are many readers who do not pause to wonder about the meaning of words like Truth and Reality in *Gayan* and *Vadan,* but just pass over them as a bit unusual, or too lofty. Or else, such words are cherished for that very loftiness and solemn ring.

protest against 'beautiful' words

To some people Inayat's teachings appealed, because they liked the noble words he used; terms like spirit, beauty, love were Good, maybe they gave some sensitive souls the safe feeling that the world was not as bad as it seemed. Another person might be irritated by the same terms and call them platitudes—which they could be out of context and without the power and meaning instilled into them by Inayat.

One day a scientist or a scholar, anyhow a man with a doctor's handle to his name, stood on the high steps in front of Inayat's house in Suresnes, among others who were waiting for a short personal talk, such as a pupil might request. He was a mureed, but, as Musharaff Khan[1] tells us, was intending to break with Inayat. The secretary[1] who received the callers heard him loudly voice his discontent.

'Love, harmony and beauty!' he said, 'He lectures about love, harmony and beauty! And what if I shot a bullet through my head in the midst of such a lecture, so that . . .' Here he used some very crude and realistic terms to describe the resulting occurrences, and continued: 'Would He still speak of love, harmony and beauty; would all these sheep-like people continue to believe in it?' He had worked himself into a fine rage by the time his turn had come to enter Inayat's room. Seven minutes later he came out, radiant. 'What a blessing,' he said, 'that it is such "godly" weather today!'

Musharaff Khan relates what happened inside. Inayat first let the man pour out all his doubt and fury, then he started talking about an entirely differect subject. The doubter became more and more calm, until only one question remained with him: 'Murshid, what magic do you have that you have disarmed me?' And Murshid answered:

Because I have already disarmed myself, that is why.'

This protesting intellectual, being a pupil at heart, understood. But the words love, harmony and beauty, very essential to Inayat's teaching, are the kind of words which are heard but seldom listened to, or, if listened to and thought about, they are apt to be misinterpreted and dismissed as unrealistically sweet. Inayat knew.

love as 'a word from the dictionary'

Love has become a word from the dictionary, a word which is used a thousand times in the day which means nothing. (I 239)

[1] This anecdote is reconstructed from two complementary sources, Inayat's youngest brother and Inayat's secretary. (Musharaff Khan, unpublished collection of speeches, and Kismet Dorothea Stam, *Rays,* p. 33 sec. ed. East-West Publ. 1975, first ed. 1927)

The word love is misinterpreted, misunderstood; we use it in everyday life without knowing what it means. When once the soul begins to know what it means, it is a word too sacred to utter. (XI 190)

It is easy to use this word, but it is most difficult to practise it through life. (VIII 239)

synonyms used to avoid misinterpretation

Often Inayat chooses a word like friendship, sympathy, heart quality and the like to avoid superficial associations, but these terms, too, are difficult to define properly, and the meaning is not always exactly identical. There are many aspects of love, and many 'grades' of it, like a scale of progressing love.

Friendship is a word which we all use in our everyday language, and yet it could take one's whole life only to realize its meaning. (VII 251)

This is from the beginning of two chapters on 'Friendship', which contains the same elucidations as the lectures on love, and at the end (VII 260) the word love itself is used.

What is called sympathy, kindness, mercy, goodness, pity, compassion, gentleness, humility, appreciation, gratefulness, service, is in reality love. (VIII 271/272)

Every kind of power lies in this one thing which we call by the simple name: love. Charity, generosity, kindness, affection, endurance, tolerance and patience, all these words are different aspects of only one thing: love. Whether it is said, 'God is love' or whatever name is given to it, all the names are the names of God; and yet every form of love, every name for love, has its own peculiar scope, has a pecularity of its own . . . . . It is love's different manifestations in different directions which distinguish themselves differently and have different purposes. (VII 74)

Within the scope of this book only a few aspects can be touched upon, preferably the unexpected ones. Chapters on 'Tuning of the Heart', 'Heart Quality', 'Love', 'Friendship', 'Respect and Consideration', 'Will and Desire' are to be found in all the volumes of Inayat's collected Works. The first thing to keep in mind is that love is not only a feeling and an attitude, but creative power. That is why will is considered an aspect of love.

love and will as creative power

Love is the only power that has created, or that can create. (VII 12)

Words such as wish, desire, love and their like mean more or less the same thing; but the word 'will' has a greater importance than all those other words. And the reason is that will is life itself. (IV 156)

Will is the active aspect of love. But receptive love, too, is creative, in human as well as in divine love. There is no aspect of love that cannot be put to use for spiritual growth, for any form of love is widening of the heart.

The same bridge which connects two souls in the world, when stretched becomes the path to God. (XI 244)

'stages' of love

A person begins his spiritual accomplishment by learning how to be a friend. (VII 252)

It is not belief in God which leads us to the goal, nor is it the analysis and the knowledge of God that brings us there. It is the friendship with God. (VI 252)

Love of form, progressing, culminates in the love of the formless. (*Gayan* 12, n. 19)

Inayat acknowledges everyone's object of love and way of loving, according to a person's evolution and character.

An Afghan soldier was once travelling with a Brahmin. The Brahmin, who was a mild and harmless man, careful not to injure the smallest of God's creation, was repeating to himself the word *Daya,* which means 'kindness'. The Afghan who was a warrior, and understood only the rough side of life, asked him what the word meant. The Brahmin explained that the word was the same as *Rahm* in his language. 'Ah', he exclaimed, 'I understand very well now what it means. I remember I was kind once in my life. For on the field of battle I saw a wounded man writhing in agony, and I was touched, and I put my dagger through him and ended his suffering'. (V 193)

The only undesirable attitudes are those where there is no love at all, and those where love is stagnant and has ceased growing.

> But love is wrongly used when it is not constantly developing and spreading. The water of a pond may turn bad, but the water of a river remains pure because it is progressing. (VIII 225), compare *Gayan* 93, n. 152.

All the same, hasty progress cannot succeed.

> Love climbs the mountain of life step by step. (*Gayan* 49, n. 82)

> What is necessary is to develop a sympathetic nature and to sustain its gradual growth. Just as it is difficult for the student of voice-culture to practise his voice and yet not to let it be spoiled, so it is with a sympathetic person. While developing, he runs the risk of spoiling the faculty of sympathy; in other words, the more loving a person, the more chance he has of being disappointed. The greater the love, the greater the fragility of the heart and the more susceptible it becomes to everything, until it can break at any moment. (VIII 282/283)

qualities of love

This means that strength of will and considerate love should develop in equal measure, until one arrives at that loving detachment described in the previous chapter. And even before reaching this attainment, a really loving person is not attached to others merely by a kind but soft affection, but he is a personality. (see p. 222)

Another weakness to avoid is superficial love, be it unstable or undeep.

> To be today friendly and tomorrow unfriendly cannot for one moment be called friendship; the value of friendship is in its constancy. (III 234)

> Love that endureth not is heart's illusion. (*Vadan* 82)

> The devotional quality needs a little direction. The love quality must be deepened first before it spreads out. If not,

> what generally happens to those who set out to love all human beings is that in the end they hate all human beings. (VIII 287)

In the same passage in which Inayat warns his audience or readers not to overrate one's power of love until it is strong enough, he states that lack of sympathy blocks spiritual growth. (VIII 283) Like so many qualities and attitudes it is both an attainment and a means to develop further. In the paragraphs on telepathy and mirroring (p. 97-101) it is said that 'all such things are natural between people who love each other.' The reverse is true also. No love, no progress.

love needed for spiritual progress

> Everything becomes spiritual once this door of the chamber of the heart is open. (VI 156)

> It would be no exaggeration to say that the reason why a man cannot achieve occult and psychic power, and the intuitive and inspirational faculty, is because he has not developed the power of love. (VII 75)

> Sympathy is the main quality to be cultivated in order to develop the spiritual faculty. (VIII 271)

> If there can be a definition of spirituality, it is in the tuning of the heart. (VIII 279)

To the question whether all kind and loving people might be called spiritual Inayat answered that they are very close to it,

> but they are unconsciously spiritual . . . . Very often we meet a mother or father or child in whom we see a deeply loving tendency; love is pouring out from them, they have become fountains of love. Yet they do not know one word of religion or of mysticism. But this does not matter. (VIII 286)

As a rule the term 'fountains of love', or 'stream of love' is reserved for the great mystics.

> The great teachers of humanity become streams of love. It is the first sign of the sage or holy man that he himself becomes love. His voice, his feeling, his presence, everything makes one realize that there is something open in him which

we do not find in everybody; this something is his deep love. (VII 76)

The fountain stream of love rises in the love for an individual, but spreads and falls in universal love. (*Gayan* 11, n. 17)

This universal love is not a vaguely professed love of all, but a gradually developed attitude and power.

Love in its beginning lives only on reciprocity; but when fully developed it stands on its own feet. (*Gayan* 37/38, n. 62

When one has risen above human love, divine love springs forth (*Vadan* 69)

This divine love, and divine manner in general, is a quality of the very advanced mystic, and is different from beginner's love in that it is free from attachment.

For in every form of human love and affection, the self is somewhere hidden, asking for appreciation, for reciprocity, for recognition; but the divine manner is above all this. (IX 113)

different objects of love

The teachers have taught us first to love from the limited, and thence to advance in love till we attain to the love of God, the Unlimited. (VII 81)

There are some people in this world whose life is absorbed in the pursuit of gold and silver, gems and jewels; they would sacrifice anything or anybody to acquire the object of their love. There are others whose life is engaged in the beautiful vision of fruits, flowers, flowerbeds, and gardens; perhaps they have no other interest besides. There are some who are absorbed in the admiration of the youth and beauty of the opposite sex, and nothing else seems to them worth more. There are others who are won by the beauty of someone's personality, and have entirely devoted to the one they love both their here and their hereafter. Everyone has his object of love according to his standard of beauty, and at the same time each one loves the perfection of the divine being . . . . Man is never capable of loving God in heaven when his sympathy has not even been awakened to the beauty of the earth. (V 179/180)

The objects of love may be different, from humdrum to exalted, but they are always worth while, admirable and beautiful to the one who desires, loves or honours the object of his love. And they are all part of the whole. Therefore the beauty a lover, or even a desirous person, sees in the object of his love spurs him on and may become a motor to bring him further. Among the Ten Sufi Thoughts one finds:

what is meant by beauty

> There is one object of praise, the beauty which uplifts the heart of its worshippers through all aspects from the seen to the unseen. (I 20, IX 267)

The emphasis on beauty is part of the Islamic contemplation of the 'signs of God' as evoked in the Quran and summed up in the Hadith (Islamic tradition): 'God is beautiful and loves beauty.' In a short commentary on this point Inayat notes:

> That which is beautiful to one is not beautiful to another. Man cultivates the sense of beauty as he evolves, and prefers the higher aspect of beauty to the lower. (I 20)

The graded evolution again.

> Who rises above the beauty of form begins to see the beauty of thought; the one who rises above the beauty of thought begins to feel the beauty of feeling, of sentiment, which is greater still; and the one who rises even above sentiment and sees the spiritual aspect of beauty, sees a beauty which is still greater. There is no end to the realization of the inner beauty; . . . yet it does not make a person turn away from the outer beauty. It only makes him appreciate it more than others do. (XI 194)

Indeed, beauty is a word to be handled carefully. It is not a merely aesthetic notion, nor an immovable Idea. In his own language Inayat had at his disposal different words for physical beauty and for beauty with less sensory connotations. There is more to this distinction than coarse versus fine. An important aspect, often brought up by Inayat, is its very subjectiveness. Beauty is created by the lover.

All that man considers beautiful, precious and good, is not necessarily in the thing or the being; it is in the ideal; the thing or being causes him to create the beauty, value and goodness in his own mind. (I 44)

When someone said to Majnun (the Romeo of a great Persian love story), 'Leila, your beloved, is not so beautiful as you think,' he said, 'My Leila must be seen with my eyes. If you wish to see how beautiful Leila is, you must borrow my eyes.' (IX 23)

A less subjective quality of beauty is its complete and balanced aspect, related to harmony.

It is useless to try and put into words what beauty is; but if anything can explain it, it is the other word for beauty and that is harmony. It is the harmonious combination of colours, the harmonious grouping of lines, and the harmonious blending of the objects of nature which suggest to us the idea of beauty. (XI 192)

aspects of harmony

This description of harmony still resembles the artistic view. But harmony, too, has many shades of meaning. It is connected with balance and with rhythm (II 29 and 80); in Urdu again there are two words for harmony, one with a musical, that is with a rhythmic, connotation; it designates the Whole, including good and bad (see chapter IX); and it may be graded into three aspects, eternal, universal and individual harmony. Eternal harmony belongs to God.

All things and beings live and move in it; yet it remains remote, undisturbed and peaceful. This is the God of the believer, and the God of the knower. (II 23)

Universal harmony is found in the created world, where all things are dependent upon and balanced against each other. (II 24) Individual harmony—and disharmony—is the aspect most familiar to us. Inayat divides this into harmony between body and soul within one individual, and the harmony between individuals. (II 25) In this realm both an active and passive training are possible, and with the great mystics lead to great results.

> The harmony of life can be learnt in the same way as the harmony of music. The ear should be trained to distinguish both tone and word, the meaning concealed within, and to know from the verbal meaning and the tone of voice whether it is a true or a false note. (II 28)

> The training of the voice consists in being conscientious about each word spoken, about its tone, rhythm, meaning and the appropriateness for the occasion. (II 29)

Outer and inner harmony can be seen or felt; that is a passive quality. But, like love, harmony has a creative side. Beauty is the more passive one of these three intertwined, inseparable concepts; love, cumulating in will, is the most active, though it has some passive aspects. Harmony is passive as a quality of beauty, active as a working quality in a soul. Beauty, especially inner beauty, is seen or felt; harmony, like love, can be developed. Neither beauty nor harmony are purely aesthetical values. All three are essential attributes of the Whole Being, as well as means for expansion and inner growth.

> The attainment of harmony in life takes longer to acquire and more careful study than does the training of the ear and the cultivation of the voice, although it is acquired in the same manner as the knowledge of music. To the ear of the Sufi every word spoken is like a note which is true when harmonious and false when inharmonious. (II 30)

Of course, this is an attainment of the great master, as is 'being a stream of love.' The accomplished mystic can control himself, his breath, his limited ego, his concentration and the active application of harmony. He has expanded so far that to him come the great attainments; communication with all, revelation and the essential final goal of spiritual endeavour: the experience of God.

communication

A certain amount of communication is present from the very first moment of awakening, as is shown in the previous chapters. The communication and understanding of the progressing mystic enlarge until he can communicate, that is understand and answer, all. This attainment is mentioned in almost all lectures on 'Awakening of the Soul' as well as in many others. For instance, in a chapter on 'Silence' one finds:

> When the mind has been made still, a person also communicates with everyone he meets. He does not need many words: when the glance meets he understands. (IV 208)

> Before the word is spoken the expression says it; before the thought has formed, the feeling speaks of it . . . And even before a feeling manifests it can be caught when one is able to communicate with the soul. This is what may be called communication: to communicate with the innermost being of a person. But who can communicate thus? The one who knows how to communicate with himself, the one who, in other words, is awakened. (VIII 305)

> If we are able to communicate with even one vein of this one life, then we are in touch with all the veins of the universe. (VIII 133)

The communication is with all, literally all. Inayat often refers to saints who are reported to have spoken with animals.

> What one realizes as the first experience of one's spiritual development, is that one begins to feel in communion with living beings; not only with human beings, but with animals, with birds, with trees and with plants. It is not a fairy tale that the saints used to speak with trees and with plants. You can speak today with them if you are in communication. (II 133)

This phenomenon, still known to those who live and work among animals, is an initial attainment; indeed it is an innate human ability that is lost in sophisticated civilization. Many classic fairy tales allude to the time 'when trees and birds still spoke'. The mystic regains this unclouded receptiveness.

Several times Inayat mentions the great communication between humans, demonstrated in the story of the apostles at Whitsuntide.

> There is the story of the Apostles who instantly knew many languages. This does not mean that they knew French or English, German or Spanish. It means that they knew the

language of every soul, that every soul began to speak to them, that they began to communicate with every person. The meaning of revelation is the understanding of the language of the soul. (VI 131)

revelation As a rule the concept revelation is used by Inayat as the highest state of consciousness. Sometimes he applies it in connection with intuition and inspiration—once even using the term 'partial revelation'—, but always stating that it is fundamentally different from the minor attainments. (IV 227) Just as unattached love is essentially different from earlier forms of love (p. 138) and essential breath differs from material breath (p. 82). There is always something like a sound-barrier to break through.

> The last and most delicate degree of intuition is revelation. This comes to prophets and perfected beings. This is a full light thrown upon the human personality, full light from within. To their eyes, ears, sense of taste or touch, all things disclose their secret. Those who have received this knowledge even partly, have by receiving it come to understand the properties of this plant or that, to know that this bitter medicine is good for this purpose, this sweet one for that . . . When they look into the mind, they know all about the mind. When they study the earth, they come to know it . . . Those who look in the higher spheres are prophets, those who look on the earth are scientists, musicians, soldiers and so on. It is from the direction in which he has studied that a man receives the revelation. In the higher spheres all things become clear to those who direct their attention to these spheres. (VII 86)

> There is one step further, and that is when the person has no longer remained simply a poet or a musician or a philosopher, but has become God's instrument only. Then God begins to speak to him through everything, not only in a melody or in verse or in colour or light, but he begins to communicate with God in all forms. Everything he sees above or below, right or left, before or behind, either heavenly or earthly is communicative. He then begins to

speak with God, and it is this step which is called revelation. (II 161)

Revelation came to the saints and saviours of humanity . . . . Those who received revelation have given us sacred books such as the Bible, the Qur'an, the Bhagavad Gita . . . . What they have given in the form of preaching, in the form of teachings, is the interpretation of the living wisdom which cannot be fully expressed in words. One can only know that living knowledge when one has experienced it oneself by the opening of the heart. (IV 227-229)

Revelation comes from within. It makes the heart self-revealing; it is just like a new birth of the soul . . . . Then a person begins to communicate with all things and all beings . . . . Every person and every object stands before him as an open book . . . . One may ask, how does one arrive at this revelation? And the answer is that there is nothing in the whole universe which is not to be found in man if he only cares to discover it. But if he will not find it out no one will give it to him, for truth is not learned; truth is discovered. (IV 214)

Thus, realization also implies the recognition of the Only Being in all beings and all things. Inayat may explain the stages of discovery in his lectures, or he may express this experience in a lyrical way in his *Gayan* and *Vadan*.

Every form I see is Thine own form, my Lord,/And every sound I hear is Thine own voice . . . . In every place I feel Thy presence, Beloved . . . . Wherever I look, I see Thy glorious vision; whatever I touch, I touch Thy beloved hand. Whomsoever I see, I see Thee in his soul; Whoever aught giveth to me, I take it from Thee. To whomsoever I give, I humbly offer it to Thee, Lord; Whoever cometh to me, it is Thou who cometh; on Whomsoever I call, I call on Thee. (*Vadan* 48, 49)

In an experience like this, which is an advanced state indeed, the mystic 'sees the one Truth in all forms'. (I 20)

A true worshipper of God sees His person in all forms, and in respecting man he respects God. (*Gayan* 41, new 70)

Fanà But there is still an 'I' and a 'You'. The unification of the mystic himself with God is a yet further development, that will be reached after going through fanà. Fanà may be compared to the Buddhist term for the ultimate goal, Nirvana, in that it represents an annihilation of the individual's limited qualities and fusion into the Whole. (II 250, VIII 42) This fusion is reached through graded experiences. First the individual personality, then the spirit, then the innermost being, the soul, accomplish fanà on their own plane of being. The initiator, the Prophet, and God are realised respectively by modelling one's being upon them. Inayat liked to illustrate the first stage as he discovered it when he himself was a pupil.

> One day I was walking in a city and met a dervish with a wonderful personality. He was dressed in a patched robe, but his speech, his voice, his thought, his movements, his atmosphere, were all most winning. At that time I was very young in the pursuit of philosophy. Youth is a time when pride has full play. So as we were walking along, and he called me 'Murshid,' I was very glad . . . . Presently we met another person, who seemed to be without any education, without any knowledge of philosophy or religion or anything out of the way, but he called him 'Murshid' too. My pride was hurt, especially when next he came across a policeman whom he also called 'Murshid.' So then I asked my teacher what could be the meaning of all this, and he said, 'Your dervish showed you the first step to recognizing God: to recognize all beings as your teacher. A foolish teacher can teach you, a wise person, a learned person, a student, a pious or a wicked person, even a little child; everyone can teach you something. Therefore have this attitude towards everybody, then it may be said that you recognize God. (XII 73)

After this assimilation of all the initiator stands for there follows—like the abstract concentration follows the concentration on an object—the fanà-fi-Rasul, which means the adept attuning himself to abstract values, the 'ideal-in-name-and-not-in-form'.

> These (adepts) have not seen the ideal, neither have they heard its voice, but they have known and loved that ideal which alone exists as far as they know. (I 42)

> The last grade is fanà-fi-Allah. The mystics who have reached thus far, are conscious of their ideal as beyond name and form, qualities and merits, which cannot even be confined in knowledge, being beyond all limitations. (I 42)

This is not the end. It marks the annihilation of the limited ego, and then the limitless Being of reality is experienced.

Baqà

> And annihilation (fanà) is equivalent to 'losing the false self (Nafs),' which again culminates in what is called Eternal Life (Baqà). (I 39)

> . . . the former is Fanà, annihilation, but the realization of the latter is Baqà, resurrection. The soul, drawn by the magnetic power of the divine Spirit, merges into it with a joy inexpressible in words, as a loving heart lays itself down in the arms of its beloved. The intensity of the joy is so great that nothing the soul has experienced in its life has ever made it so unconscious of the self; yet this unconsciousness of the self becomes in reality the true consciousness of Self. It is then that the soul realizes fully, 'I exist.' (VIII 180)

> It is an expansion of the outer personality to the width and the height of the inner personality. Then man becomes God-man, God-conscious; outwardly he is in the universe, inwardly the universe is in him. Outwardly he is smaller than a drop; inwardly he is larger than the ocean. And in this realization the purpose of belief in God, of worshipping God, and of loving God is accomplished. (XI 164)

Inayat did not discuss these last stages before every audience. He knew too well that people are not only attached to their ego and visible limitedness, but that the greatness of the God-vision may induce fear by its very immensity.

fears of all-oneness

One should remember, however, that there are very few who enjoy reality compared with those who are afraid of it, and who, standing on the top of a high mountain, are afraid of looking at the immensity of space. It is the same sensation. What frightens them is the immensity of things; they seem lost and they hold on to their little self. (XI 164/165)

In order to reach this stage the soul must become so mature that it is able to enjoy it. For an infant soul would not be able to enjoy this particular consciousness of all-oneness. (X 210)

One has to surrender something—the limited ego—, just as in human love one begins to experience that forgetting oneself brings happiness. No wonder that mystical poetry uses the symbols of love.

symbols of oneness

Inayat often cited the Persian poets Hafiz, Saadi, Rumi and others, and explained the symbols they used (for instance I 42/43, X 216). Very often he refers to the love story of Majnun and Leila to clarify the identification of lover and beloved. All his life Majnun has been longing and searching for his Leila who is kept away from him. At last, all he says and sighs is 'Leila'—just as the mystic repeats one of the names of God. When, after a thousand difficulties Leila comes to him and says, 'I am here as I promised, O Majnun,' he answers, 'I am Leila.' (V 178) The lover has identified himself with the beloved. This is, says Inayat,

love, lover and beloved

the love of souls who are no longer the possessors of love, but who have become love itself. (XI 104)

The identification of love, lover and beloved is a basic notion in Sufism.

The greatest principle of Sufism is, 'Ishq Allah, Ma'bud Allah' (God is love, lover and beloved). (V 17)

Given the basic idea of God the Only Being, the creator also is the created and the creative power. Intellectually it may be called the unity of subject, object and their origin. In the

Vedanta it is usually referred to as the unity of knower, knowledge and the known. To Inayat, as an Indian Sufi, this was a familiar notion. But for the forever analysing western audiences he had to go slowly.

> What keeps the soul in perplexity is the threefold aspect of manifestation, and as long as the soul remains puzzled by this, it cannot arrive at the knowledge of the One. These three aspects are the seer, sight and the seen; the knower, knowledge and the known . . . . One aspect is the person who sees; the second aspect is the sight or the eyes, by the help of which he sees; and the third aspect is that which he sees . . . . these three aspects seem to be separate . . . . When this riddle is solved by the realization that the three are one, then the purpose of the God-ideal is fulfilled. For then the three veils that cover the One are lifted . . . and they are found to be One, the Only Being. (IX 103/104)

The God-ideal referred to has been mentioned in chapter III, p. 36. The adept needs an ideal to begin with. But the mystic whose beloved is God may reach the state wherein he, the longing lover, identifies with the beloved and becomes love—which is the foremost attribute of the Only Being. (VIII 138) This is a high realization indeed.

The initial realization is difficult; one has tasted something perfect and cannot hold it for long. All mystical literature, including Inayat's *Minqar-é-Musiqar* and *Vadan,* is full of longing. There is a long poem in *Vadan,* starting with the words 'Riding on the horse of hope' and ending:

the longing of the mystic

> I went through the thick forests of perpetual desire,
> I crossed the running rivers of longing.
> I passed through the desert of silent suffering,
> I climbed the steep hills of continual strife.
> Feeling ever some presence in the air, I asked 'Are you there, my Love?'
> And a voice came to my ears, saying, 'No, still further am I.' (*Vadan* 19)

Even for the advanced mystic there are obstacles and he has

to regain his soul's freedom again and again. Inayat remembers a poem made by his own murshid, Abu Hashim Madani. The verse is addressed to the limited self and Inayat quotes:

> 'When I feel that now I can make peace with myself, it finds time to prepare another attack.' (VI 94)

perfection and perfectedness

The inherent problem is that even the greatest mystic is a man, a created being. However he widens his consciousness to God-consciousness, there always remains an element of limitation in him. In the text quoted on page 146 (VII 86) it is said that revelation comes to 'prophets and perfected beings.' Perfected is not yet perfection. God alone is perfect, and the nearest approach is divinity or godliness. But even this divinity reached in God-consciousness, is different from God.

> No man has a right to claim divinity as long as he is conscious of his limited self. Only he who is so absorbed in the contemplation of the perfect being that his limited self is lost from sight, could say this, but in most cases he will not say it. (IX 110)

> Divinity is reduced God and enlarged man. (IX 116)

> In reality divinity is the expansion of the human soul. (IX 116)

> No doubt, compared with God divinity is the imperfection of God, but it is still the perfection of man. It is just like a drop of water which is entirely and absolutely water, and yet it is a drop in comparison with the ocean. The ocean is God, but the drop is divine. (IX 119)

> The soul that rises to that stage where manhood ends and godhead begins, enters the initiation of the spiritual hierarchy, and then he is neither man nor God. He is not God, because he is limited man; and he is not man, because he is God-conscious. (IX 131)

This subtle division between the Whole Being and the mystic who has approached it, should not be forgotten. In Sufi tradition there are but very rare occasions that a mystic is recorded to have said 'I am truth.' As said in chapter III (p.

29) Inayat strongly warned those superficial philosophers who professed 'to be God' (for instance VI 96 and 189, X 69/70), but he relates, also, the legend of Mansur who was executed because he said so, and after the beheading his blood wrote the word 'I am truth.' (IX 110) Whatever may have been the historical facts, the poets and their legend evoke what it means to reach the highest plane of realization.

> Then the mystic is no longer the knower of truth, but truth himself. (X 27)

> When we are face to face, beloved, I do not know whether to call Thee me, or me Thee. I see myself when Thou art not before me; when I see Thee myself is lost to view. I consider it good fortune when Thou art alone with me, but when I am not there at all, I think it the greatest blessing. (*Gayan* 78, n. 126)

> I searched, but I could not find Thee; I called Thee aloud, standing on the minaret; I rang the temple bell with the rising and setting of the sun; I bathed in the Ganges in vain; I came back from the Kaaba disappointed; I looked for Thee on the earth; I searched for Thee in the heaven, my Beloved, but at last I have found Thee hidden as a pearl in the shell of my heart. (*Gayan* 81, new 131)

> What the Sufi strives for is self-realization, and he arrives at this self-realization by means of his divine ideal, his God. By this he touches this truth which is the ultimate goal and the yearning of every soul. It is not only realization; it is a happiness which words cannot explain, it is that peace which is yearned for by every soul. (IX 266)

from emotion to peace

When Inayat was not hampered by the limited associations of his audience who might interpret self-realization as mental or artistic self-expression (XII 75), parts of his lectures on realization border on those passages in *Gayan* and *Vadan* where the unfathomable melting in the Only Being is evoked lyrically. The greatest attainment is peace; before peace the experience is happiness. And the initial stage of ecstasy is emotion, often accompanied by tears or movement. It is remarkable that this initial state, which is only the first liberating moment, is usually regarded as characteristic of mysticism and ecstasy.

> Exaltation is a purifying process. (IV 117)

A few pages earlier (IV 115) Inayat points to forms of exaltation in daily life.

> Even reading a beautiful poem can produce exaltation; good music gives exaltation, and a feeling of great joy does so too. It all breaks up congestion. (IV 115)

The mystical ecstasy also breaks up congestion. See Inayat's description of the *sama* meetings of the Chishti Sufis, who use music as a means.

> Ecstasy manifests in various aspects. Sometimes a Sufi may be in tears, sometimes it expresses itself in *raqs,* motion . . . . The sighing of the devotee clears a path for him into the world unseen, and his tears wash away the sins of ages. All revelation follows ecstasy; all knowledge that a book can never contain, that a language can never express, nor a teacher teach, comes to him of itself. (II 61)

Though not all orders use music as the Chishtis do, the liberating tears are a common enough experience. Many of Inayat's pupils, especially some who entered his order very young, proud of being strong and not given to tears, were astonished at their weeping after their first meeting with him. (SK, 14, 15, 44, 45, 48, 54, 70 and 81) Such tears not only wash away sorrow and sins, but also mean a complete experience of life, of which joy and pain, catharsis and exaltation are all part.

> As the whole process of daily life consists of both joy and pain, so the life of the dervish is also filled with both joy and pain in the presence of God. By the help of concentration, poetry and music, joy and pain are felt more deeply. Therefore God becomes living to him; His presence is before him in all his moods. When once his pain has had an outlet in some form or other in the Sam'a, the musical ceremony, the condition that follows it is that of deeper insight into life. (II 95)

On good and bad, sorrow and joy, more will be said in Chapter IX. In this short survey of the highest attainments—in as far as they can be reduced to words—a few more points should be mentioned. Firstly the joy that follows the initial crisis.

> All pain is significant of change; all that changes for better or worse must cause a certain amount of pain, for change is at once birth and death. (*Vadan* 116)

> Sorrow enables a man to experience joy. (*Nirtan,* first edition)
> My heart drinks its own tears and puts them forth as pearls. (*Nirtan* 25)

> By creating happiness one fulfills one's life's purpose. (*Vadan* 118)

> The joy, therefore, of the one who experiences the inner life is beyond comparison greater than that of the average man living only as a captive in this mortal body. (I 80)

But more than joy is peace, positive peace. And once peace is attained words become more and more rare. Peace can be mentioned, it can be prayed for, one can put into words what is needed to reach it, but to experience it one has either to go the whole way, or to share the radiation of a great mystic.

> Perfection is attained by five achievements: Life, light, power, happiness, and peace. (*Vadan* 118)

> Draw us closer to Thee every moment of our life, until in us be reflected Thy Grace, Thy Glory, Thy Wisdom, Thy Joy and Thy Peace. Amen. (*Gayan* 71, n. 111)

> Once peace is developed in a soul, that soul feels such a great power and has such a great influence upon those who approach it and upon all upsetting conditions and jarring influences coming from all sides, that just as water makes the dust settle down, so all jarring influences settle down under the feet of the peaceful. (X 113)

Peace belongs to the ultimate stage of attainment. It comes after idealization, after recognizing, after communicating and after realization. To all these subjects many passages are devoted, to perfection only a few lines.

> Divine perfection is perfection in all powers and mysteries. All these are manifested without specially striving for them. Perfection and annihilation is that stage where there is no longer 'you,' where there is what there is. (XII 75)

> Let They Perfection be mine, and my imperfection be cleared away as the mist in the sun. (*Nirtan* 10)

VIII Life After Death and Life Before Life

doubts about after-life

'Is there any real knowledge of the life after what we call death? Shall we know our dear ones? The questioner thinks there may be an imaginary knowledge and doubts the reality of this knowledge.'

Inayat answered:

> There are three ways of knowing about this. 1. intellectually, by theory. 2. by meditation, 'dying before death,' to attain that state which is the state after death during one's lifetime. 3. to die. (*Sufism,* September 1921, p. 13)

speculations

Let us consider the intellectual theories first. Probably it was the validity of these speculations that raised doubts in the enquirer. We do not know who he or she was: a Christian who had suffered from too severe concepts of after-life, and wanted to prove them untrue; or a sceptic who watched western seekers adopt eastern ideas like karma and reincarnation, fitting them to their own outlook on life. There are, of course, many other speculations about after-life, such as ancestor and spirit worship, and awareness of these may have added to the enquirer's scepticism. For the sceptic as well as for those outgrowing old forms, for those mourning their dead, those afraid of death, and those seeking it as an escape, for all those answers have been given by Inayat.

These answers were inspired by three things: his experience as a mystic, which he called 'dying before death,'; his conceptions of good and bad and how to handle a wrongdoer (see chapter IX); and his considerateness in not saying more than the questioner could take in. Such an individual approach is not possible in a survey like this book. For some persons—as is the present author's experience—it is a relief when they learn of Inayat's view; dying people have asked me to explain his views. On the other hand, some do not want to discuss the subject of what comes after. For those I should repeat:

Take from these ideas what seems to you best, and forget the rest. (Edinburgh-interview, see page 10)

For many modern men Inayat's answer referring to the mystic's experience of death lacks comparison with anything familiar to them and they consider it not an experience but a speculation they are unable to believe. For them there is some more Inayatan advice to precede this outline:

Believe as much as your intelligence allows you to believe, as much as you can reach; do not believe what your intelligence does not allow you to believe. (VIII 38)

Though in Inayat's day there was already a great deal of typically twentieth century scepticism, there was still more fear of hell-fire and hope of a golden heaven. To people struggling with fears of postponed punishment (not to those who were simply content in their expectation of heaven) Inayat imparted his mystic's experience that heaven and hell are not places, but states of consciousness.

heaven and hell

There is the question of what has been called in the scriptures heaven and hell. What are they? Heaven and hell are our world, our consciousness, that in which we live day after day and year after year, and which continues in another world. (IV 233)

It is the state of mind which is heaven; it is the state of mind which is hell. (VII 52)

This does not imply a denial of a hereafter, not in the least.

Those who deny the hereafter, deny themselves that knowledge which is the essence of all learning. (VIII 176)

It implies that there is no awsome figure hovering over us, brandishing threats or promising sweetness, but that man creates heaven and hell, here and in after-life.

Heaven is not a place where the virtuous are sent. Heaven and hell are both within man. All the higher spheres of which man talks are within, but he never realizes nor imagines that he can find the higher spheres within himself. (VII 243)

There are many teachings, doctrines, speculations, and ideas as to the hereafter to be found; but if there is anything that could explain the nature and character of the hereafter it is one word, and that is reflection . . . . The hereafter of each one is what his soul contains. (IV 269)

All the things promised for the hereafter you will have to take from here. They are not kept ready for you; you will have to bring them with you. (VII 128)

If one has learned while on earth how to create joy and happiness for oneself and others, in the other world that joy and happiness will surround one; and if one has sown the seeds of poison, one must reap those fruits there. (XI 231)

karma Does this imply that Inayat preached Karma? Not exactly. He did pay attention to causes and consequences.

It is quite evident that what one sows one reaps. (VIII 163)

But in the same paragraph Inayat compares Karma with the moral doctrines of punishment and recompense in the three religions of Bible and Quran, and elsewhere (II 35) with Fate. He considered it wise to handle all such concepts carefully.

One of the reasons why one should not think too much about previous causes, that are unknown to us as well (VIII 166), is that such thinking may paralyze a person's efforts and stand in the way of growth and progress.

In a way it is a virtue to take everything patiently and call it Karma; but that is not sufficient. We should realize that happiness is our birthright. God does not rejoice in our sorrow, God is not pleased by our pain; and therefore we must do everything in our power to escape from illness and other difficulties, instead of lying patiently waiting, as if under a rock, 'because it is our Karma.' (VI 123)

Coming to the philosophical point of view one may ask whether man is a machine or an engineer. If he is a machine, then he must go on for years and years under a kind of mechanical action of his evil deeds, in which case he is not responsible for his actions. But if he is an engineer then he is responsible for his actions, then he is master of his destiny,

> and makes his destiny what he wishes it to be. (VIII 164/165)

Here, and in other lectures, called 'Man, Master of his Destiny' (VI 216-233) Inayat assumes the existence of some destiny, an outline or plan for each life, but at the same time man's freedom to use that plan in different ways. And:

> There is always the possibility of change. (V 57)

reincarnation With karma usually goes the idea of reincarnation. Inayat considered the different representations of other worlds or a later life on earth as methods used by religious leaders to serve spiritual, ethical and psychological purposes: to give people some idea of greater worlds; to teach them morals and adherence to morals, (I 59, X 52) and to console the many in need of consolation.

> Ideas, such as that of the other world and of different planes, are taught by the philosophers in order to give people some notion of the inner world. (XI 54)

> When they said to a good person, 'Your good actions will bring you back as a better person,' it was said so that the man who did not know the two extreme poles of his soul (the limited and unlimited) might understand that no good action could be lost; and for the man who did not know what to hope for in the hereafter, and who only knew about life as it is lived on the earth, it was a consolation to know that all the good he had done would come again (VIII 177 = I 175)

The consoling aspect was important in India, where the social conditions were rigid. A single individual might become a Sannyasi, a mystic, and outgrow all inner and outer boundaries, because only return to the Source is his aim. But the majority had to live and die within the bounds of its caste.

> For every chance of progress was barred for the lower classes. Their only consolation was the idea that they would reincarnate and be born in a higher class; there was no other way. (IX 157)

The same applies for the old promise of heaven for those unhappy on earth. But Inayat showed the possibilities to reach heaven, happiness, in this life; that is the mystic's realization. Therefore, he saw a danger in too rigid speculations about punishment and recompense. Besides, our conceptions of good and bad are limited, not the same everywhere, and change with our evolution. (limited and man-made: I 57, VIII 148, 163, XI 238; not the same everywhere nor always II 22, V 31, VII 200, 249, VIII 165, 233, X 52, IX 256); changing with our evolution (VI 64, VIII 110, 164). Above all, the image of a severe god of retribution, breeds fear or protest, and not the love needed to widen the consciousness.

> The thought 'I am suffering now because of my sins in a past life,' may bring an answer to the enquiring and reasoning mind and stop it from rebelling for the moment. But will this take away the irritation that the misery is causing his heart? Will that mind ever excuse God for having so severely judged him? He may own his mistakes of the past, but will he ever believe in God as a God of love and compassion, as a God of mercy, or a God of forgiveness? (I 138/139)

> It is all right for someone to say that because in the past incarnation he has done so much evil, in this life he has a bad time with much suffering; or that in the past incarnation he has done so much good, that this time he has become rich. And it is all right for others to say that when they go to hell for their sins they will be whipped and thrashed and put into the fire. But when you look at the grace of God, you forget all these things; no rules, no laws, no deserving or undeserving can be distinguished any more. There is only one thing, and that is love; love that stands above law. (VII 260)

> Many of the dogmatic religions have taken away the love element which makes God sovereign; instead they make a God who is limited, who is bound by the book, and who cannot show compassion. (X 151)

> The judge is the slave of the law, the forgiver is its master. (V 128)

Inayat considered that the idea of a loving God was needed for trust and progress. People who are weighed down by feelings of guilt or sin, passively accepting bad conditions, or immobilized by dreams of happiness in heaven or in a later life on earth, cannot move and cannot grow. The expectation of another life on earth might, also, give fuel to limitedness in another way:

> The idea of reincarnation often comforts those who think that it is too soon to renounce the pleasure of life in order to commune with God. (V 124)

Though Inayat sometimes compared a certain conception of Karma with Judgment Day and Fate (V 48-59, VI 225-232), and some interpretations of reincarnation with a certain image of heaven and hell, he also observed that those who no longer wanted to believe in heaven and hell, found a solution in the belief of reincarnation.

> The idea of reincarnation has made a great impression in the present age, because it appeals at once to the scientific faculty and reasoning natures and it also satisfies those who wish to keep a fast hold on their individuality. (V 123)

> The doctrine of reincarnation's claim to truth rests chiefly on the law of action, (karma) and this at once appeals to the intellect. (VIII 168)

But this very preference for the 'logic' of this speculation Inayat saw as a human and limited standard and therefore as a hindrance to spiritual attainment. (V 124)

> From a business point of view this is very just, but from a spiritual person's point of view it can be looked at differently . . . . For in every soul there is the power of the Almighty, there is a spark of divine light, there is the spirit of the Creator. (IV 46)

> For a Sufi to think: what was I and what shall I be, takes him away from the ever springing stream of life. (*Autobiography*)

> The Yogis . . . do not for one moment believe that

> reincarnation is for them. If one asks a Yogi he will say, 'No, I am striving for Mukti, salvation.' (VIII 168)

Mukti (release, liberation) means to be free from the 'wheel of rebirths,' to become free from return to this limited life. To Indians attached to earthly life and to many poor, low-caste, or casteless Indians the belief in karma and reincarnation means hoping for a better future in this world, whereas most Western concepts of karma are directed to the past. Many enjoy toying with alleged previous lives, as Napoleon, Beethoven or an Egyptian pharaoh. Inayat once witnessed a ball where people were invited to come in the costume of a former incarnation. It amused him, and he used the scene in his play *Una,* where he let two would-be consorts of one pharaoh confront each other. (XII 224) But mostly he was careful about this subject. For some it was a real consolation, for instance for parents who had lost a child and hoped to see it again in another child. (V 124) However, according to his notes in his unpublished *Autobiography,* he saw the Westerner's ready acceptance of reincarnation firstly as a streak of their rational make-up and he did not want to disturb this, as long as a person was not ready for another outlook. Often he underlined that his Sufism did not prescribe doctrines (VIII 170, XII 104) and that everyone should choose what suited his temperament best. (XII 104) He tried not to speak against reincarnation (VIII 171/172), but those who wanted a conclusive answer 'like a brick to hold', or those who wanted a confirmation of their own views, were not satisfied. Inayat knew this.

> People have often asked me what the Sufi had to say about reincarnation, and my silence at times, and Yes and No at times have made it vague. Some perhaps thought that I did not believe in it, and then naturally the Sufis in general would not believe in it. This is not the case. Every Sufi is free to believe what he understands as right and what he can understand. Self-realization is the aim. Beliefs in doctrines are pills given to sick people for their cure . . . . All things are true to a certain point, but compared with the ultimate truth they fall short in proving themselves existent . . . . If I speak to my view it will confuse you just now. (*Sufism,* September 1921, p. 14)

In this answer to a point-blank question Inayat inserted his own view saying 'self-realization is the aim.' On a similar occasion he could be a bit more explicit.

> I have never spoken against the doctrine of reincarnation, as I do not see the wrong of it; but neither do I see the right of it. When the purpose is the realization of the unity of life, or the unity of God, then the idea of reincarnation, which is based upon the false ego, is not fruitful. (VIII 172)

Inayat did see a coming and going of souls,but not as the selfsame individuals. Sometimes he explained the doctrine of reincarnation as an interpretation of this 'travelling' of souls towards manifestation and back to their origin.

the journeying souls

> The reincarnation as meant by them (the thinkers) was the partaking by the fresh soul descending towards manifestation of the attributes of the souls which are ascending towards their original source, which give their load of impressions to the willing souls met with on the way . . . . The truth of the reincarnation theory can be understood in this way: that the selfsame proportion of Consciousness which has once been a soul *might* happen to form again as a soul; but in general there is no such possibility . . . . In any case the soul has to merge into the Consciousness before it is sufficiently alive to manifest again. That is why we cannot call it the same soul, for it is quite purified from its previous conditions. It is just like a drop of ink: when it falls into the ocean the water merges into water and its inky substance sinks to the bottom. (VIII 169/170)

In other words: the divine part merges into the divine, the impressions and experiences may be transferred to other souls on their way to manifestation[1] and in this way one can

[1] A good representation of this interchange between an earth bound and a home going soul is given in *The Cloak,* by Clifford Bax. This one act play formed part of the repertory of a travelling company and made a great impression (See *Seven Famous One Act Plays,* edited by John Ferguson, Penguin 1937, 1938, 1950, p. 31). Clifford Bax participated actively in the receptions at Inayat's London home in 1915 (*Sufi,* February 1915, p. 2) and his wife was a friend of Havelock Ellis's wife, Edith Ellis; the latter was a mureed.

assume that the attainments of an individual return or reincarnate, but not the individual person, nor what was once his ego, as composed of acquired qualities and characteristics.

> Souls which are passing . . . towards the physical plane . . ., meet with other travellers who are on their journey back home, and they learn from them a great many things. (I 129)

> If it happens to be the impression of one personality, falling upon the mind going towards manifestation the distinct characteristics of a certain personality who has lived in the past will show clearly in the life of that person. It is in this that the secret of the doctrine of reincarnation, which the Hindus hold, can be recognized. (I 154, compare VI 229)

This journey of the souls is described with many details in *The Soul Whence and Whither* (I 111-185), and summed up briefly in many places, for instance III 261, IV 269-271, IV 191, VI 240, VII 240-241, VIII 153-180. The idea is that the souls go out from the Only Being 'like rays from the sun.' On their way to manifestation they meet and absorb many impressions; all these impressions become like veils, covering the original 'clean' soul so thickly that, in most cases, it forgets its origin and identifies itself with the veils of feeling, thinking, and the body, which is the last cover. When returning it must give back that garb. That is death.

die before death

How can one assure oneself of the truth of this theory? By becoming a mystic.

> By studying all the philosophies and metaphysics all through his life, a man may prove to himself by reasoning that there is continuity of life; yet this realization gained by effort of mind will not give him the feeling of certainty which he would wish to have. The Sufi, therefore, practises the process by which he is able to touch that part of life in

Clifford Bax had been interested in Indian Philosophy since his eighteenth year (Clifford Bax, *Ideas and People,* London 1936, p. 231), that is some years before Inayat's arrival in the West. Whether *The Cloak* owes something to Inayat's ideas or influence is difficult to say, but the contents are different from the usual western ideas on reincarnation and very much like Inayat's concept of passing on one's impressions.

himself which is not subject to death; and by finding that part of life he naturally begins to feel the certainty of life. (VI 272)

Many people reject the notion of an after-life. There was an old agnostic whose son and daughters all three were mureeds, but he was not. All the same, he liked and respected Inayat and often invited him to his home. Once he said placidly, 'Believe me, Murshid, I am an old man, and I can tell you there is no life after this life.' Inayat smiled and replied, 'I am a mystic, and there is.' (SK 29)

The process of widening one's consciousness and approaching God-realization, as described in the previous chapter, is an experience of after-life.

'In the other world' means in a world which is veiled from our eyes, our physical eyes; but it does not mean a world far away from us beyond our reach. Both the living and the dead inhabit the same space; we all live together. Only a veil separates us, the veil of this physical body. (X 39)

Man has become motionless, stagnant, by attaching himself to this world in which he is born and in which he is interested. If he can make his soul more supple and thus be able to turn away from all this, he can experience all that has been said of the various planes of different worlds, which are in reality different planes of consciousness. (VIII 321)

In the scriptures (the Hadith) it is said, 'Die before death.' (Mautu qabla an tamautu) What is this dying? This dying is playing at death. The mystics have all through their life on earth practised playing at death; by playing at death they were able to see what death is. Then it was not only intellectual knowledge; they actually saw that the soul stands independently of this physical garb. (VI 27)

The mystic does not wait until the hereafter, but does all he can to progress now. (*Gayan* 11, n. 17)

'The hereafter I see here; it is not afterwards. I see the past and present and future all at the same moment.' (IX 58)

But even Inayat had not seen like that always. He knew,

also, that not many were as coolly philosophical about death as the old gentleman who denied after-life. Inayat recognized, from studying life and from remembering his thoughts as a boy, that most people fear death and are sad about parting.

fear of death

I remember, when, at an early age I first knew of death, how for hours I was sad, thinking, 'This, my body, the only means of experiencing life, will one day be in the grave. I shall be away from all things and beings that are the interest of my life to me today. This whole environment which interests me and keeps me engaged all day long will one day be a mist; neither shall I see anybody nor will anybody see me; all whom I love now will one day be separated from me.' Now my own experience in the past clearly tells me how others must feel at the idea of turning into what seems nothing after being something . . . . Such is the case of all those who are so much interested in the dream of life that the idea of death, which is a more real state of being, is horrible to them. (V 123)

When the thought comes to a man, 'Some day I must leave all this and go down to the grave,' a great sadness comes upon him. With some people this fear lasts part of their lives; with some it lasts the whole life. The proof of how great the fear of death is, is that death has been made out to be the worst punishment, although it is not nearly so bad as the pains, sorrows and worries of life. (V 44)

It would be a wrong conclusion to presume, that Inayat, or any other mystic, might advocate suicide. This same page V 44 continues with a tale about a man who complained all his life and wished himself dead; but when death came he asked for postponement. Inayat met many who felt unhappy and contemplated suicide.

suicide

There are numberless people, unhappy, depressed, or in great despair, perhaps wanting to commit suicide, who after having done this eventually realized that life is worth living after all. (VI 104)

However unhappy or feeble a man may be, his life is too

dear to him to sacrifice. Suicide is only possible under great stress of emotion. All work, all struggles are in order to live. (VII 184)

euthanasia

Passive euthanasia Inayat did not consider as suicide or killing, but he did not approve of active euthanasia.

Is it wrong to let a person die who is suffering very much, or should one use artificial means to keep him alive? It is not advisable that a doctor, or a relation, or anyone, should kill a person who is suffering very much in order to save him from pain; . . . every moment that one passes on this physical plane has its purpose. We human beings are too limited to judge, to decide to put an end to life and suffering. We must try to make the suffering less for that person, to do everything in our power to make that person feel better. But to use artificial means of keeping someone alive for hours or days is not a right thing to do; because that is going against nature's wisdom and the divine plan. It is as bad as killing a person. Man's tendency is always to go further than he ought to; that is where he makes a mistake. (IV 46)

Passive euthanasia is accepting death when it comes. Inayat saw that people either did not accept life in all its forms, including pain and sorrow (see next chapter), or clung to it blindly, unconscious of the inner life that continues, but that could be experienced here and now.

continuity of the inner life

Once man has experienced the inner life, the fear of death has expired; because he knows death comes to the body, not to his inner being. When once he begins to realize life in his heart and in his soul, then he looks upon his body as a coat . . . . The fear of death lasts only so long as man has not realized that his real being does not depend upon his body. (I 80)

death of those dear to us

But there is one thing those living the inner life, too, will not be able to avoid. It is no good to get 'hardened by piety' and every human being will naturally be sad when realizing that a person he or she has loved will not be with him (her) any longer in the old, familiar form. But there are ways of mourning.

Inayat lived in London during the first world war and there, in those grief-stricken days, he gave his lectures on 'Life after Death'. (*Aqibat,* V 37-78) He consoled survivors and taught them, the widows and bereaved parents, and the many struggling unhappy ones, how to understand death and how to help those departed. Not by calling them back.

> . . . call not back the traveller, who is on his journey toward his goal; for you know not what he seeks . . . . By weeping for the dead you will make sad the souls who cannot return to earth . . . He is happy in the place at which he has arrived; by wanting to go to him you do not help him; your life's purpose still keeps you on earth . . . . Verily, death is a veil behind which is hidden life that is beyond the comprehension of the man on earth. If you knew the freedom of that world, and how the sad hearts are unburdened of their load; . . . and what freedom the soul experiences as it goes further from this earthly life of limitations, you would no more mourn those who have passed, but pray for their happiness in their further journey and for the peace of their souls.

These are a few lines from a burial sermon, separately printed, to console the bereaved. Inayat also left prayers and blessings for the dead to be said in the first days or weeks after their passing. To quote one:

> Heal his spirit, Lord, from all the wounds that his heart has suffered through this life of limitation upon the earth. Purify his heart with Thy Divine Light and send upon his spirit Thy Mercy, Thy compassion and Thy peace. Amen.

He explained the effect of such prayers in *Aqibat.*

> The dead feel the thought, the good wish of the living. Prayer and religious rites focus the mind of the living on that of the dead, so that the dead may be helped by the living, or the living may be blessed by a saintly spirit. (V 69)

spiritualism

Though the living may help the departed by prayer and loving thoughts, Inayat advised against spiritualism. Not only because it is better for a soul beyond to proceed on his way home, but because raising spirits is dangerous for the medium.

> We are not doing spirits any good by calling them back when they have no body. Why not let them forget the experiences of this world of illusion rather than attract them? (VII 151)

> In regard to spirit communion, which is a subtle subject, I will say that it is better to have more connection with the beings living upon earth than to be obsessed with the desire to meet with people on the other side of life. It is here that we are meant to evolve, and by being absorbed in those who have passed on we are taken away from the life we are meant to have. (V 70)

> It was for the benefit of some mediums who were used by the great explorers of spiritualism that I showed my disapproval of that line; not as an unbeliever nor as someone who makes fun of these things, only for the welfare of those simple ones who are made use of, and whose lives are ruined in order that the others may find out some secret of it . . . . If they want to experience, they must experience themselves and take the consequences. (IV 249/250)

> When people see a ghost, it is part illusion and in part they may really see it. When the inner eyes see, these outer eyes think that they see. (V 69, compare I 119)

The war book on *Life after Death* is the only published work of Inayat in which he sets down some cases of ghosts and haunting he had met with in India. As to not raising a spirit, there is one exception. There is no harm in calling upon a departed master, for his inner being is connected with the Spirit of Guidance, which is, in its essence, always the same, and always ready to help. (I 118, V 45, VIII 178/179, IX 142, 145)

> Sometimes there are visions of the murshids, the higher beings; these come to the initiate. They come to guide and to help in all difficulties. Someone who is quite absorbed in the thought of a prophet or murshid may be so lost in him, that if he calls upon him in any difficulty, the one upon whom he calls will always come and help him. (V 70)

Inayat recorded the times when his own murshid had helped

him, the first one immediately after his death, when Inayat was much absorbed in him. Of the disciples of Christ he says:

> It is told in the gospel that after his resurrection Christ was seen several times by his disciples. It is the experience of every person who has practised concentration and who has meditated, that he sees that which he has held in his consciousness, not only inwardly but outwardly before him. This is the first experience that every mystic has. The disciples were lost, absorbed in the thought of Christ; how should they not see him? (VIII 183)

Those who have lost their beloved often see his or her likeness in an unknown person passing in the street. The prayers for the dead, mentioned above, direct the thoughts of the living and the journey of the departed towards the greater world known to the mystic.

Sometimes Inayat was asked to help a person who indulged in self-centred or otherwise harmful mourning. In general he reawakened those people to their purpose in life, but he also relates the case of a widow who was happy in her memories. Her relations wanted Inayat to tell her to mix with others again, and he went to see her. But he discovered that only the memory of her happy life with the departed husband brought her joy.

> I thought it would be a sin on my part to take her away from her joy. If the memory had been a misery for her, I would have spoken to her otherwise. But is was a happiness for her, it was the only happiness. (II 231/232)

our own death

Such a dedicated but uncomplaining attitude is an exception. Most people are upset by death. Most of all by the idea of their own death. But it is different for the adept, for the agnostic, and for those afraid of punishment.

> All souls return to God, some with open eyes, some blindly. (V 105)

> Desire to live continually is a desire of the spiritual person as well as of the material person (VI 19)

> Death for the spiritual souls is only a gate through which

they enter into that sphere which every soul knows to be its home. (XI 241)

Those who hope to die conscious of spiritual life may have asked Inayat what they best could think of at the moment of dying.

What thought should the mind hold at the moment of death? The thought should be in accordance with the evolution of the person, either of God or the object of his devotion, or of pleasant surroundings and whatever he likes and has idealized. (V 44)

Many are the answers to unspoken questions as to those dying blindly. There are, also, words of advice to hasty followers,for instance VI 20, where Inayat remarks that one should make people rise above the fear of death gradually and not suddenly, for otherwise this knowledge would frighten a person more than death itself. Especially sensitive persons, who have just freed themselves from traditional threats of hell and punishment, for some time will feel safer in denying after-life. Another fear springs from a misinterpretation of Nirvana, which. may take to mean 'becoming nothing' instead of becoming all.

Very often people are afraid of reading Buddhistic books, where the interpretation of Nirvana is given as 'annihilation.' No one wants to be annihilated. (II 250)

In this condition of Nirvana or highest consciousness, however, one is conscious all through of the body as much as of the soul. During this experience a person lives fully. (VIII 312, compare end of previous chapter)

Also, tact is needed with people who deny after-life not because they are afraid, but because they are only conscious of the world they can see, touch and smell; a life other than that of the senses is inconceivable to them.

life after death

One might think it uninteresting to live as a spirit and not as a body. It might seem uninteresting to one who has not experienced to live independently of the physical body. (X 40)

> How to die before death is something that man today does not know; and he does not care to know. (VII 191)

Inayat's descriptions of the first experiences of those who are confronted with after-life without understanding it, are rather realistic. (V 63, 68) Those souls who do not know that they are souls go through an oppressive muddled state, but after some time they will recognize their new situation and their possibilities. That is why, in the first days, the living can help the departed by praying and concentrating on the greater inner world.

> If the soul has had a horror of death, it carries that horror with it. If it has agitation at the thought of death, it carries that feeling with it; also, the dying soul carries with it the impression of the idea and regard for death of those surrounding it in life, especially at the time of its passing from the earth. This change paralyzes every activity of the soul for some time. The soul which has become impressed by the idea it held of death, and by the impression which was created by those around the deathbed, is kept in a state of inertia. (I 166/167)

> After death, as he recovers from this impression, he gradually finds himself alive; for the life which kept him alive in his physical garb, of course feels strange in the absence of that garb. (V 42)

But once the traveller is accustomed to his changed circumstances, he discovers his greater freedom.

> At death comes leisure; after death the mind comes to greater life, a life more real than here. (IV 107)

To Inayat this greater life was natural and real indeed. Sometimes, almost casually, he tells how a mystic attains his knowledge of after-life, and in a place where he enumerates all the powers and inspirations of the accomplished mystic, the experience of after-life is just one of these.

> If there are men living in the world today who while standing on earth witness the inner planes of existence, if there are any who really can communicate with the higher

spheres, if there are any who can convince themselves of the life in the hereafter and of what it will be like, it is the master of breath, and not the students of intellectual books. (IV 193)

Therefore the one who lives the inner life is all things; he is as a physician who knows things that a physician cannot know; . . . . He becomes the artist of the entire world, the singer of the divine song . . . . He does not need outer things as the signs of knowing the eternal life. His very life is the evidence of the everlasting life. To him death is a shadow; it is a change; it is turning the face from one side to the other. (I 86/87)

In the books and chapters on after-life Inayat answers scores of questions just as a traveller describes a country to those who have not seen it. What does the soul and mind do without the old body? The same as on earth, work is continued. (I 169, 172, II 250, VIII 177) Children and infants who died come to spiritual maturity (V 109); the methods of the mystic are the same as on earth (II 250), but found sooner. (V 106) On the question whether there is a difference of sex Inayat answered 'yes', almost 'of course', for this is implicit in the male and female aspect of creation. (V 33, 93) Does one meet those whom one has loved? Yes, said Inayat, and also those whom one hated, so better not hate. (IV 258) A great difference is one's speed, one is as quick as one's thoughts. (I 178) In general things are lighter, there is a greater freedom of movement, and things are less painful. (I 178, IV 211) But a certain kind of difficulties must be solved there too, even something analogous to being ill (I 176, 177, 179), and at last another departing, a change or death. (I 178/179, V 110) This departing includes a change of form, a leaving behind a mantle, for as long as the soul has not melted back in the Only Being, it always has a form. (IV 211) Inayat mentions the change of form, from one rather resembling the body until, at a much further stage, what remains is a purely luminous being.

Its body then consists of radiance; it is light itself. The difference is that light as we understand it on the physical plane is of another character. For here it is visible, but there

> it is both light and life in one, so the light is audible as well as visible, besides being intelligent. (I 181)

The descriptions of these higher developments are difficult to convey, but in all mystic literature one finds similar reports of light, sound and several planes. Where such descriptions are hearsay instead of experience, all manner of rather rigid speculations regarding the exact number of 'heavens' is the result. Inayat knew this, and when people asked him to state the right quantity, he answered that detailed divisions are arbitrary.

> For instance, if one asks a meditative person, 'Are there seven planes of existence? he will say, 'Yes, it is so.' But when another person says, 'I have read in a book on Greek philosophy that there are nine planes of existence; can it be true?' he will answer, 'Certainly.' Then another comes and says, 'I think that there are only three planes,' and again he will agree. He does not say this to please; he is able to see these planes as five, seven, nine, in as many forms as he likes, because he actually sees them so. (VII 264)

Inayat compares this with the beginner in music who only recognizes seven tones in an octave, and the experienced musician who knows there are many scales and many ways to arrange tones and notes. As to the division of manifestation and return in stages or planes, Inayat sometimes referred to the numbers he had learned in his Muslim tradition (VIII 321, V 24/25), but he remarked that such divisions are only 'for convenience' (IV 198) and he himself mostly talked of three principal planes or conditions: angelic, that is the world of light, sound and feeling; mind (jinn, genius), that is the world of thought and imagination; and physical, our well-worn earthly world.

> These three spheres: angelic, jinn, and physical, have each a particular garb. This garb may be called the body of that sphere, which the soul has to adorn. And when returning, it must give back that garb to the same sphere from which it borrowed it. (VII 241)

This accounts not only for our physical death, but for later changes too. The level-headed precision with which Inayat described these worlds is remarkable. Sometimes he notes that to many such accounts sound like fairy-tales (II 86), or he repeated that all ideas of the inner body or the hereafter are actual experiences of the mystic and not speculations. (XI 146, I 127)

People's doubts in this connection are not purely intellectual. Many should like to understand and know about death, but they know of no other standards and instruments than those of the earth.

> The objective world is so concrete before his eyes that he cannot see beyond it. (VIII 215)

> People want to see the face of reality with the eyes of illusion. (XI 17)

spirit and matter

They have no idea of the possibility of gradual discovery. The great barrier—apart from the emotional ones mentioned above—can be found in the deep-rooted concepts of spirit and matter. In general spirit and matter are regarded as being irreconciliably opposed, so that to choose the one means to renounce the other. Another wide-spread notion is that only matter exists, that thoughts and feelings are 'merely' reactions of brains and nerves. In fact, this fervent rejection of spirit is also based on a dualistic feeling, just as is the attitude of those who only want to recognize spirit.

> There is the man who says, 'Spirit is one thing and matter is another thing; matter is not spirit neither is spirit matter.' This is a religiously inclined person. There is another, a materialist, who says, 'There is no such thing as spirit; all that is there is matter.' And then a third person comes along who says, 'Do not mention the word matter to me; there is no matter. It is only an illusion; only spirit exists. (XI 57)

All three may be slightly shocked at hearing Inayat pronounce:

> It is not only spirit that is the being of God; matter is the being of God too. (XI 66/67)

As God the Only Being comprises all, material creation is not excluded.

> Just as ice and water are two things and yet in their real nature they are one, so it is with spirit and matter. Water turns into ice for a certain time, and when this ice is melted it will again turn into water. Thus matter is a passing state of spirit; only, it does not melt immediately as ice melts into water, and therefore man doubts if matter, which takes a thousand forms, ever really turns into spirit. (XI 57)

All the same, spirit remains the more powerful primal aspect of these states of aggregation.

> Matter is a state of spirit. (*Gayan* 47, n. 79)

> Matter is an action of spirit which has materialized and has become intelligible to our senses of perception. (XI 57)

> Spirit and matter are the two names of one life. The primal aspect of life developing into denseness remains spirit, and its development into dense form is called matter. (XI 63)

life before life

The latter sentence touches on the question of life before life, which is not put as often as the one about life after death, though it is its natural counterpart. One cannot understand the return journey well, if one is not acquainted with the voyage out. The first question should be, 'How does spirit turn into matter?' or 'What do they have in common?'

What they have in common is vibration, a concept not so incredible today, when the electric properties of the brain, and the movement inside atoms have been established as it used to be before, when all material things seemed solid and immovable. Also, we have the notion of sound and light waves to which Inayat could refer. The power of breath is less generally known, but the control of breath enables the accomplished mystic to follow vibrations of all sorts.

creation: how

Whereas the mythical explanations of creation widely differ and are subject to cultural evolution, the mystical descriptions have much in common. There is always a memory, a hint of sound and of light, originating from an unfathomable whole.

If creation can be explained, it is the phases of sound or of vibration, which manifest in different grades in all the various forms in life. Even what we call matter or substance, and all that does not seem to speak or sound, is in reality all vibration. (II 85)

The first step towards manifestation is contraction. That contraction is seen in all living beings and in all objects. It is first contraction that takes place, and then expansion, which comes as a matter of course, as a reaction. The former tendency is the desire of inhalation, and the latter exhalation. (I 113)

The Bible says, 'In the beginning was the Word, and the Word was God;' and it also says that first was the Word, and then came the Light. (II 123)

If we said, 'First was the breath,' it would be the same as saying, 'In the beginning was the Word.' (II 159)

Yogis had worked with sound for thousands of years before any such researches (those of Professor Froissard in Paris, who treated gas casualties of the First World War with experimental breathing exercises) were thought of or undertaken. The school of Mantra Yoga is concerned with this science. The one belief that started this was that vibration is creative and that the whole universe was produced by sound, by the Word; as it says in the Bible, first was sound and then was light. This contains the mystical thought that one may understand vibrations as spreading in two directions; when audible they become intelligible, and coming from the form of the Being they become visible. (XII 118/119)

'The Mysticism of Sound' is one of the first and most recurrent themes of Inayat's lectures; most of these are collected in volume II of the *Sufi Message.* Passages on light are found, among other places, in I 117, 122, 128, 181, VIII 153, XI 38-41. Light is also used as a simile. Inayat, like many others before him, uses the example of the sun and its rays to visualize the process of creation.

The picture of God and of souls is that of the sun and its rays. The rays are not different from the sun, the sun is not different from the rays. Yet there is one sun and many rays. The rays have no existence of their own; they are only an action of the sun. They are not separate from the sun, and yet the rays appear to be many different rays . . . . So it is with God and man. What is God? The spirit which projects different rays; and each ray is a soul. (IV 191)

As these rays go forward the first plane they strike is the angelic plane; the second plane they strike is the plane of the jinn; and the third is the physical plane . . . . they have passed through all three, and while passing through they have received all that can be received from each place, learned all that is to be learned, gathered all that is to be gathered; but they still exist on those planes although they do not know it. They are only conscious of that plane where their ray has opened its eyes; . . . we only see what is before our eyes and not what is behind our back. Thus every soul has at the back of it the angelic plane and the jinn plane, but before its eyes is only this physical plane. Therefore it is only conscious of the physical plane and is unconscious of the planes from which it has turned its eyes, though even after manifesting on earth it is still connected with the higher spheres . . . . Thus the soul, deprived of the heavenly bliss, becomes conscious of the troubles and limitations of life on earth. It was not that Adam was driven out of the Garden of Eden; he only turned his back on it, and that made him an exile from heaven. (VIII 154/155)

Not all 'rays' travel with the same speed, nor do they busy themselves with the same things. Many do not journey as far as the physical plane, but remain in the angelic or genius condition. (I 115, 171)

It is not the angels who have settled in the angelic heavens who come to earth; for these rays have finished their creative power in manifesting as angels. (I 122)

The soul that goes as far as the sphere of the jinn as a current coming from the heavens functions in the body of the sphere of the jinn . . . . it becomes necessary for the soul coming with the angelic body into the world of jinn to adopt a body of that particular world in order to withstand the weather of that plane . . . . That is the condition for going into another sphere. (I 128)

Some concept of angels is found in most traditional religions. Inayat explains that there is quite a difference between the ray returning from the earth and the one that remains settled in another plane. (I 119, 122, 124, 125) As said above, the 'bodies' of other spheres are difficult to describe.

> Man always pictures the beings he imagines and cannot see with his physical eyes as something like himself. (I 126)
>
> All the teachings given by the great prophets and teachers are only interpretations of what they have seen. (VIII 293)
>
> The picture of the angels that we read of in the scriptures as sitting upon clouds and playing harps is but an expression of a mystical secret. Playing the harp is vibrating harmoniously; the angels have no actual harps, they themselves *are* the harps. (I 116)
>
> It is mentioned in the ancient scriptures that angels came with messages to the prophets of Beni Israil; but the explanation of this from the metaphysical point of view is quite different from what an ordinary person would imagine. No man on earth is capable of communicating with the angels in heaven, nor is an angel from heaven inclined to communicate with man. But in the exceptional lives of the prophets what happens is, that they rise above all the planes which keep man removed from the angelic heavens, and by doing so they are able to touch these heavens. (I 118)

As mentioned above in his lectures on *The Soul Whence and Whither* Inayat was called on to satisfy much idiosyncratic curiosity. But there remains one question of more general purport too. Why was the world created, why did the Only Being manifest itself in many forms?

creation: why

To this question Inayat gives three answers, which are closely interconnected. The first one is that a human cannot know that, because God is by nature greater than he is. Only the greatest mystic may experience the answer in a state of highest unification.

No one can say how God looks upon the world, how God sees life. Yet there are souls who attain to the divine vision, in other words, their outlook becomes God's outlook. (XII 17)

The creation is, because it is. (I 24)

Why does the sun shoot out its rays? Because it is its nature. And the same answer applies to the question of why the supreme Spirit manifests. Because it is its nature. (VIII 154)

Many ask what was the reason at the back of this manifestation, of this creation. The reason is beyond all reasoning. There is no reason. It is nature itself; love cannot but manifest. When poetically expressed, the great ones have said that God was lonely, and in order to realize his predisposition which is love, in order to experience it, He manifested. It is poetic and it is true. (VII 240)

The latter quotation includes the two traditional answers: creation out of love and creation for experience. Creation as an act of love is inferred from the fact that the nature of creation is the doubling of one. (II 85)

Whereas the human lover longs to unite, to become one with the object of love, he or she could not have this longing if they were not two. Therefore the first act of love is creation of an object to love.

Love is the power that is the original cause of creation; it is the battery working behind the mechanism of the universe. (III 144)

Someone asked a Sufi the reason for this creation, and he answered, 'God, whose being is love itself, desired to experience the nature of His own being, and in order to experience it He has to manifest Himself.' (X 149)

God knows Himself by his manifestation. Manifestation is the self of God, but a self which is limited. (XI 238)

The Knower had to manifest Himself, thus becoming an object to be known, and by this knowledge the Knower arrives at perfection. It does not mean that the knower

> lacked perfection, for all perfection belonged to the Knower; only he became conscious of His perfection. (I 232)

The idea is this: we can only know a thing by comparing it with its opposite; one could not know light if there were no darkness. But God, being perfect, has no opposite. (VIII 97)

> All things existing have their opposite, except God; it is for this reason that God cannot be made intelligible. (*Gayan* 63, n. 100)

But the very limitedness of everything created can be seen as an opposite to the unlimitedness of its Origin. (IX 101) The notion of a devil as an opposite to God is a moral and psychological aspect of another God-conception. (see chapter III)

purpose of life

> The purpose of life, in short, is that the Only Being makes his Oneness intelligible to Himself. He goes through different planes of evolution, or planes through which he arrives at different changes, in order to make clear to Himself his Oneness. And as long as this purpose is not accomplished, the one and only being has not reached His ultimate satisfaction, in which lies His divine perfection. (I 237)

> The experience of every soul becomes the experience of the divine mind; therefore the divine mind has the knowledge of all beings. (IX 139)

> It does not bring anything new to God; it only makes Him conscious of what He is. (V 94)

The experience of all creation contributes to this divine self-knowledge. In more than one place (IV 231, VI 24, VIII 294, XI 235) Inayat remarks that animals, birds, plants, rocks, all things count, and that all created beings have their own form or expression of spiritual life. But the most valued experience is that of a human who arrives at being conscious of limited and unlimited life both—that is to say, the experience of the great mystic. (I 144/145, IV 119, VI 259, VIII 157, 162)

The purpose of this whole creation is fulfilled by attaining at that perfection which a human being is intended to attain. All the saints, sages, prophets, and masters have been human beings, and they have shown divine perfection in fulfilling the purpose of being human. (IX 175)

In man the purpose of manifestation is fully accomplished; especially in the man who has on his return journey become more and more conscious of the purpose, by widening his outlook and by living a fuller life; the man who has reached that stage of realization which is called divinity, in which is the fulfilment of the purpose of this whole manifestation. (I 112)

The 'fuller life' and 'all the planes' infer that all human experience is needed, that of outer life too. The many passages discussing the reason of creation as God's experience, generally go on to explain the purpose of life as well. There is a book on *The purpose of Life* (I 187-240) and several chapters (I 23-26, VI 16-44, VII 204-211, XII 76-78). On page 42 I already referred to the minor and major purposes of life. Here I add a few quotations in connection with the 'Why' of creation and the meaning of life.

There are as many different aspects of that purpose as there are people in the world; but behind all of them is one purpose . . . And that purpose is accomplished when the inventor looks at his invention working, when the architect builds a house which he has designed, and he enters it and sees how well it is made; the purpose is accomplished when a play is produced, and the producer watches it . . . Every man seems to have his own purpose, but all these purposes are nothing but steps to the one and only purpose which is the purpose of God . . . the fuller experience of life within and without, the fuller knowledge of life above and below. (VIII 127)

Seekers after different things, seekers after wealth, seekers after ideal, seekers after pleasure, and seekers after paradise, must have their own ways; . . . One may contradict another, although they are all making their way to the goal. (I 229)

This conception of creation to which every unique experience contributes is in itself an answer to the deep-felt questions about the meaning of life. And it makes Inayat not only a guide on the ways back home to the origin, but also a helper who accepted and respected daily life.

meaning of life

What all souls seek is to know the meaning of life. . . . Whatever different interests people may have, their only real inclination is to find the meaning of life. . . . Thus in either a material or a spiritual way every soul is striving for what it longs for all the time, each in its own particular way. (VI 145)

Life is interesting in every phase; on the journey towards manifestation as well as on the soul's return towards the goal. Every moment of life has its particular experience, one better than the other, one more valuable than another. In short, life may be said to be full of interest. (I 165)

There is the journey from the goal to the life in the world, and there is the journey from the life in the world to the goal, and both journeys are natural. (VII 204)

The purpose of life is fulfilled in rising to the greatest heights and in diving to the deepest depths of life. (I 231)

There is always a steady compass focussing Inayat's outlook on life, also when he acknowledges the sordid and trivial aspects of daily life.

It is in the knowledge of self that there lies the fulfilment of life. The knowledge of self means the knowledge of one's body, the knowledge of one's mind, the knowledge of one's spirit; the knowledge of the spirit's relation to the body and the relation of the body to the spirit; the knowledge of one's wants and needs, the knowledge of one's virtues and faults; knowing what we desire and how to attain it, what to pursue and what to renounce. And when one dives deep into this, one finds before one a world of knowledge which never ends. And it is that knowledge which gives one insight into human nature and brings one to the knowledge of the whole creation. And in the end one attains to the knowledge of the divine Being. (I 235/236)

IX Sufism in Daily Life, An Art of Living

What the world needs is the mystical outlook. (XI 186)

life a struggle and life an opportunity

Man is not only scared of badness but also of goodness; man not only dreads war but also peace; he is not only tired of enmity but also of friendship; he not only suspects his adversary but even his own brother. It seems as if the mind of the world is not only tired but ill; as if humanity has had a nervous breakdown. Individually or collectively man does not know his life's purpose or goal. The Sufi message warns humanity to get to know life better and to achieve freedom in life; it warns him before every action to note its consequence by studying the situation, his own attitude and the method he should adopt. (IX 255)

Man may be taught to do good, he may learn righteousness, but this is virtue forced upon him as the result of a certain teaching; real virtue comes by understanding the oneness of life, thus binding man to friend and enemy alike. (VIII 133)

We are able to do anything if we choose to make the effort. (XI 83)

You need not do a thing today because you did it yesterday. (*Vadan* 80)

The soul has not come on earth to die the death of helplessness, nor continually to suffer pain and misery. (XI 255)

Life is an opportunity, not only of accomplishing one's desires, but of fulfilling even the deepest yearning of the soul. (*Gayan* 55, new 91)

Not that one should expect everything to be good and beautiful and, if one's expectation is not realized, think there is no hope of progress. (IX 74)

> Because life means a continual battle. One's success, failure, happiness, or unhappiness mostly depend upon one's knowledge of this battle. (VI 77)

> After all, life is a struggle and we must be ready to struggle. Only, struggle must not make us drunk so that we lose the way of peace which is the first thing to consider. We must not be like a boxer who is always looking for another person to box with. (VI 76)

These are a few of Hazrat Inayat Khan's remarks concerning daily life. He was used to consider all circumstances, all sorts of characters and all grades of development, but for all its adaptability his view on life is firmly rooted in his philosophy of unity. In a letter to a pupil who busied herself with the printing of his books he expressed his wish to have his first book on the art of living (*Moral Culture,* III 229-262) published together with *The Unity of Religious Ideals* (IX 5-279), because he saw them as matching one another (unpublished correspondence with Miss J. Dowland, letter from Geneva, autumn 1924 or 1925). He described himself as 'an optimist with open eyes', (VI 81) and did not shun the problems of sadness, difficulties and evil. As a mystic he could see the passing, temporary nature of much sorrow (II 87). A deep sense of the illusory nature of earthly life was ingrained in him as in every Indian philosopher. But he advised many others not to advocate these theories as long as one had not really experienced them.

life real and unreal

> When a person says to another who is in pain, 'It is all illusion,' the one who is suffering will say, 'It is a reality to me. If you were the one who is suffering you would not say that it is an illusion' . . . . To call something that our senses perceive an illusion we must first understand its nature and character, in order to prove to ourselves and to others that it is an illusion. (XI 15)

For Inayat himself most outer things were so fleeting that once he was amazed at visitors who had, for hours, talked business and fashion. 'Strange that they think all this is real.' But he studied daily life in all its forms from the very day he started trekking through India as a young adept who was also a professional musician.

> My tour not only secured my professional success, but the greatest advantage I derived there from was my constant contact with people of the highest to the lowest classes and from the best to the worst. I associated with personalities ranging from the saint to the sinner, and had the great privilege of studying human nature in reality.

This passage from an autobiographical record composed in 1915 has been left out in the recent edition (XII 125-164) where it should be found on page 138. Maybe the editor decided to omit this conclusive remark because of his own conception about perfection that will be looked into below. But the passage does not stand alone.

> The purpose of life is fulfilled in rising to the greatest heights and in diving to the deepest depths of life. (*Vadan* 131)

'why does God allow suffering'

It is a common human trait to reject 'the deepest depths' when first confronted with them. For all of us, the time comes to pose the fundamental questions about good and evil, and the injustice of suffering. It is this problem that will be the main subject of the following few pages, though deserving of much more than such summary attention. The question came to Inayat in his childhood. During a lecture (Leeds 1919, manuscript by Dr O. C. Gruner, in *Fondation Nekbakht*) he recalled how he was puzzled because the good hero of a story was treated badly. Young Inayat would not stop asking questions about it, until the grown-ups in the big household of his youth lost their patience and sent him away. He tried to find an answer in an old book of ethics, and listened to the conversation of visiting philosophers. When he was about twenty he went through a crisis when everything seemed lost to him. Those nearest to him had died, his country and his art seemed to be held in contempt. A few years later his murshid, Syed Hashim Madani, taught his pupil Inayat, without many words, how to find his way in the world behind our limited knowledge and to discover the 'reasons behind reasons.' (see below). But he always continued to understand, from observation in others and in his old self, the protest, the arguing, the indignation of those who accuse God of injustice because of human suffering.

> If God were separate from man, and if he rejoiced in the suffering of man, then one might blame him. But as the Sufi realizes, he is the sufferer and the suffering (compare page 150); yet at the same time he is beyond all suffering. This fact can be understood by not merely believing in God, but by knowing him. Suppose our hand dropped a heavy weight on our feet and hurt them, are our hands to be blamed? No, for they share the pain with the feet, and although the feet seem to be hurt, yet that which feels the hurt is our being, our absolute being, and therefore the hand shares the hurt with the foot. So it is with God: all our lives are his and he takes part in every feeling of joy and pain which we feel, but at the same time his perfect being keeps him above all earthly joys and pains, whereas our imperfection limits us, so that we become subject to all joys and pains, however small they are. (VIII 134)

> If one would ask what is the cause of all the misery in life, the answer would be that there is one cause only and that is the limitation of life . . . . When Buddha was young he saw that there was great pain in the world, and his first thought was to find out what was behind it; and so it has been with all the great teachers. They all wanted to solve this one question, to find out what is the cause of all misery. (XII 47)

the masters called by suffering

> Human suffering is the first call we have to answer. (*Gayan* 32, n. 53)

Inayat respected all who tried to help their fellow-men, but he considered the great saints and sages, prophets and mystics as best fitted for this. All these great teachers knew suffering by experience, though they were able to rise above the pains of limitation and share the peace of the Only Being.

> The bringers of joy have always been the children of sorrow. (*Vadan* 90)

Causes for the suffering of the master may be found in outer circumstances and the reactions of others. People may reject his teachings (I 31, 84, IX 237), misunderstand him (IX 127, 234, 145) and he is never able to express himself fully (I 86, X 73, XI 146, 150). He may be sad because of the lack of general evolution (*Gayan* 22, n. 35) and he always has to live in two worlds, 'like a fish on the land.' (VIII 55) Or, the reverse:

> The work of the prophet in the world becomes as hard as if a person were asked to jump into the water and then come out dry. He must live in the world and not be of the world. (A Hallajian image, IX 134)

At the same time, his sensitivity is bound to be greater than that of most people.

> And if one asks how a mystic, who has been so kind and helpful, gets on among the crowd in everyday life, since the rough edges of everyday life rubbing against him must necessarily make him heartsore, the answer is that they certainly do, and the heart of the mystic is even more sore than that of anybody else . . . . But just as the diamond by being cut becomes brilliant so does the heart; and when the heart has been sufficiently cut it becomes a flame which illuminates not only the life of the mystic, but also that of others. (X 30)

Here we touch on something that goes deeper than outer circumstances and the actions of others. Also, it is not only the mystic who matures through sorrow. Whilst certain people grow bitter through suffering, others will become stronger.

> As fire can cook or burn food, so also does pain affect the human heart. (*Gayan* 31, n. 50)

> By going through sorrow we rise above it. (*Vadan* 91)

suffering though deep feeling

For we should not forget that the ultimate purpose is happiness. But:

> If there were no pain one would not have the experience of joy . . . . Without pain the greatest musicians, athletes, discoverers, and thinkers would not have reached the stage

they have arrived at in the world. If they had always experienced joy, they would not have touched the depths of life. For what is pain? Pain in the true sense of the word is the deepest joy. If we have imagination, we can enjoy tragedy more than comedy: comedy is for children, and tragedy is for grown-ups. It is by pain alone that somebody becomes what is called an old soul, one who may be young in age but whose thoughts are deep.

If sorrow and sadness have no reality, why then did Christ say, 'My soul is exceedingly sorrowful?' We must distinguish between the human side of the Master's life and the divine side . . . . Why does God send his message to humanity by a man and not by angels? Because only a human being knows human beings. He knows them from having experienced human limitation. That he felt sadness is the most beautiful side of the master's life. If he had not, how could he have sympathized with those who are sorrowful? (VI 122, 123)

In this passage and several others (*Nirtan* 27, II 195, IV 85, VIII 325/326, X 209) we find a reason for a spiritual master's suffering, and at least one reason for our own sorrow as well: a certain experience of pain can work to develop the capacity for deep feeling which is utterly different from suffering inflicted from the outside. The latter can be fought, but the pain of feeling and the closely connected pain of change are not to be feared, though, as a rule they are. Everyone who has been in love, or has known a long-awaited home-coming or has attained a great goal, is aware that tears and laughing are close neighbours, converging in one reaction. And the one who never has felt sad may know fun or pleasure, but not happiness, not real joy.

What is to be revived in the present generation is the capacity of feeling. (XI 74)

In every experience, good or bad, the soul finds a certain joy, and that joy is in the fulfilment of life's purpose. That joy is not only experienced in pleasure but even in pain, not only in success but also in failures; not only in the cheerfulness of the heart but even in the breaking of the heart there is a certain joy hidden. For there is no experience which is worthless. (I 232/233)

People who have had deep experience of any kind, of suffering, of agony, of love, of hate, of solitude, of association, of success, of failure, all have a particular quality, a quality which has a special use for others. (VIII 269)

In talking about the capacity for feeling Inayat had to dispel the pre-conditioned interpretations of the solemn and long-faced as well as of the superficial and sweet.

Emotional people are not always loving people. (VIII 280)

Man is not born into this world for depression and unhappiness. His very being is happiness, depression is something unnatural. By this I do not mean that sorrow is a sin or that suffering is always unavoidable. We all have to experience both in life, in order to accomplish the purpose of life. We cannot always be smiling, and there is no spiritual evolution in ignoring either side of life. (X 144/145)

how to fight unnecessary suffering

'Depression is unnatural.' Depression is one of the forms of sadness one can learn to outgrow. Pain and joy, when genuinely felt have a widening effect and so make a person stronger. But there are many kinds of suffering that can and should be resisted. There is suffering through circumstance, through others, and through our own attitude.

In order to understand this struggle one must see that there are three sides to it: struggle with oneself, struggle with others, and struggle with circumstances . . . . What is needed is that all three should be studied and learnt, and one must be able to manage the struggle in all three directions. (VI 89)

This is a passage from *The Alchemy of Happiness* (VI 3-277). The title of this collection of lectures is a current simile in classical Sufi literature. This volume VI, like volume III and much of the volumes IV, VII and VIII, deals with problems of daily life. The basic idea of Inayat's art of living is always the mystical outlook, which means the acceptance of the unity of being. (XI 186) Because for most people this can be an abstract idea only, Inayat takes our limited perception into account by giving many bits of advice for ordinary people.

> We know intellectually that all are one. But when someone insults us, we cannot bear it, we no longer think that he is the same as we are. (VIII 229)

> The life which everyone knows is this momentary period of the soul's captivity. (XI 241)

> Every difficulty in life is owing to man's limitation which covers the divine spark in him until in time it becomes obscured from his view, and this culminates in the tragedy of life. (XI 235)

> The true ego does not know sorrow; its true being is happiness, for the real ego is God and God is happiness. (XI 236)

> One might ask, what is the best way to take in everyday life to lead one to life's ideal? The best way is to consider harmony as the first principle to be observed; . . . it is easy to say, but most difficult to live. (X 53)

To master daily life one needs an unbiased perception, strength of will, strength of purpose, and a beginning readiness to understand. Apart from the fact that 'looking inside helps looking outside' (IV 221), several of the mystic's initial methods can be applied to the fight against suffering. Once started in this way, one will find all sorts of causes and reasons for suffering. Some of these causes are so common that we forget to notice them. Time and again Hazrat Inayat reminds us to discern the role of suggestion working through circumstances, through others and above all through ourselves.

suffering through suggestion

Among the suggestions from circumstances and others are conventions, customs and attitudes.

> If we consider our knowledge, a thousand things we seem to have experienced, we find that other people have told us most of them and we believed them at once. (VI 95)

> No one can escape being affected by another person's mind. (VII 53)

> There is much in our lives that depends upon suggestions which come from outside, either consciously, or unconsciously, as well as suggestions which come to us from ourselves. (XII 38)

> The whole of life in this world is built on conventions and accepted ideas, and conscience is erected on this edifice. (VIII 199)

> Blinded by conventions and by the laws of his time and the customs of his people, man has ignored and opposed the truth. (IX 237)

> We hardly realize how much we depend in our everyday life upon suggestion, especially in forming our opinions of other people. . . . And at this time when our life in the world is very automatic and we all depend upon what the newspapers say, we collectively change our opinion of people, day after day. We neither know the cause of their being praised, nor do we know much about why they are blamed. (XI 75)

Wherever one discovers the working of undesirable suggestion one can try and inactivate it. The adept can use the results of his inner development (VI 90/91, VIII 220), but there are many other methods.

> The battle of each individual has a different character; it depends upon a man's particular grade of evolution. (IX 161)

Counter-acting and counter-suggestion can help, if one knows how to apply these (IV 254, 255, XI 78, VIII 48, X 33). A person should not take a heavier load than he can carry easily (*Vadan* 77), but he must not say 'I can never'. (VI 218, XI 80, 81) Failure does not matter (*Gayan* 29, n. 47, IV 256), that is a general principle. One can always try again. Inayat's own life is an example of beginning again, three times over, and succeeding at last.[1]

[1] Elisabeth de Jong-Keesing, *Inayat Khan, a Biography*, p. 81, 86, 137, 165

As always, resisting suggestion is firstly a matter of attitude. In the lectures on suggestion (XI 75-96) many of these attitudes and methods are discussed, and also the slips one may make when applying them.

> The best way to react against suggestion is to try and find out the facts. But very often what a person does is to try and find out the facts in the light of that suggestion. It is just like the story of Othello, who when he begins to enquire about Desdemona interprets everything in the same light as it was suggested to him. (XI 77)

Like the beginning adept, a person commencing his struggle against ill-luck, failures or unhappiness, needs self-knowledge first.

> Just as for every illness there is a remedy, so for every disaster there is a reconstruction. , . .But we shall not understand the outer life if we do not understand ourselves. (VIII 56)

And this will make clear that much misery may be caused by ourselves.

> Man is afraid of every distress that comes to him, and he partakes of it without first having faced it and studied it analytically. (IX 166)

> There are many who develop the habit of worrying about things. The least little thing worries them very much. They cherish whatever little sorrow they have; it is a plant they water and nourish. (VI 136)

> Every little pain and discomfort often continues through the power of suggestion. As soon as one feels discomfort or pain the mind repeats, 'I have a pain. I am uncomfortable', and this suggestion adds to that pain, like fuel to the fire. (XI 86)

> The wretched always look for some excuse to be miserable. (*Gayan* 46, n. 77)

> Thus miseries are attracted by those who fear miseries; disappointment is brought about by those who expect a

disappointment; failure is caused by holding the impression of a failure. Often people say, 'I shall never succeed, I shall never succeed. Everything I do goes wrong, there is something wrong.' It is a very good thing that there are stars, so that they can attribute their miseries to the stars. But these miseries belong to them, it is they in reality who are holding them in their minds. When a person is continually thinking, 'Nothing will happen right; nothing good will come,' failure is anticipated; and even if all the stars of heaven were in his favour he would still meet with failure. In this way man is the creator of his condition, of his fate. (IV 253)

> Also, ... when they have forgotten something, which is a natural thing for a human being to do, they repeat to themselves, 'How stupid! How forgetful on my part!' and that idea repeated twice or thrice deepens their forgetfulness. (XI 80)

suffering through actions

> When a person looks for evil then he can see nothing but evil in every person. In this way he grows so accustomed to it that his world becomes full of evil. He has contemplated it and looked for it and created it. (VII 215)

Of course, there is suffering inflicted by others. But even there one can exert an influence, beginning with difficulties arising out of personal relations. In his book *Moral Culture* (III 229-262) Inayat systematically considers our actions and reactions towards friends, strangers, enemies, wrongdoers, towards ourselves and towards God. For the moment let us take the subject of enemies who cause suffering. One should neither constantly dwell on the faults of the enemy, which makes them worse, nor underestimate him. Both attitudes are ego-increasing.

> Complaining about the harm caused by the enemy is weakness; avoiding it by taking precautions, facing it with strength and checking it with power are the things worth doing. (III 235)

The best thing, Inayat continues, is to try not to make enemies, and, if possible, to modify existing enmity by not reacting rashly, or even by a friendly attitude. But to answer enmity with kindness is not everybody's work. Even for the mystic there are cases where he must not show kindness (III 251), only tolerance, though a mystic may have evolved to a stage in which he really can love his enemy. One should not, Inayat says, profess to love one's enemy, unless we really consider him as another God-part and no longer in his limited quality of an enemy. (XII 72)

Moral Culture

Moral Culture systematically deals with the fact that everybody's fighting power, endurance and tolerance are in accord with his grade of evolution. One cannot prescribe the same methods, attitudes and virtues for all, just as one cannot expect the same God-conception to be valid for a child and a philosopher, a peasant in ancient Egypt and a churchman in a modern city. This may be one of the reasons why Inayat considered *Moral Culture* as matching *The Unity of Religious Ideals,* in which gradations also present in religious motives and expressions are considered. Another is that to Inayat the building-up of human personality is the essential preliminary to the transcending of human limitation into the mystical consciousness.

Moral Culture gives a general division of the art of living on three main levels. For most people a sound start is to let their acts be guided by the principle of reciprocity, which means to give and take in even measure. Observing this implies a beginning attention for the rights and feelings of one's fellow-men and not for one's own condition only. Some may grow to the stage of benificence, which brings a considerable widening, for then one considers one's fellow-man's needs spontaneously, without paying much heed to oneself; but the benefit in happiness is great, for 'the world is a dome' (a recurrent image) and what we do comes back to us like an echo. (II 22, V 30, VIII 204). The last principle, renunciation, we already encountered in previous chapters as the attainment of the few able to live in communication with all. To them 'I' and 'others' are not really different. Their renunciation is not a constricting virtue but a natural action. (III 261, VI 237-239, XI 180-182)

It is often confusing that some of the results of inner

evolution can only be alluded to by means of terms evoking the well-worn virtues which have been taught and even enforced—if only by suggestion!—by religious and other leaders throughout the ages. To avoid confusion Inayat often had to draw clear distinctions between formal virtues, forced virtues and superficial imitations of great results.

good principles cannot be enforced

What virtue is that, o righteous man, which gives not happiness? (*Vadan* 127)

Nothing that is artificial has any power. (XI 106)

Self-denial cannot be a virtue when it is the result of helplessness and culminates in dissatisfaction. (VIII 71)

A person who pretends to be unselfish is generally foolish-selfish. (VII 122)

One should not force one's nature. A man once asked another man to lend him his raincoat. It was immediately given but at the same time the giver was very much annoyed that the other should have asked for it, and when he himself was obliged to go out in the rain he was vexed at having to get wet. It would have been much better for him to have said at once that he was sorry not to be able to lend the coat. Once having given it, however, he should not have grudged it. (VIII 69)

Often fine principles can be practised to great disadvantage. (VIII 70)

When virtues control a man's life they become idols; and it is not idols that we should worship; it is the ideal behind the idol. (VIII 79)

Whatever we consider at the time to be right, just, good, and virtuous, that is the thing we ought to do; but we should not impose or urge what we consider right or good or pure upon others who do not consider it in the same way as we do. (VI 250)

I try to do the right which seems right to me at the moment; at another moment the same may seem to me wrong.

> Therefore I do not attempt to impose my right upon the one who does not see the right of it. (*Vadan* 65)

In Inayat's days the standard virtues of the nineteenth century still held sway, although there was growing doubt as to their value. Shortly afterwards a total rejection of 'morals' sprang up in some circles where people had become disgusted with the misuse of virtues that had become idols. Nowadays these freedom fighters' children grope for a new hold. Moreover, all of us must at some time struggle with the same question that puzzled Inayat when he was a child. He did not ask only 'why is there so much suffering?' but also, 'why did this good person suffer?' How many have not exclaimed that God cannot be just, if he allows innocent people to suffer. We tend to regard suffering as punishment. And God should be *'is God just?'* good—that is, his works must please us.

> Many blame God, many judge Him, and many think it is unfair on the part of God to create, and to destroy. (I 114)

> They think what they consider good is the will of God, and what they consider not good is not the will of God. (IV 181)

> Many have been resentful towards God for having sent them misery in their lives, but misery is always part of life's experience. Some may become very angry and say, 'This is not just', or 'This is not right, for how could God who is just and good allow unjust things to happen?' (VIII 101)

These protests are based on the presumption that we know what is just and good. We do not. As said in previous chapters (page 5 and 161) the concepts of good and bad are man made, they are subjective and not the same for everyone, nor in all times.

> It is not true that virtue is one thing and sin another. The same thing which was once virtue may become sin. (VIII 233)

> The standard of right and wrong, the conception of good and evil, and the idea of sin and virtue are understood differently by the people of different races, nations, and

religions; therefore it is difficult to discern the law governing these opposites. (II 22)

Mankind tends to consider that all that is pleasant has come from the mercy of God, and all that is unpleasant either from the wrath of God or not from God at all, because he thinks that God is just and merciful. In reality God's goodness and mercy are hidden under all pleasant and unpleasant experiences in life. We call things unjust when we cannot see their justice; things are unpleasant to us when the standard of our pleasure is limited; things appear unmerciful when we restrict and limit mercy. (IX 104)

When I look back on my past I see that every happy and unhappy experience I had to go through, however bitter or sweet at the time it appeared, was for some definite purpose. (*Sufi,* April 1918, p. 4)

Evil and ugliness exist in man's limited conception. In God's great Being they have no existence. (XI 238)

good and perfect not identical

There is another difficulty. When we are angry with God, or puzzled by the incongruities of life, we not only subject God to our limited judgment, but we confuse the words good and perfect. There are several ways to arrange our thoughts about good and evil: philosophical speculation, practical ethics and mystical experience. But the first thing is to find out what the word 'good' means to us.

As we have seen perfection means comprising all and not even the mystic who come nearest to God can be called perfect, but only perfected (p. 152) for he exists in a limited human form. (X 67) Nonetheless, our common association with the word 'perfect' is 'completely good, without any evil.'

Some people who admire piety and goodness want everyone to be an angel, and discovering that this is impossible they are full of criticism. Man has in him both a devil and an angel. (X 87)

The whole interest in life is in journeying towards perfection. If man were born perfect there would be no joy in life. (XI 250)

Inayat, as a mystic, saw beyond limited conceptions. As a student of life, and as a human being who himself had gone through many difficulties, he understood puzzlement and indignation. As a philosopher he drew a conclusion that he knew would shock many.

> God cannot be good and perfect at the same time; it takes good and bad both to make perfection. (*Vadan* 131)

> It would puzzle a believer who considered God to be all goodness and all beauty if he were told that God also contains everything that is bad and evil. (VIII 97)

All the same, in the practical passages concerned with the art of living, Inayat describes how to discern evil and how to counter-act it. For though one may accept that both good and bad have a place in the temporal world, this does not mean that one should not fight evil. The principle underlying this seeming contradiction is the perfection and completeness of the Only Being and the limitedness of all creation.

> God is we, but we are not gods. The difference between God and our being is not of the being; in being, God and we are one. The difference lies in our limitation and in the perfection of God. (IX 101)

> All that is in our nature is in the nature of God. The only difference is that God is great and we are small; we are limited and God is unlimited; we represent imperfection, God represents perfection. (VI 182)

> Life can be pictured as a line with two ends. One end of the line is limitation, and the other end of the same line is perfection. As long as one is looking at the end which is limitation, however good, virtuous, or pious one is, one has not touched what may be called perfection. (VI 192)

temporal ideas of good and bad are needed

As the limited view is the view of most people, temporal ideas of good and bad are needed.

> In religious terminology one often makes use of pairs of opposites, such as God and devil, heaven and hell, sin and virtue. Man begins acquiring knowledge by learning about

pairs of opposites, and he cannot rise at once to that level where he comprehends life without these. In one way the idea is not correct; it is not right to conceive of God, who is all-powerful, as having another personality, an opposite power which one calls the devil. But . . . . a devotee whose object is to raise his ideal of God as high as he can . . . , is hindered by being made to see that all that he considers wicked and ugly is also a part of God. However, this idea diminishes God, making Him limited, and producing a power, if not equal, yet all the same opposite to God . . . . nevertheless, it gives a picture, it is more comprehensible and tangible to distinguish between the God of good and the Lord of evil. . . . If we did not distinguish between the two, if we arrived directly at the conception of unity, we would be missing a great deal in life. It is only after having distinguished between them that we can come to the idea of unity which raises us above it all. For instance, when a person says he will not look at anyone else's faults and closes his eyes, he has missed a great deal. But the one who has seen them and yet risen above them is the person who deserves to close his eyes from all that is evil. (VIII 97, 98)

Nothing but good can be praised, and none but the good can be worshipped. (IX 178)

Different religions have taught different morals which were right for the people at that time. No doubt the law of the masses must be respected, but the real conception of right and wrong lies in one's deepest self. The soul is not pleased by what is not right. (X 52)

This deepest self is not the psychologist's *über-ich.* We have seen that for the mystic our deepest soul is both beyond our conscience and beyond our subconscious, which are limited; it is our God-part, which is revealed to us through mystical training; whereas the conscience acts directly, and the subconscious is known through the help of psychological insight. Though the latter provides some widening, of course it cannot reach as far as the mystical experience.

good and bad in creation

Now follows the question: if this God-part likes goodness and rejects evil, then what about the teaching that both good and bad belong to perfection? The answer is that evil itself is bound up with limitation, and, though present in the created world, has no existence in reality; that is, reality as experienced and defined by the mystic.

> As the shadow is evident, yet non-existent, so is evil. (*Gayan* 87, n. 140)

> In ancient times many have tried to help the imagination of those who sought goodness by teaching them belief in Satan. . . . This was in order to explain to those who could not understand where badness came from. In reality badness is only the shadow of goodness; and as shadow is non-existent so evil is non-existent. Good is always going forward; what is left behind is less good, and what is gained on the journey forward is more good. But when we compare things then we call one thing evil and the other good . . . . it was simply a method of teaching the people of ancient times. In reality God is beyond comparison, though of course we compare God with something when we call Him good, as many do. What is our own goodness? It is very small; it is not something to judge God by. (VIII 129, 130)

The subject is connected with the purpose of life, as mentioned at the end of chapters IV and VIII.

> One (the advancing mystic) begins to see that the whole universe is a mechanism working towards a certain purpose. Therefore the right one and the wrong one, the good and the bad are all bringing about one desired result, . . . a result meant to be, which is the purpose of life. (IV 126)

> In order to find goodness one must find wickedness to compare it with. When we have found both, then both become clear; wickedness will show what goodness is. In order to find reality we must gather the knowledge of what is unreal. . . . All this existence which is before us and which is subject to change and death is not reality; . . . but we can only see this when we have acquired some knowledge of reality. (XI 152)

As we have seen (p. 122 and p. 144) this awareness of the mystic's reality includes knowledge and experience of balance and harmony. Therefore balance and harmony are also connected with the subject of good and evil.

> The question of balance explains the problem of sin and virtue, and he who understands it is the master of life. (V 213)
>
> Ultimate good is harmony itself. (II 148)
>
> How uninteresting the world would be if all men were perfect; it would be like a piano in which all the tones were the same. (IX 244)
>
> The one who always does right need not be here. This is the place in which to do both wrong and right. (IX 43)

This view of balance as including both good and evil throws a light on two recurrent themes in Hazrat Inayat Khan's lectures; there is something good, that means God-connected in the greatest wrongdoer; and nothing is only good or bad. As Inayat never stopped at intellectual understanding only, he often adds that it is easy to posit a pretty theory, but difficult to give it reality in our actions. (VI 99, XI 134) To him as a mystic the outer surface was naturally transparent.

> There is a right side to every wrong, and a wrong side to every right. (*Vadan* 95)
>
> Life is always different from what one thinks it to be, and this applies to pain, pleasure, happiness, success, and failure, everything. (VI 120)
>
> When people say that someone is bad, it really means that the surface has become bad. The depth cannot be bad. . . . The very fact that he is living shows that there is a spark of goodness in him. (VIII 107)
>
> There is an English phrase: a lost soul. But the soul is not lost; the soul is only buried. When it is dug out, then the divine life breaks forth. (IX 24, 25)
>
> One cannot say that an evil person has no good in him, nor a

good person no evil. (VIII 201)

There comes a time in the life of a man when he can see some good in the worst man in the world. (IV 103)

There is always a possibility of progress for every soul, even for the most wicked. (V 114)

When Inayat's centre-leaders in America asked him whether 'even a gross person' could become spiritual and progress to the goal, he answered 'yes' emphatically; if only the wish to proceed was sincere and such a person did his exercises, especially the zikar (dhikr) regularly. (unpublished *Instruction-interview,* Detroit, June 1926). As for those who do not want to change, do not know that they may change, or do not persevere in trying there are many different ways to handle them. The last thing one should do is to fight and repress, for that only feeds evil, (see below). One can keep clear of the wrongdoer if possible, and if counter-action is needed, one should act with forethought and with an eye for the consequences.

In the same instruction-interview and in several reminiscences (SK 1, 9, 15, 21, 33, 41, 44, 48) we witness Inayat dealing with undesirable situations or unbalanced people. He did not close his eyes for unpleasantness nor did he give fuel to the fire of a strong and thick limited ego. For though in his philosophy evil belongs to the created world and even has a function temporarily, evil should be overcome, and good should prevail.

how to recognize desirable (good) actions

But if good and bad are different for everybody and at all moments, and there is good in evil and evil in good, then how can one recognize what is good and desirable? For our tendency to look for one simple standard for good and its opposite is great.

Is there any particular action or thing which one can point out as being evil? No doubt man is always apt to do so, but nothing can be evil according to a fixed principle. Then what is it? It is something which is devoid of harmony, it is something which lacks beauty and love, and above all it is something which does not fit into the accommodation of life. (VIII 104)

What determines that something should be called right or wrong? Four things: the motive behind the action, the result of the action, the time and the place. (VI 235)

Virtue is what brings real happiness. (VI 29)

how to handle evil

When one feels sure, if even for the time being, that something is wrong, one may start to counter-act, fight, neutralize, or starve it. Neutralizing evil can be done by an advanced mystic, who may conquer the most wicked 'by being quite the opposite'. (VII 112) But the present chapter deals with the possibilities for everybody, and everybody can counter-act evil in one way or another. A good way would be to try and rise above it (*Vadan* 69), but as a rule one takes to fighting first. If the fight is not a blind hitting out, but an effective use of weapons and methods, it certainly has its place in the art of living.

Every impression of an evil nature should be met with a combative attitude. (*Gayan* 27, new 44)

The one who goes into life's battle without first acquiring the knowledge of warfare loses in the end. But one who learns about this warfare of life first, learns its reason and its causes, becomes more capable of fighting the battle of his life. (VI 78)

Most of the methods offered by Inayat resemble those of the incipient mystic. And that is precisely the point, for it is the rudiments of the mystical outlook that will open up new possibilities for the management of life. Thus, we recognize the study of life, compressed into a bit of practical advice.

It is not necessary for us to be great or good, pious or spiritual. The first and most necessary thing is that we become observant. (VI 106)

Apart from the philosophical view of good and evil, discussed above, observation will produce psychological insight. One finding will be that suggestion can sustain evil as well as suffering. And just as we ourselves create some kinds of suffering, there may be evil of our own creation. For instance, we may see badness when it is not really there.

> The badness is not always in the objects and persons, but it is often in our way of looking at them. (X 149)

This may be a result of the well-known psychological habit of projecting our own unconscious wishes and attitudes into others.

> Man sees in another his own fault. (*Nirtan* 32)

> When we blame another person, when we dislike somebody, we overlook the same element in ourselves. (VI 95)

But there is another important way in which evil is created unconsciously. By talking and thinking about evil one increases its stature; hence very often an attempt to fight something bad has the opposite effect.

not to feed bad tendencies

> By accusing another of his fault you only root him more firmly in it. (*Gayan* 17, n. 27)

> When we say to someone who is in a rage and who has just been quarrelling, 'You have done wrong,' we have not given him a good thought, but have only added fuel so that he might fight with us too. One often sees that when two people are fighting and a third approaches them with the best intentions, they will both turn on him, and that will make three persons fighting at the same time. (XI 47)

> No sooner do you begin to see the bad side of man's character than you automatically throw a cover over the good side of his nature. (*Vadan* 130)

The latter maxim points to a still subtler way of adding fuel to badness. It is one thing to irritate a wrongdoer, and quite another to accept something bad as being bad. Here, by acceptance of evil is meant receiving, guarding and nursing it. Inevitably, one has to admit the existence of bad things, but one need not continually bear them in mind. To listeners who doubted the desirability of ignoring badness, Inayat said,

> One might ask if there does not exist animosity in people if one does not think about it. It may exist, but by taking notice of it, by acknowledging it, one gives life to it; if one does not acknowledge it, it will die in time. For animosity is a fire, but not a perpetual fire; it is the acknowledging which gives fuel to the fire. If one does not acknowledge it, the fire will be extinguished. (VI 264)

> To resist evil usually means to participate in and be guilty of the same evil. (III 130)

> Resist not evil, the scripture says. When there is resistance to evil in the other person do not become angry with him. When you foster the same emotion you add to his, and you also increase the same fire in yourself. It is like infecting yourself with a contagious disease instead of curing it. (XII 92)

Controlling one's angry, impatient reaction is not a weak and negative passivity, but a positive one, based on will-power and concentration. (VI 83, 102, V 236)

> If one were passive from weakness it would be weakness. But if one is passive from will-power then it is strength. (VI 166/167)

A good teacher does not further his pupil's progress by forbidding things, but he lets a wrong tendency peter out by itself. (IV 235) We may recognize an instance of such inoffensive help in the way Inayat, in a lecture, spoke about our tendency to see more faults in others than in ourselves.

> It is natural for people to take interest in the faults of others. (V 155)

And we may note one of the ways in which he made his listeners aware that we had better start doing something about our own shortcomings.

> Man does not realize how important is his own life, his self; and the study of his own life and his own self is a study of the greatest importance. (VI 78)

To begin with our own faults is not only 'good', like an old-fashioned 'virtue', but it is easier and makes us stronger to cope with others later.

> Generally one starts by struggling with others, and then one struggles all through life, and never finishes. The one who is somewhat wiser struggles with conditions, and perhaps he accomplishes things a little better. But the one who struggles with himself first is the wisest, for once he has struggled with himself, which is the most difficult struggle, the other struggles will become easy for him. (VI 90)

This is from the chapters 'Struggle of Life', and 'Life, a continual Battle', which contain much and varying advice on all sorts of struggle. To abstain from action is not the only method.

> There are moments when one must be persistent, and there are moments when one must be easy. (VI 82. Compare 'Our Dealings with Enemies', III 235, 236 and 251, 252)

One should consider circumstances, our own abilities and the likely results. (III 235, 236, XI 138) There is no rigid principle, though not to give fuel to badness is often advisable, and its positive counterpart, to 'water the plant of goodness' still more so.

> The one who sees good in others will see more and more good. The one who has a fault-finding tendency will find so many faults that at last the good will seem bad in his eyes. (VIII 61)

rearing good tendencies

> Sufis believe that if evil is contagious, goodness must be even more so. (IX 255)

These two methods, starving the bad tendencies and fostering the good ones can be applied to self-correction as well as to one's attitude to others.

> One should acknowledge in one's friend, in one's companion, in those one wishes to help, the good part in their character. By acknowledging it, by noticing it, one will fortify it; it will become greater. And do not think it is against humility to acknowledge even one's own merits; for

if one is unconscious of one's merit, the plant is suffering there without water. It does not mean that by acknowledging one's merit, one's virtue, one becomes proud or conceited; if one wants to one can keep oneself free from pride or conceit. But by recognizing one's merit one certainly waters the plant which is worth rearing. (VI 266)

The way to overcome error is, first to admit one's fault, and next, to refrain from repeating it. (*Gayan* 12, n. 18)

Does a person become less by finding faults in himself? No, he becomes greater, for he not only finds that all the faults which are in others are also to be found in him, but that all the merits of the others are also his own merits. (XI 198)

There are several warnings against false modesty and against the undesirable suggestion created by harping on one's own faults. (I 205, VII 115, XI 80, 86)

We should never allow that spirit of mastery which is in us to become blunted by a feeling of inability, for the essence of life is hope, and when we hope for the better, we shall be better. (XI 83)

It is never too late in life to improve; there is always scope for the man who wants to improve himself. But the man who is content with himself, or so discouraged that he does not want to improve, falls flat. (VI 220)

The sinner can become righteous at any moment if he makes up his mind—the difficulty is to make it up. The next thing is to carry it out. (VII 51)

When Inayat's pupils came to him complaining about somebody's conduct, he used to answer in this vein:

Now you have told me what he has done; can you tell me, also, what he will do? (SK 1)

Last month is too long ago to judge. Even if he were wicked yesterday, today there is hope for him, wickedness is a cloud over him; our very trust will disperse the cloud. (*Sufism,* December 1924, p. 11)

We saw in the previous chapter that Inayat did not agree with the philosophy of sin and punishment, because belief based on fear impedes the growth of faith. (I 139, VI 243, IX 142) Another reason is that the preoccupation with sin breeds evil in both the wrongdoer and the moralizer. Whereas the thought of forgiveness makes forgiving more probable and more powerful. (IV 116, 117)

> When a man asks forgiveness, that forgiveness develops in his own nature too, and he becomes ready to forgive others. Christ says in his prayer, 'Forgive us . . . as we forgive those that trespass against us.' . . . By asking forgiveness of God, we give up the desire to demand that our fellow-man should ask our forgiveness, and instead we want to forgive him. (IX 45)

As to the sinner, the real question is, whether his request is earnest enough. (I 60) As to the forgiver, he must have reached some inner evolution, for to forgive or to overlook means standing above things. (VIII 241-243) Inayat, very often, describes the wide outlook of the mystic which makes him less critical than ordinary man.

reasons behind reasons

> It is easy for an ordinary person to say what is good or bad, just or unjust; it is very difficult for a wise man. (VIII 224)

> One might naturally think that by virtue of one's evolution one would see more wrong, but that is not the case; the more one evolves the less wrong one sees, for then it is not always the action itself which counts,it is the motive behind it. (VIII 164)

The motive, or the 'reason behind reason' as Inayat usually calls it, may be seen by the mystic as the deeper meaning of an occurrence, its necessary place in the symphony of the whole (to use another of Inayat's similes). But there is also the simple acknowledgement of, and insight in another person's psychological make-up. Complete understanding is a mystic's result. (IV 141, VI 64, X 18, 154, IX 257) He has gone through all the grades (VI 236, 237) from first fault-finding with others, then turning to the faults in himself, thirdly to the phase of righting the wrong regardless of who caused it; to seeing the relative value of good and bad, and at last recognizing good and bad, that is unlimited and limited, as two ends of one line. The first three stages are not beyond an ordinary person's reach. Even the first stage is necessary and should not be bypassed, though not of course a phase to be tied down to for a whole lifetime.

> To see a person and say, 'That person is wicked, I dislike him,' that is learning. To see further and recognize something good in that person, to begin to like or to pity him, that is unlearning . . . . You have unravelled that knot. (II 151)

> The third person is the one who says, 'What does it matter if you did wrong or if I did wrong? What is needed is to right the wrong.' (VI 237)

The step from finding fault with others to a first understanding of their reasons is the most difficult one, not only because it is a first fundamental change of attitude, but because it goes against conventions one has taken for granted. Several times Hazrat Inayat Khan described the bewilderment of those who, for the first time, discover some of the 'reasons behind reasons', the disturbing fact that good and bad are relative values, only dependent on different points of view.

> People think that life is simple: the things that seem good to them they believe to be good; the things that seem bad they just think are bad, and so on. But the time comes when a person asks himself in a bewildered manner whether the ideals of his people are really high or low. (XII 65)

All social, moral, national, cultural and religious standards of good and bad are local, temporal, subject to change, external. They belong to the limited world. But this very limitedness, combined with the concept of the unlimited offers a standard that can be applied to all grades of evolution.

limitedness the cause of suffering and evil

> There is one sin, if ever sin existed . . . As soon as the soul begins to say 'I', he is exiled from heaven, for all blessings belong to that state which the soul experienced before he

claimed to be 'I', a separate entity, separate from the others. (XII 30)

The whole idea of the Sufi is to cover his imperfect self even from his own eyes by the thought of God; and that moment when God and not his own self is before him, is the moment of perfect bliss. My murshid, Abu Hashim Madani, once said that there is only one virtue and one sin for a soul on this path: virtue when he is conscious of God and sin when he is not. No explanation can describe the truth of this except the experience of the contemplative, to whom, when he is conscious of God, it is as if a window is open which is facing heaven, and when he is conscious of the self the experience is the opposite. For all the tragedy of life is caused by the consciousness of the self. All pain and depression are caused by this, and anything that can take away the thought of self helps to a certain extent to relieve man from pain; but God-consciousness gives perfect relief. (IX 115, VIII 231)

Inayat was well aware that for most people this realization is almost unimaginable.

It is very difficult for man to realize his true self, because the self he knows is a most limited self. (VI 188)

Therefore one cannot say that for ordinary man 'to be God-conscious' is 'the only virtue'. To begin with everybody has to build up a certain amount of limited identity to fulfill his small purpose of life. But most egos overabound in limitedness, and, unknowingly, we tend to feed and foster limitedness and thus we close the way to widening and the solution of our problems. Self-indulgence, of course, is an active fertilizer for limited egos. But the dangerous attitude Inayat mentioned most frequently is self-pity.

dangers or self-pity

There are many miseries in life, but the greatest misery is self-pity. (IV 170)

Self-pity is the cause of all the grief of life. (*Gayan* 23, n. 37)

Self-pity is the worst poverty. (VIII 113, 285, XI 235)

Worrying comes from self-pity and fear. (VI 58, XI 258)

> It (the over-fed limited ego) knows itself as an entity separate from friend and foe. It concerns itself with all that is transitory; it is blind to the future and ignorant of the past. It manifests in the form of self-pity. It expresses itself in the form of vengeance. It lives by feeding upon bitterness and its life is always spent in obscurity. Its condition is restlessness and discontent. It has a continual appetite for all that is there; it is never satisfied. (VI 94, 95)

> A person who is always concerned with his own feelings, is so absorbed in himself that he has no time to think of another. His whole attention is taken up with his own feelings. He pities himself, he worries about his own pain, and is never open to sympathize with others. (IX 19)

The remedy for self-pity is love, a sincere interest in the weal and woe of a fellow-being. This love or friendship or sympathy comes first: selflessness, that well-thumbed old virtue, comes after.

> Much can be learned by study, but not unselfishness. Unselfishness can be learned by one thing only and that is by treading the path of friendship. (VII 253)

Even thus, the word 'selflessness' may meet with wrong associations. It used to be recommended by those in power to the defenseless. Others may have a vague notion of becoming nothing, because one does not acknowledge the greater self concealed in the limited self.

> What is the soul? If there is any explication that can be given of the soul, it is the feeling of 'I am'. The feeling of one's existence, this is the soul; . . . And what is the ego? Ego is what is gathered around the soul, . . . When a person says or feels, 'I exist,' that is the feeling of the soul. But he goes further and says, 'I exist as what? I exist as a physical body, as hands, as feet, as head, as a tall person, as a short person, as a thin person, as a stout person.' It is that feeling of being a tangible and visible being, it is that knowledge surrounding the soul, which makes the ego. (VII 268/269)

> Self-effacement does not in any way lessen; it only makes one limitless. (*Vadan* 122)

Further we should not forget the conventional and social obstacles against self-effacement. In Inayat's own Indian culture pride and honour were foremost qualities. Transformed into self-respect and dignity they can help in outgrowing limitedness. In some sectors of western culture self-advertisement is a must.

> The central theme of life today is self-assertion. When a person speaks about himself he wants to make himself ten times more important than he is. He cannot help it; if he does not do so the others will not understand. I even heard one man say to another 'Your modesty is your greatest misfortune.' (VII 191)

Today, in some circles, it is *bon ton* to get the better of another. Those who are subject to this custom may expect that the same may happen to themselves. To that extent, the interpretation of the word reciprocity is familiar to them.

reciprocity Reciprocity, for Inayat, is a subject of such importance that he included it among the basic Sufi Thoughts.

> There is one law, the law of reciprocity, which can be observed by a selfless conscience, together with a sense of awakened justice. (I 17, IX 267)

Reciprocity as 'fair business' (VI 237) is very much a principle for an average person only aware of his limited ego and its wants. But someone applying the law of reciprocity consciously and voluntarily may grow. The very attention needed to weigh the opponent's rights and to discover that they may be as justified as one's own, may open a door to a greater world. It can be interesting to discover something about other people's reasons and backgrounds and feelings. In one place Inayat even suggests to try being kind and watch the results out of curiosity. (VII 113)

Of the many reciprocity-places I can only choose a few. A general one; one answering objections, and a few pointing to results.

Life is the outcome of reciprocity and reciprocity can be created by changing the attitude from a selfish to an unselfish one. (III 95, 96)

Man thinks that an unselfish person is incapable of guarding his own interests in life; but however much it may appear so it is not so in reality. A selfish person is a disappointment to others, and in the end a disadvantage to himself. Mankind is interdependent, and the happiness of each depends upon the happiness of all, and it is this lesson that humanity has to learn today as the first and the last lesson. (III 88)

He who does good and waits for a reward is a labourer of good; but he who does good and disregards it is the master of good. (III 239)

One who returns more good for less good, is a good man; one who returns less good for more good, is selfish; one who tries to be even in the exchange of good, is a practical person; but the one who returns good for evil is a saint. (*Gayan* 90, n. 148)

As said, we need not become saints, only to make a liveable world. But when we apply ourselves to reciprocity we may share some of the mystic's results. One of the mystic's characteristics is his widened outlook. (VIII 127, 297, 319, XI 147) This wider outlook begins with looking from the point of view of another as well as from one's own (*Gayan* 40, n. 67), and that is within everyone's capacity—if only one sets oneself to try. How to try and combine daily life and some spirituality is discussed in *Mental Purification.* (IV 95-237) This perspicacious book shows the average man a way to a wider outlook.

looking from more than one point of view

By trying to look upon life not only from one's own point of view but also from the point of view of another, one loses nothing, but on the contrary widens the horizon of one's view. (*Vadan* 118)

When a man is able to see both from his point of view and from that of another, he has complete vision and a clear insight; he so to speak sees with both eyes. (VI 52)

The one who is able to listen to another is the one who will make another listen to him. (VIII 243)

And then there is another stage of expansion, and that is trying to look at everything from another's point of view also, trying to think also as the other person thinks. This is not an easy thing because from one's childhood one learns to think so that one stands upon one's own thought. . . . Yet, by seeing from his point of view you do not lose your own; your own point of view is still there; but the other point of view is added to yours, therefore your knowledge becomes greater . . . And the third aspect is to feel another person. (IV 124, 125)

We often hear Inayat discern five stages of development. The attainment of the first three is not confined to the mystic only. Here on IV 124, 125 Inayat pays attention to the difficulty of 'stretching the heart'. Elsewhere he says,

As soon as one begins to consider the feelings of another, one begins to worship God. . . . Every moment of life brings an opportunity for being conscious of human feeling, in prosperity, in adversity, in all conditions. It costs very little; only a little thought is necessary. (VI 96)

The same attitude is called difficult in one lecture, and easy in another, but both remarks are encouragements. Inayat had to show widely different people that the expansion of one's view by focusing one's attention on other people's thoughts and feelings is essential.

He who takes notice of the feelings of another person with whom he comes in contact, practises the first essential moral of Sufism. (IX 19)

This moral leads up to one of the basic ten Sufi Thoughts.

the only moral

There is one moral, the love which springs forth from self-denial and blooms in deeds of benificence. (I 19, IX 267)

This rather compact formula manages a load of three topheavy words and one unusual one. The latter, beneficence, has been mentioned on p. 197, and love and self-denial are considered in previous chapters, p. 136-142 and p. 70-72. Inayat knew that many other conventional associations burdened the word moral.

> Regarding ethics, this important word is used here, but in reality, the greatest ethics or morals that one can learn in life are friendliness, which culminates in generosity; and it is never too soon to cultivate this seed of moral in the child. (III 18)

> The greater your love, the greater your moral. If we are forced to be virtuous according to a certain principle, a certain regulation, certain laws and rules, that is not real virtue, it must come from the depths of our heart; our own heart must teach us the true moral. Thus the mystic leaves morality to the deepening of the heart quality. . . . There is no greater teacher of morals than love itself, for the first lesson that one learns from love is: I am not, you are. (X 16)

> Sincere courtship is in itself a religion . . . The lover begins to lose his selfishness through thought for her. (III 146)

> Love in its first stage may be called affection, a tender feeling towards someone, be it mother or father or child or brother or sister, be it friend or mate . . . . even in that first awakening one will see the phenomenon of selflessness. (XI 188)

> Charity begins at home. We should first begin to practise our sympathy with those who are related to us. . . . The best way would be gradually to widen our sympathies, gradually expanding them from those who are nearest to us to those who are most remote. (III 233)

As most aspects of love have been covered in chapter VII, there remains only one aspect to be discussed here, because it belongs to daily life. At least, it used to belong to it. Nowadays, especially in the West, respect is a controversial subject. But respect ranks high with Inayat, and that is not only because of the courtly dignity of his cultural background. Being able to feel respect is an important psychological development, and it is indeed a necessity for spiritual advancement. (X 99)

> The one who has no respect for himself, has no respect for others. (III 221)

> No love-offering can be more precious than a word or act of respect, for the highest expression of love is respect. (*Gayan* 58, n. 95)

ideal Respect is connected with another almost mistrusted concept, ideal. Ideal is not a vague notion or a good principle frozen into an idol. (XI 255)

> What is missing in modern education, in art and science, in social, political, and commercial life, is the ideal, the ideal which is the secret of heaven and earth, the mystery hidden behind both man and God. (IX 249)

We already saw (p. 36) that an ideal is needed to make God comprehensible, since one cannot love the abstract. But the God-ideal is not the only one.

> An ideal is something to hope for and to hold on to, and in the absence of an ideal hope has nothing to look forward to. It is the lack of idealism which accounts for the present degeneration of humanity in spite of all the progress it has made in other directions. There are many kinds of ideals: principles, virtues, objects of devotion; but the greatest and highest of all ideals is the God-ideal. (IX 97)

> If a person has no ideal before him to reach up to then he has no way in which to progress. (XII 34, 35)

There are chapters on ideals. VI 246-252, IX 26-29, 63-100, 264-266. A comprehensive one is XI 173-178. There the first ideal is described as the ideal which one has for oneself; a child already dreams of having 'an elephant or a horse' (in today's terms: a car or a yacht), or of becoming famous, or maybe of becoming very good. The second aspect is when a person makes an ideal out of a principle, and when he succeeds in carrying out his principle, 'then he has accomplished a great thing'. The third ideal is the ideal of bettering conditions, the fourth is idealizing a person, and the fifth concerns the God-ideal.

The first three will be easily acknowledged. The latter two are eyed with mistrust by many. But to admire and honour someone else does not mean humiliating oneself. (XI 160) On the contrary, the ideal is a means of growing.

> As great is a person's ideal, so great is that person. (XI 176)

The fear of domination has been dealt with on p. 59. There remains one cause of the fear of love and respect to be discussed here, and that is its connection with feeling. Recently in some circles, the importance of feeling has been rediscovered. But the majority still may reject feeling for its own sake (its possible pain), or because it is not done, or in apparent contrast with reason. Feeling is considered weak.

> Delicate ideas such as this (respect and consideration) are most difficult to learn and practise in life, and today many wonder if they are not weaknesses; but something that can only be practised by mastering oneself can never be a weakness. (VIII 237/238)

> There exists, especially in the Western world, a false conception of the strength of personality. Many have understood this wrongly, and under the guise of strength they want to harden their hearts. (VIII 280)

power But gentleness is a power. The advanced mystic is an example of strength and feeling.

> With all his gentleness and tenderness, inwardly he becomes strong. (XI 163)

Strength, power, self-reliance, mastery, magnetism are essential attainments, not only for a mystic, but for everybody. Only, one should take care to develop strength in a right way.

> In training an infant one must remember that his mind-power, which means will-power, must not be diminished, and yet the infant must be controlled. (III 15)

> Power is necessary and should be developed; but when man is anxious to develop power, either of body or mind, he ought to remember that the will-power is behind it all. (VII 59, 60)

A man who lacks money misses little; but the man who lacks power of mind misses everything in life. (VI 254)

There are many chapters on all sorts of power, and the connected subjects of mastery and magnetism: II 141-146, 212-215, IV 72-87, 119-125, 148-151, 175-187, VII 57-72, 139-141, VIII 206-210, XI 103-128, 220-224, XII 82-93. The subject is referred to in other lectures as well. It should always be borne in mind that this power does not imply hardness or bogus strength. He who wants power out of love for power, or to cover up his inner uncertainty will make a show of strength and meet with no real response.

True power is not in trying to gain power; true power is in becoming power. (VI 21)

Power most often costs more than it is worth; the man who attains power, not knowing its proper use, loses in the end, for all that is held by power will some day revolt. (*Gayan* 59, n. 96)

On the other hand, it is not kindness only, there should be a balance between feeling and will-power. (VI 85, 203) In developing any mastery whatever, will-power comes first, for without it other forms of power cannot be developed. (VI 199, VII 62, XII 84)

Will is not *a* power, but it is *all* the power there is. (II 236)

As we have seen (p. 138), will is an aspect of love. This creative, self-reliant and open way of loving is not of the surface, it is the working of our God-part. (VIII 118-127, IV 181-187, VI 21, VII 57, 60)

Inner expansion, consciously or unconsciously arrived at, is the secret of all magnetism. When a person possesses magnetism people listen to him, are attracted to him; his work will last or make a deep impression. (IV 36, 37; 66, VII 76)

Everyone sees how great is the influence of personal magnetism upon success in everyday life, profession, business, family, and daily occupations. Sometimes we notice that we go to a shop to buy a certain thing, and there is something about the manner of the salesman that impels us to decide to visit the same shop the next time we need that kind of article. Even if it is a long way to the shop, we prefer not to go to one which is nearer. Similarly it sometimes happens that a person goes to a hotel or boarding-house or restaurant, and someone treats him in such a way that he decides to return to that place rather than visit another. So with doctors, solicitors, barristers, scientists, professors and teachers of all kinds. (VII 65)

Magnetism is closely connected with one of the most important aims of Sufism, first in daily life and, eventually afterwards, as an adept. I mean the development of personality.

personality

It is as important to think about the development of personality as it is to think about spirituality. (XII 33)

The development of one's personality is the real purpose of human life. (*Gayan* 35, n. 57, III 215, XI 251)

The whole of religious, spiritual, and philosophical teaching leads us towards the development of personality. (X 143)

Inayat devoted a book as well as several independent lectures to the subject, *Character Building and the Art of Personality* (III 197-228 and VI 44-59, VII 110-118, VIII 234-236, XI 134-141). It is also referred to in many other places. We find personality described as different from individuality. Man is born as an individual, his character is made, in part consciously, in part unconsciously; personality is developed.

Personality is like a cut diamond. (XI 138)

Character may show artificial traits (XI 137), but the power, of personality is in its sincerity.

Nature is born, character is built and personality is developed. (XI 134)

The qualities of Sufi personality are not unlike the qualities we expect of someone whom, in common parlance, we call a personality. Both are autonomous and strong, self-reliant, self-confident; they have self-respect and a clear insight in their relations with others. Their attitude is cheerful, they do not fuss, their work has impact, they can be relied upon (III 43, 56, 104, 201, 206, 207; VI 55) But there are spiritual overtones in Inayat's description of personality, like dignity, nobleness, wide outlook, reflection of the greater worlds. Often people tended to prefer talk about occult power to 'simple things like this'. (VI 55) But respect for ordinary life was inherent in Sufism and Hazrat Inayat Khan used this to build a bridge between daily and spiritual life. Himself he never lost touch with greater worlds, nor did he close his eyes for daily human life. To be human, also, has a special meaning, it is almost identical with personality.

to be human

> It (the Sufi-school) is not only a spiritual development, it is the culture of humanity: in what relation man stands to his neighbour or friend, to those who depend upon him and those who look up to him, to strangers unknown to him; how he should feel and act through life and yet keep on progressing towards the goal which is the goal for every soul in the world. (X 75)
>
> The human quality manifests when he (man) develops personality. (XI 156)
>
> To become like an angel is not very difficult; to be material is very easy; but to live in the world, in all the difficulties and struggles of the world, and to be human at the same time, is very difficult. (VIII 236)

Being human, in this sense, approaches being spiritual. As said at the end of chapter IV, Inayatan Sufism does not turn its back upon the world but emphasizes the service of humanity.

> The end and the sum total of all mysticism, philosophy, and meditation, of everything one learns and develops, is to be a better servant to humanity . . . . If there were two people before me, one with great power of wonder-working . . ., and another humble and kind and gentle and willing to do anything he could for his fellow-men, I would prefer this last man. I would say: the first is wonderful; but the other is a sage. (VI 69/70)

The magazine Sufism of December 1921 opens with a letter from Inayat to his pupils.

Dear Friends on the Path,

The progress, happiness, and peace of each individual depends upon the progress, happiness, and peace of all. This is the central theme of the Sufi message. For some time during the present age man has thought that might was right; but time will always prove that, on the contrary, right alone is might. There are different ways by which people are striving to bring about better conditions in the world. Although every sincere thought given to this object and every action done towards it accomplishment is of value, and in this way all must contribute something toward the ideal spoken of above, yet, principally, the thing most necessary just now is to awaken in humanity the spirit of what we call in Sufi terms Tauhid, meaning the oneness of the whole being, which is the key to the present problem of humanity, and it is this key that has, it seems, been lost. (*Sufism,* December 1921)

Inayat considered it his task, and that of his pupils, to show to all helpers of humanity where and how that key could be found.

X Sufism in Daily Life, Service of Humanity

wordly and spiritual means for bettering conditions

When an adherent of another spiritual movement asked Inayat about the difference between his school and Sufism Inayat, of course, answered that there are different ways to the Truth but all leading to the same goal. He added:

> The need of the world at the present time is so great that if there were a thousand times more societies than there are, they would be too few to meet it. The main object of life is to do some good to oneself and to others; and whoever, individually, or collectively, does so is blessed. (*Sufism,* December 1923, p. 13)

He also observed the more worldly attempts to better conditions. He appreciated their intention but did not see that outer change could have a lasting effect. (XII 27)

> No doubt every activity like the League of Nations, every institution of this kind is good, but not sufficient. (VII 177, 178)

> Every attempt made today to better the condition of humanity through politics, education, social reconstruction, and many other ways, all these, however excellently planned, can only be fulfilled if this something (inner life) which was missing is added to them; but in the absence of this, all the efforts of many, many years will prove to be futile. (VI 156)

> All the methods by which humanity tries to bring about better conditions fail if the psychology of the ego is not studied. . . . In the name of reconstruction a great deal of cruelty is taking place; yet all think that they are doing it for the best of humanity . . . One person who has risen above the false ego can do much more than a thousand people blinded by their false ego, pretending to do good. . . . One

must know what kindness is before trying to be kind. (XI 202)

psychology Inayat discussed two of the worldly methods for helping humanity in an appendix to his *Autobiography*: psychology and socialism. Of psychology he remarks that it is quite different from ancient psychology, as known in the East, but 'enormously useful in medical science being used as hypnotism, mesmerism and psychoanalysis'. But he considered it dangerous without moral culture. The over-emphasis on material causes 'drowns the spiritual idea'. In a public lecture he said:

> The psychology which is considered nowadays as a new philosophy is still in a primitive condition; what I mean by psychology is the bridge between material science and esotericism. (XI 73)

Some forms of modern psychology aim at looking for reasons behind reasons and at establishing a non-artificial personality, freed from forced virtues; and science has rediscovered psychosomatic causes of diseases. Of such things Inayat could approve, but he disliked the obligatory outspokenness, which to him seemed blunt and rude. There may have been a cultural bias to this judgment, but he himself, indeed, healed people with few or no words, by balancing an attitude, by his own example, by ignoring an undesirable trait. Of course, his power and personality were exceptional. His other objection is the one quoted above. Psychologists such as he met stopped short at anything beyond their rational perception. They need not. At least one psychiatrist and one psychologist known to the present author, use their Sufism to enrich their work with their patients. This is just what Hazrat Inayat meant with Sufism in daily life; material and spiritual work can be combined.

> Spirituality is in no way a hindrance to worldly progress. A worldly success when gained through the power of spirituality has a stronger foundation. (XI 236)

> What is most necessary is to connect the outward action with the inward journey. (VIII 151)

The world of today would have been much better than it is if there had been a spiritual ideal placed before it as well as a material ideal. (III 111)

political means That is the long and the short of it. It is also the essence of Inayat's remarks concerning socialism.

There are two sides to socialism, a wrong side and a right side. The right side is its practice as consideration to others, and the wrong side is its practice owing to self-pity, as it produces envy, jealousy, rivalry, competition and all manner of bitterness. (*Autobiography, appendix*)

Where can this spirit (of independence), this true spirit, be learned? From socialism? Only a little. From politics? Only partially. The view of the politician is a partial view. (VII 174)

There is a great deal of talk going on in the world just now about communism. Yet if communism is devoid of a spiritual ideal, it could be only a change of condition on the surface. (XII 56)

Inayat considered both capitalism and socialism as worship of 'the same god', materialism. (VII 166, 247, XII 54) In adherents of either 'creed' he valued those qualities that made them 'really human'. He used to mention a rich merchant who had applied himself to his work with concentration and had become wise and softened. (I 219, X 31) Beside the selflessness of some socialists he respected the worker's pursuit of a modicum of human dignity. But he considered the desire to amass more and more possessions as an intoxication in any person. (VI 111, 139, VII 218, IX 74, 75) The nineteenth century attitude promising heaven to those poor on earth and enforcing piety on this ground was entirely foreign to him. He did not expect interest for spiritual things unless a person had succeeded in obtaining something like a living wage.

One has seen the working day of workmen, and even of children, sold for next to nothing, so that the misery of their conditions cried aloud; and again at another time they have received a wage for the same work, that enabled them to lift their heads with some of the dignity that human kind should show. (III 188)

There are vast sections of humanity whose lives can be called little else but lives of slavery, who are caught and wedged in the wheels of a civilization that crushes and destroys so much beauty of ideal, of personal freedom and expression. (III 176)

But once a person had enough to live on and some spare time besides, Hazrat considered it a waste of time if one did not seek for, at least, some spiritual development.

Among those who have a little freedom in life, who have time to think about gaining some knowledge, there are many who seek only after novelty. (VI 26)

Every moment lost in waiting for spiritual attainment is the greatest loss conceivable. (II 176)

education All the same, nobody should be forced, and Inayat often warned that one should not 'wake those who slept'. But from the very beginning of his trekking through the world, he emphasized the importance of providing for an inkling of spirituality in school. In India he had tried to have music included in the curriculum; in the West he often pointed out that children should be taught more than arithmetics and other surface knowledge. (III 110, 111, X 242, 243, 250) He had visited factories and seen the deadening monotony of the conveyor belt.

What is most necessary now is to introduce into education the spirit of providing for oneself all that one needs, and arranging for oneself all that is necessary in one's everyday life. The mechanical life of our times may show progress, yet it is not a complete progress. Imagine a person spending from morning till evening in a factory and only making needles. Perhaps he does this for twenty years and what does he know of life? Only how to make a needle. (X 246, 247)

The first knowledge we must gain is the knowledge of the purpose of our life. It is a great pity that education as it is today pays very little attention to this question. (VI 33)

The child should not only be taught to read and write but to have an all-round idea of life and how it can best be lived. (III 96)

For the betterment of humanity people should be taught to understand from childhood what the automatic working of the mind is, and what a difference there is between it and the working of mind with will. (XI 79)

the third aim of Inayatan Sufism

Though for Inayat himself the realization of spiritual life came first, and he was happiest in the company of other mystics, he had a better eye for the imminent dangers in the world than most people. In a radio address (Detroit, 24th April 1926) he warned against the resentment and bitterness in Germany. He had been there only for a short time, and did not read newspapers; but he did read people. At another occasion he reminded his audience of the ostrich policy adopted by many before the First World War.

> Did they not say in every country when the war came: we did not know? Yes, it was so for those who slept, but the awakened one had seen the preparation. (IV 211)

The relations between peoples and nations had been one of his initial concerns. First, he had sought to establish a creative understanding between Moghul and pure Hindu musical culture in India. (see page 18) Soon the exploitation of the East by the West became a problem to him. In the three aims of Sufism, drawn up in 1918, we still read that East and West should come closer to each other. (see p. 19) But after years in Europe and America, having witnessed war between countries, groups and individuals, when asked whether he taught Sufism because of the misunderstanding between Christians and Muslims, he answered, with an allusion to a well-known Quranic simile in the final phrase:

> It is not only the misunderstanding between Christians and Muslims, but the misunderstanding among Christians themselves, and between individuals and between fighting nations which has brought Sufism to the West.

> Furthermore, Sufism as a school . . . is not from the East or the West, but from above. (*Sufism,* June 1923, p. 15)

A few years earlier he had answered similar questions.

> Leaving the East aside, even if we think only of Europe, of the hatred and prejudice existing; so much that if it goes on one cannot think what will be the end, for it is already paralysing social, political and commercial life. (*Sufism,* May 1921, p. 11)

Hazrat Inayat's answers, remarks and lectures on this kind of subject are collected in the book *The Problem of the Day* (X 237-270) and in chapters like 'The Desire of Nations' (VII 162-169) and 'The Birth of a New Era'. (VIII 216-218) There are many chapters on democracy (VII 170-179) but that is less political than it might seem. Democracy is one of those confusing terms with many, rather different, connotations. Even the western political, social, administrative and ethical implications are obviously not the same everywhere. Muslims in general identify democracy with their concept of egalitarianism, because Islam is meant for all. Tauhid, the unity of origin and purpose for all souls, it the mystic's democracy. Thus, a spiritual interpretation of democracy is the only one that matters for Inayat.

> In point of fact democracy is always spiritual; there cannot be a material democracy. People call any system democracy which appears or claims to be democratic, even if it proves upon examination to be only a shadow of democracy. (VII 176)

Of course Inayat was no student of politics or economics. He did not deny the necessity of industrial or commercial development (VI 147) and took it for granted that 'for the general good there are political and commercial problems to be solved'. (IX 255) But whenever he had to consider these subjects he added that spiritual progress, insight in life and knowledge of the purpose of life could be of greater help. (VI 146, 147, VII 168, 195, VIII 295, IX 255) But although Inayat was no politician or economist, an economist or diplomat can be a mureed. In fact, there are some, and in prominent positions. In high positions and in modest ones as well, Sufis may do some good and have done some good. For the followers and pupils all rely on Hazrat Inayat Khan as their example and inspiration, and adhere to his philosophy of unity that should lead to brotherhood and better human relations.

brotherhood, the word and the meaning

Brotherhood is another of those well-meant words, which are easily spoken but seldom looked into. There are several chapters on 'Brotherhood' (X 261-270, XI 183-187) and many admonishments about the real meaning of the term.

> Mysticism need not teach brotherhood, for a mystic becomes a brother by nature; mysticism culminates in brotherhood, a brotherhood unlike any other institution of brotherhood in the world. (XI 183)

> It is mostly interest in worldly things that unites man with another in order that they can make more profit. How great would be this power if man would unite in true brotherhood . . . The world, in spite of any success it may seem to have today, is suffering from the wrong application of a right principle. (IX 13, 14)

> I had the pleasure of meeting Abdul Baha (leader of the Bahai Movement) when he was in Paris, who showed great interest in my music and with whom I had an interesting talk about our experiences in the Western world . . . . (He asked,) 'You are also preaching the brotherhood of nations?' I said, 'I am not preaching brotherhood, but sowing the seed of tauhid, the unity of God, that from that plant of Sufism may spring up fruits and flowers of brotherhood.' (unpublished *Autobiography*)

Another common misunderstanding came from those who supposed that anything connected with religion meant a new sect. We saw already on p. 20 that Inayat warned against this misinterpretation. (see also IX 256-258, X 257, 269) And quite often he had to correct another superficial conclusion: inner unity does not mean outer uniformity. (IX 11-14) Nor does his respect for each person's God concept mean syncretism.

The main object of the Sufi Movement is to bring about a

better understanding among the different classes, among the followers of different religions and the people of different races and different nations; but by this we do not mean mixing them up. (X 269)

If anything, one could call his endeavours, oecumene *avant la lettre,* emphasizing not only respect for another people's conviction, but understanding as well.

The Sufi Movement has members belonging to many different faiths and who have not given up their own faith through understanding the faiths of others. (X 257)

In 1919 he assisted at an embryonic oecumenical attempt in London. (*Sufi,* January 1920, p. 8, League of Religions) At the end of October 1924 he paid a visit to Archbishop Söderblom in Siguna, (Sweden), who was preparing his first oecumenical conference out of which the present oecumene of Christian churches has been born.

I had the pleasure of seeing the Archbishop Nathan Söderblom from Upsala, and was pleased to know that he was working to bring together all different Christian faiths. And I was glad to hear him say that this was the first step; that showed me that he believed in the second step also. (*Autobiography*)

Inayat's talks with western churchmen

His enjoyment of talks with serious students of religion and mysticism is apparent from the few remarks on such meetings preserved in the *Autobiography.* While in Russia, in the winter of 1913-1914, the Finnish philosopher and physician Dr. E. W. Lybeck took Inayat to see a group of monks who remained severely anonymous.

I was requested to speak on my ideas. I accepted the kind offer most thankfully, and gently began to explain my ideas. At times, when I went a little beyond the boundaries of their religious conventionalities in which they were accustomed to talk, I found them slightly chilled, but I have never seen such comprehensive minds, in which all that is spoken as wisdom and truth so easily finds accommodation. They were interested by the idea, (Truth, see p. 134) and the only

> wonder to them was how could the truth exist in such a perfect form as I did present outside their church, which alone they had so far believed to be the centre of all truth. They were wise people, with awakened sympathy, with the love of Christ and appreciation of truth. To me their contact was a wonderful experience. No end of questions were cast at me, but politely and the answers, gently given, went straight to their hearts and sank into their souls. No further arguments ensued after they had received one satisfactory answer. (*Autobiography*)

His visit to the Vatican (1923) aroused mixed feelings in Inayat and in his hosts, monsignor Cascia and Cardinal Gasparri. They asked, ' "What did I mean by wisdom." '[1] (*Autobiography*) The explanation was 'hesitatingly admitted with consent and half-consent.' Indeed, though they invited the foreign mystic to a ceremony—which he liked—his works, emphasizing the meaningfullness of all religions, were put on the index.

Culturally, as a Sufi for whom a murshid, a spiritual guide is essential, Inayat was more apt to appreciate Catholicism than Protestantism, of which a book was the sole support. But he was rather disappointed by most services he attended in Rome.

> I learned from it that it was all a preparation (for that)which a service is meant to be, a perfectly organised drill by which to learn and respect man, above all a spiritual man . . . I thought it is the very sentiment that is needed to be awakened in man, though it is done in a narrow way, and yet in no other way it can be very well done. (*Autobiography*)

Probably the most congenial soul Inayat found in the West (apart from some musicians) was a French mystic, l'abbé Clain.

> I once met a Catholic priest who is a well-known man in Paris, l'abbé Clain. He asked me if I would tell him some ideas of the Eastern thinkers which they get in their meditations. He listened to what I said attentively. Every

[1] For Inayatan definition of wisdom see pages 17 and 147

word I said seemed not foreign to him, not against his ideas. He was so pleased with all he heard and with all we spoke together and with that which we could not speak in words, but can only be exchanged in silence, and in the end he only said: 'What you say is not different from what we believe, except for the difference in terminology.' (*Appendix* to *Autobiography*)

the companions

But closest to him, spiritually and mystically, were his three brothers, who formed his immediate sounding board. These lifelong companions were his really accomplished trainees, his most understanding disciples. To Inayat, they always remained his 'asli' (original, genuine) Sufis. After his death in 1927, they continued his work, each according to his own special gifts. Shaikh Pyaromir Maheboob Khan, saintly and aristocratic, was loved and respected for what he was; Murshid Muhammad Ali Khan, the powerful healer, for what he achieved; Murshid Musharaff Moulamia Khan, with his artless charm and lively stories of the past, for what he represented. Until the latter's death in 1967, fifty seven years after Inayat's departure from India, these three formed a direct link with his cultural background, and during his life they were the only ones who really knew what Inayat saw and felt when he spoke about India.

Between 1907 and 1910, and at the end of 1926 Inayat had many talks and silences with holy men of all creeds in India. We know that he deeply enjoyed these, some names of these men are recorded, but the actual talk or exchange of ideas are not. Of course, these sages were not the kind to ask much.

For the mystic everything all the time is answering his questions. (XI 213)

Of one meeting the exchange of opinions has been handed down in part. But the questions of this Brahmin priest, the first mystic Inayat met after the death of his own murshid, were more like a friendly examination on the final aims of Sufi and Yogi mysticism, which is *mukti, moksha,* freedom of the soul.[1]

The circle of his Western followers has included Swiss,

[1] Elisabeth de Jong-Keesing, *Inayat Khan, a Biography,* p. 68, 69.

Dutch and English clergymen. Ministers and priests are meant to be helpers of men, or 'servants of humanity' as Inayat expected his mureeds to become. He set great store by the application of his philosophy in practice. Though he loved a discussion with a knowledgeable expert in one of his own disciplines, mysticism, music or poetry, a merely theoretical approach did not meet with his approval. He acknowledged the need of a scientific framework, but the artist's presentation was what counted. Such was his approach to Indian music, and, according to his view, the same goes for theology. Inayat was a keen student of religions, concentrating on their inner sense. Occasionally he might point to an essential difference of form between Buddhism and Hinduism, or between Sufis and Yogis, but he was careful to end such a passage on a note of understanding, and always alluded to the final goal of unity. This explains how he disagreed with a certain form of university teaching, called 'neutral' at the time.

> I met a professor in Switzerland who was studying theology. He came to see me and he said, 'I would like to know the difference between the Hindu and the Buddhist idea, wherein they differ.' I said, 'Our work is to find out where they unite; where we differ we do not want to look because that which divides us is not true (limited, temporal). When we are seeking for truth we should not divide.' He answered that at the university they have another point of view; 'We are not told to study these religions with interest; we must be neutral in studying religion.' I said, 'If you are neutral to your friend or neighbour you will never understand him all your life. You may live together for years; as long as you are neutral there will be a wall between you and the other person, you will never understand. It is only sympathy that will make you understand your friend. It is by sympathy that you will understand the religion of another, therefore it is proven futile to study religion with a neutral point of view.' (*Instruction Interview,* Detroit 1926)

Hazrat Inayat's aim was to bring fresh, real, living God concepts to believers and unbelievers as well. For to him, those seemingly opposed groups were both victims of a dead God-concept, and therefore a long way off from God.

> Not only unbelievers in God, but even believers, who look upon God as a heavenly being who dwells in heaven, are both absent from God to the same extent. (VII 213)

> The object of Sufism is uniting life and religion. (IX 255)

> Its central theme is to produce the consciousness of the divinity of the human soul. (VIII 20)

to see God in man

A few years ago an agnostic posited that he did not believe in a God in heaven, but in God in man. Probably he meant the limited side of man, but his actual words were almost identical with one of Inayat's recurrent aphorisms.

> If you do not see God in man, you will not see Him anywhere. (*Vadan* 89)

This is the essence of Hazrat Inayat's philosophy, provided one keeps the difference between limitedness and unlimitedness in mind.

> God is God and man is man, yet God is man and man is God. (*Vadan* 79)

> What pleases man that pleases God, and therefore if we please all around us, we please God. (VII 34)

> If a man can do anything to please God, it is only to please his creatures. There cannot be a better prayer and a greater religion than being conscientious in regard to the feeling of other men, being ready to serve them, to please them, in every way, to forgive them, to tolerate them. (VI 69)

> The service of God means that we each work for all. (*Gayan* 30, new 49)

'is all this possible?'

Very often people came to Inayat, saying that they liked his ideas and wished that the world could be changed, but they doubted if it could be done. Inayat acknowledged the difficulty (VI 52, VIII 286, IX 99), but always continued with encouragement and reminders that 'if we all worked in our small way, we could accomplish a great deal'. (VIII 286)

Inayat answers

Inayat knew from experience what working in a small way

can do. Maybe the most direct answer to our doubts is his own life story. He began his work in the West from scratch, uninvited, unknown, with no backing at all. At his death he left behind a world wide movement. But not only this. In his *oeuvre* he left a rich deposit for his own culture and ours and updated the methods of mysticism for the modern mind.

The other answers to the questions whether 'all this is possible' are found everywhere in his work. For whatever Inayat said and did, was meant to uncover and bring to life possibilities unknown to many. Whenever he points to these possibilities, be it the attainment of God-realization or the understanding of others, he may add that the end cannot be reached in one leap, that the work may be difficult, that there are traps of mere speculation and superficial use of words—but the great purpose is for all, and there is always a meeting ground. If only our wish to progress is sincere. It is up to us either to nurse limitedness and grudges, or to set out and discover our unlimited possibilities of widening.

> The same word has reached the ears of the one and the heart of another. (II 87)

> Man has the key of life in his own hands, if he only knew it. (XI 249)

A Chronological Survey of Hazrat Inayat Khan's Works

I *India 1897*-1910

a. musical text-books:

Apart from articles in Barodan newspapers and two musical text-books for Western instruments dating from a transitory interest in Western music about 1897 (*Inayat Harmonium Shikchak* and *Inayat Phidal Shikchak*), there are two other text-books already bearing his mark. One is *Balasan Gitmala,* a work meant for girls' musical education, which was controversial at the time. The other is *Inayat Git Ratnavali,* containing lessons on theory and methods, and seventy five songs; most of these are in Urdu, but a few in Hindi and Gujarati, with some English folk songs added. The Indian songs are extremely varied: gay, serious, devotional; also of very different styles, the North-Indian *khyal* prevails but a few songs are in honour of Hindu gods. The introduction points to Indian musical culture as a reason for national self-respect.

b. an important musical treatise, *Shaorey-é-Minqar-é-Musiqar* (Indian Press, Allahabad 1912). This work, in three parts, was completed during Inayat's stay in Hyderabad (1903-1907), where he worked as a musician and was trained as a Chishti Sufi. *Minqar-é-Musiqar* contains a description of ragas, mostly *dhrupad,* Hindustani poems and Kathak dances, both in their outer form and inner meaning. The book takes most of its inspiration from Islam, but Krishna too makes his appearance. Some of the songs and poems are Inayat's own compositions; these express mystical longing and attainment, very much like his later English *Vadan* and *Nirtan.*

c. gramophone records (His Master's Voice, Calcutta, 1909 and 1910)

The late Mr Vibhukumar S. Desai—who, among other

books, wrote a biography of Inayat in Gujarati—provided the following numbers of records, formerly belonging to Pundit N. S. Gurtu of Dharwar.

1. GC 8-12417/18	6. 8-12427/8-12396	11. 8-12440/8-12441
2. 8-12419/20	7. 8-12428/8-12433	12. 8-12356/8-12390
3. 8-12422/24	8. 8-12430/8-12392	13. 8-12387/8-12389
4. 8-12423/29	9. 8-12432/8-12355	14. 8-12391/8-12303
5. 8-12426/37	10. 8-12436/8-12439	

Of these records number 2 is preserved in the Archives of the Faculty of Music and Fine Arts of Benares Hindu University, Varanasi 5, U.P. It contains a Tarana Darana and an evening song of which the English transcription gives a corrupted title: Deen Jo Nahin Jani Hai. *

II *Europe and America*

a. 1910-1920

It has been my lot, especially in the beginning of my work, that I had to build the whole building with unaccommodating vessels and broken tools. It was like playing on a piano which is out of tune . . . Later things turned out for the better. (*Autobiography, Appendix)*

Inayat considered the first ten years as a time of preparation, and he summed up the difficulties he had to deal with: he was not a missionary for a certain faith, nor a representative of a maharaja; he started without friends and recommendations, and found the cultural imponderabilia, the things everybody unconsciously takes for granted, causing no end of misunderstanding; he met prejudice against colour, against anything Eastern, against Islam, and fear of his very goals, mutual understanding and discovery of greater worlds. In the beginning he was also hampered by his own difficulties with the English language. As a champion of Indian culture he did not belong to the anglicized Indian circles.

He himself could mend part of the difficulties he encountered. He made friends, some of whom recommended him as a musician from one country to another, whereas others helped him in his first attempts to make his ideas known in print. Later his English had greatly improved, but up to 1920 all the books are work of varying degrees of co-operation.

The first Western book *A Sufi Message of Spiritual Liberty* was compiled by Inayat himself in 1913, with the help of the Parisian publisher and bookseller E. Bailly, a French author (?) Mademoiselle Jorys, a Belgian nobleman Tserclaes living in England, and H. Balakin, a Russian officer. The Theosophical Society printed the English edition in 1914. In this book there is much traditional Sufi philosophy arranged systematically, but already Inayat's characteristic improvisory method can be traced as well as his keen observation of and adaptation to Western ways of thinking. The book has been reprinted V 9-36, without the original Preface and without the biographical note by Tserclaes.

From the Russian tour (December 1913-May 1914) dates a sketch called *Sakuntala before Shiva* or *Sakuntala in Surarga,* an adaptation of a theme from Kalidasa's *Sakuntala.* Seventeen of Inayat's Indian melodies were harmonised and orchestrated for Western performance by Sergei L. Tolstoi and Vladimir I. Pohl. The piano version of these westernized songs was published and they were twice performed by an orchestra at the Sokolniki Circle.[1]

During the First World War and the two ensuing years Inayat lived in London. There a Sufi Publishing Society was established. One of the first books issued was the fruit of an earlier association. In 1911, in New York, Inayat met a New York librarian, C. H. A. Bjerregaard, a prolific author on esoteric subjects. Prompted by Inayat, Mr Bjerregaard revised and rewrote his previous book on Omar Khayyam (*Sufism and Omar Khayyam,* New York 1902) as *Sufism, Omar Khayyam and E. Fitzgerald* (Sufi Publishing Society 1915). The result is a mixture of Mr Bjerregaard's style and Inayat's elucidations. One cannot regard this work as a book by Inayat, but it is one of his attempts to inform the West as to what Sufism and mystic poetry—wine included—means.

To introduce himself to the public Inayat authorized the printing of his so-called *Confessions* (Sufi Publishing Society 1915). The title is chosen in imitation of some well-known

[1] *Tolstoy Remembered* by his son Sergei Tolstoy, translated from the Russian by Moura Budberg, p. 188 and 189.

Western autobiographies. and it may have been the brain child of a minor poet, Miriam Regina Bloch, who actually edited the book. She had the somewhat stilted literary style of those days. The book is partly an adaptation of the more concise Tserclaes biography, with the pronoun 'he' changed into 'I', but Inayat provided valuable new information. Regina Miriam Bloch also helped to edit the first four issues of *Sufi,* a quarterly. In 1916 Mary Williams took over the direction of the Sufi Publishing Society. She was a parson's daughter and probably a teacher of English (as such she advertisied in *Sufism* 1923). She was a mureed since 1912.

In *Sufi,* April 1916, p. 18-23 there appeared Inayat's dramatical sketch *Tansen.* This has not been reprinted, but VIII 13-332 almost forty lectures announced in *Sufi* between 1915 and 1925 are published for the first time. Their importance and the reliability of the text is highly disparate, the more so as a third of this volume consists of lectures belonging to the 1925-1926 period. The same procedure has been followed in editing *The Mysticism of Sound,* II 9-68. Inayat gave innumerable lectures on Music and Sound, at first as an introduction to his concerts, later in a wider context. In *Sufi* 1915-1919 *The Mysticism of Sound* is announced several times, but the first book bearing this title appeared in 1923. The recent edition contains old and incomplete lectures on Sound and Music, and exhaustive treatments from a later period. A few seem answers to very specific questions, some are bordering on the apocryphic, others are essential.

In 1915 Inayat was invited to speak at the first All-India Musical Conference in Baroda. As he was not in a position to leave London, he wrote or dictated his speech *The Music of India,* which was read at the Conference, and published in its proceedings, and reprinted in the *Journal of the Oriental Institute,* MS University of Baroda, Vol. V, No 1, September 1955. In Europe the same article was published *Sufi* 1916, April p. 8-18, and reprinted in the nineteen fifties in Dutch and German musical magazines.

Whereas VIII 13-332 offers hitherto unpublished lectures and scrapbook material, other lectures from the 1916-1919 period were published contemporarily in a series *Voice of*

Inayat. The editors were Mary Williams (*Pearls from the Ocean Unseen,* 1919) and another faithful co-worker, Lucy Goodenough (*Aqibat, Life after Death,* 1918, *Love, Human and Divine,* 1919 and *The Phenomenon of the Soul,* 1919) The editors used their own names as if they were the author, and indeed, their rendering of Hazrat Inayat's words is not complete and they sometimes unconsciously, added their own interpretation. Though Inayat considered these books rather poor, they have been reprinted V 37-256. I have only quoted from them when a passage was supported by more reliable texts on the same subject. In spite of the corruption of these lectures the underlying contents and sometimes the way of expression are recognizably Inayatan and worthwhile.

In *Sufi* January 1920 and October 1920 a book 'Sex' by Inayat Khan was announced. The followers did not publish the manuscript until 1938 and changed the title into *Rasa Shastra* (III 115-195). The work combines traditional Indian views with Inayat's keen observation of Western attitudes. It would have been valuable and extremely original in its own time; now it is mainly of historical interest.

During the last two years in London Inayat enjoyed the help of Dr O. C. Gruner who advised on Inayat's improving English and did not alter or add to his texts. The results of this cooperation are *In an Eastern Rosegarden,* 1921, and *The Way of Illumination,* 1922. Dr Gruner was a blood specialist, and Inayat introduced him to the work of Avicenna (Ibn Sina 980-1037), the Persian physician and mystic philosopher who influenced Arab and Western medicine and philosophy for centuries. This resulted in Dr Gruner writing *A Treatise on the Canon of Medicine of Avicenna.* Three years after its publication (Luzac, London 1930) the standard Avicenna edition of Dr Annemarie Goichon appeared, and the Inayat-inspired treatise is almost extinct.

Ever since 1915 *Sufi* published occasional translations of Hindustani and Persian poems by Mrs Jessie Duncan Westbrook. In 1918 at the latest there appeared three collections of Mrs Westbrook's translations. They were much used in the 1918-1920 classes, but are not reprinted. The titles are *Hindustani Lyrics, Songs of India* and *The Divan of Inayat*

Khan. Apart from the latter the songs of India also contain some of Inayat's own poems. Often the source is *Minqar-é-Musiqar,* though the attempt at English verse caused much deviation from the original wording.

According to custom, Inayat's best Hindustani verses and compositions were not published. But in the late nineteen fifties they have been tape-recorded as sung by his youngest brother Musharaff Khan, and the tapes are preserved in the *Collection Musharaff Khan-de Koningh.*

In 1919 *Character Building* and *The Art of Personality* were announced, but they were not published until 1931.

Between 1915 and 1920 there were several lectures on *Moral Culture.* These were arranged as a book by Inayat himself. With the corresponding *Unity of Religious Ideals* it is mentioned in his correspondence with Miss J. Dowland. Inayat set great store by their simultaneous publication. But the first edition of *Moral Culture* is dated 1937, whereas *The Unity of Religious Ideals* appeared in 1928.

b. 1920-1923

From 1920, until The Geneva Headquarters of the Sufi Movement took over, Miss Dowland of the Polygon Hotel in Southampton took upon her the publication of Inayat's work in the Sufi Book Depot, Southampton. She herself made an anthology of Inayat's sayings, which was authorized by him, and published as *The Bowl of Saki.* Another pupil-compiled collection is *Aphorisms* (XI 225).

Different from these pupils' choices are GAYAN, VADAN and NIRTAN. These collections of maxims, poems, advice, prayers, views on life, on personal problems, expressions of mystical longing and attainment are the only books written directly by Hazrat Inayat Khan himself. He wrote and revised on scraps of paper he carried with him, and made the division in chapters which, like the three books themselves, were given titles adopted from Indian music. *Notes from the Unstruck Music from THE GAYAN* was first published in 1923. According to the secretary D. K. Stam, *The Divine Symphony* or *VADAN* was completed on the eve of Inayat's departure for America in December 1925. Miss Stam also collected and arranged the last scraps of paper Inayat left at his death in

February 1927, and they were published as *NIRTAN or The Dance of the Soul.* These three books have been translated into many languages and reprinted, separately or together, many times. The last English *Gayan* dates from 1975 (Sufi Publishing Company, London/Geneva). The Rainbow Press edition (California 1976) is a photographic reprint of all three in paperback.

In 1920 the ruler of Baroda, Sayaji Rao Gaekwar, visited London. He advised Inayat—whom he had known as a grandson of the famous singer, veena-player and musical scholar Maula Bakhsh—to write an autobiography. This he did. The unpublished *Biography* consists of: I. a story of Inayat's life in India, preceded by a genalogy and the life stories of Maula Bakhsh and Inayat's father Rahemat Khan. This compilation was made by Mehr Baksh, Inayat's brother-in-law in India. II. an *Autobiography,* covering the years 1910-1923. III. a *Journal,* consisting of short notes on travels and meetings from 1923 onward, and *Appendices* on several subjects.

c. 1923-1926

In these last years the secretaries S. N. Furnée and D. K. Stam conscientiously noted place and date of each lecture they recorded. The actual archive of lectures covers much more than has been published. Cataloguing is in progress.

TITLES of BOOKS and ASSEMBLED LECTURES,

Collected in the twelve volumes *The Sufi Message*, Barrie and Jenkins, London, 1960-1970.

Indian edition [including Index] by Motilal Banarsidass, Delhi 1988-1990.

Volume	Title	page	approximate date
I	The Way of Illumination	9	1920
	The Inner Life	61	1922
	The Soul, Whence and Whither	107	1922-1923
	The Purpose of Life	187	1924
II	The Mysticism of Sound	9	1915-24
	Music	69	1915-24
	The Power of the Word	153	1915-24

	Cosmic Language	197	1924
III	Education	9	1922, 1925, 1926
	Rasa Shastra	115	1919
	Character-Building and the Art of Personality	197	1919, 19ü
	Moral Culture	229	1920
IV	Health	11	1924, 1925
	Mental Purification	95	1926
	The Mind-World	239	1922, 1924
V	A Sufi Message of Spiritual Liberty	9	1913
	Aqibat, Life after Death	37	1917–18
	Love, Human and Divine	139	1917–18
	Pearls from the Ocean Unseen	189	
	Metaphysics	225	
VI	The Alchemy of Happiness	11	1922 (5 chapters), 1925 (4), 1924 (4) 1925 (11), 1926 (10); not yet placed 6
VII	In an Eastern Rose Garden		1920 and 11 additions 1923–6
VIII	Sufi Teachings		36 not yet identified (=old); 1916 (1) 1918 (1), 1921 (1), 1922 (3), 1923 (5), 1924 (6), 1925 (7), 1926 (4)
IX	The Unity of Religious Ideals	11	1921
X	Sufi Mysticism	9	1922, 1925, 1926
	The Path of Initiation and Discipleship	57	1921, 1923, 1924
	Sufi Poetry	115	1922, 1924, 1925, 1926 and old lectures
	Art, Yesterday, Today and Tomorrow	155	1926 with older additions
	The Problem of the Day	237	1921, 1922, 1923
XI	Philosophy, Psychology, Mysticism	15	1925

Of this work a philologically sound edition appeared in the nineteen fifties

	Aphorisms	225	before 1922, see page 243
XII	The Vision of God and Man	9	1923 and after
	Confessions	125	1915
	Four plays:		
	The Bogey-Man	169	
	The Living Dead	195	
	Una	215	
	Amin, the Faithful Trustee	233	

These plays have been dictated by Hazrat Inayat on board ship between 1923 and 1926

* The set of records taken by Hazrat Inayat Khan to the West were lost in France during World War I, and all attempts at recovering copies of them in India, efforts redoubled during the nineteen fifties and sixties failed. Part of the problem was that enquirers sought after records of Pir-o-Murshid Hazrat Inayat Khan rather than of Professor Inayat Khan R. Pathan Tansenzaman, the name under which the recordings were brought out. Their rediscovery is a recent surprise we owe to two musicologists with special qualifications in Indian music. The Australian Michael Kinnear found them at EMI Archives, London, and alerted his colleague, the Dutchman Joep Bor, who at once recognized their significance in relation both to Inayat Khan's music and its Indian background, and to the important musical and aesthetic aspects of his contemplative philosophy.

They then set to work on reproducing this classical vocal music on CD's and cassettes that were published by another author of Indian music, Ger Storms, for the Panta Rhei, Katwijk, Holland publishing house in December 1994, together with The Gramophone Company of India. The booklet accompanying the CD is of particular interest, including a full discography by Michael Kinnear, an extensive introductory survey and several striking specimens of song texts in translation and a number of rare photographs. Both the music with its unusual style and beauty and the accompanying elucidation cannot be recommended too highly to those interested in either classical Indian music in itself, or in Inayatan Sufism as bringing out a by now no longer familiar but essential aspect of Inayat Khan's personality, work and values.

APPENDIX

THE AIMS OF THE SUFI MOVEMENT

The Movement is based upon the Sufi Message brought to the Western world by Hazrat Inayat Khan in 1910.

In his studies as an initiate in one of the ancient Sufi orders, Inayat Khan recognised the basic love and wisdom through which humanity may realize the purpose of life. He saw these two principles as enshrined in the ideals of all religions. He held that by honouring all, and respecting their differences, a basis for mutual understanding could be reached which would not be possible by seeking to convert one to the views of another.

In pursuance of his vision he came to the West, and taught in Europe and America until 1926 when, shortly before his passing, he returned to India. He called his teaching the Sufi Message and to propagate it he founded a body called the International Sufi Movement. In the constitution are enshrined the following Sufi Thoughts:

1. There is one God, the Eternal, the Only Being; none else exists save He.
2. There is one Master, the Guiding Spirit of all souls, who constantly leads his followers towards the light.
3. There is one Holy Book, the sacred manuscript of nature, the only scripture which can enlighten the reader.
4. There is one Religion, the unswerving progress in the right direction towards the ideal, which fulfils the life's purpose of every soul.
5. There is one Law, the Law of Reciprocity, which can be observed by a selfless conscience together with a sense of awakened justice.
6. There is one Brotherhood, the human brotherhood, which unites the children of earth indiscriminately in the fatherhood of God.
7. There is one Moral Principle, the love which springs forth from self-denial, and blooms in deeds of beneficence.
8. There is one Object of Praise, the beauty which uplifts the heart of its worshipper through all aspects from the seen to the unseen.
9. There is one Truth, the true knowledge of our being within and without which is the essence of all wisdom.

10. There is one Path, the annihilation of the false ego in the real, which raises the mortal to immortality and in which resides all perfection.

The Movement has the following Objects:

1. To realize and spread the knowledge of unity, the religion of love and wisdom, so that the bias of faiths and beliefs may of itself fall away, the human heart may overflow with love, and all hatred caused by distinctions and differences may be rooted out.
2. To discover the light and power latent in man, the secret of all religion, the power of mysticism, and the essence of philosophy, without interfering with customs or belief.
3. To help to bring the world's two opposite poles, East and West, closer together by the interchange of thought and ideals, that the Universal Brotherhood may form of itself, and man may meet with man beyond the narrow national and racial boundaries.

Regarding the aims of the Movement, we quote as follows from the words of Inayat Khan:

"The purpose of the Sufi Movement is to work towards unity. Its main object is to bring humanity, divided as it is into so many different sections, closer together in the deeper understanding of life. It is a preparation for a world service, chiefly in three ways. One way is the philosophical understanding of life; another is bringing about brotherhood among races, nations, and creeds; and the third way is the meeting of the world's greatest need, which is the religion of the day. Its work is to bring to the world that natural religion which has always been the religion of humanity: to respect one another's belief, scripture, and teacher. The Sufi message is the echo of the same divine message which has always come and will always come to enlighten humanity. It is not a new religion; it is the same message which is being given to humanity. It is the continuation of the same ancient religion which has always existed and will always exist, a religion which belongs to all teachers and all the scriptures.

"Sufism in itself is not a religion nor even a cult with a distinct or definite doctrine. No better explanation of Sufism can be given than by saying that any person who has a knowledge of both outer and inner life is a Sufi. Thus there has never at any period of the world's history been a founder of Sufism, yet Sufism has existed at all times.

"The present-day Sufi Movement is a movement of members of different nations and races united together in the ideal of wisdom; they believe that wisdom does not belong to any particular religion or race, but to the human race as a whole. It is a divine property which mankind has inherited; and it is in this realization that the Sufis, in spite of belonging to different nationalities, races, beliefs, and faiths, still unite and work for humanity in the ideal of wisdom.

"The Sufi message warns humanity to get to know life better and to achieve freedom in life; it warns man to accomplish what he considers good, just, and desirable; it warns him before every action to note its consequences by studying the situation, his own attitude, and the method he should adopt.

"Sufism not only guides those who are religious, mystical, or visionary, but the Sufi message gives to the world the religion of the day: and that is to make one's life a religion, to turn one's occupation or profession into a religion, to make one's ideal a religious ideal. The object of Sufism is the uniting of life and religion, which so far seem to have been kept apart. When a man goes to church once a week, and devotes all the other days of the week to his business, how can he benefit by religion? Therefore, the teaching of Sufism is to transform everyday life into a religion, so that every action may bear some spiritual fruit.

"The method of world reform which various institutions have adopted today is not the method of the Sufi Movement. Sufis believe that if evil is contagious, goodness must be even more so. The depth of every soul is good; every soul is searching for good, and by the effort of individuals who wish to do good in the world much can be done, even more than a materialistic institution can achieve. No doubt for the general good there are political and commercial problems to be solved; but that must not debar individuals from progress, for it is the individual progress through the spiritual path which alone can bring about the desired condition in the world.

"The Sufi message is not for a particular race, nation, or church. It is a call to unite in wisdom. The Sufi Movement is a group of people belonging to different religions, who have not left their religions but who have learned to understand them better, and their love is the love for God and humanity instead of for a particular section of it. The principal work that the Sufi Movement has to accomplish is to bring about a better understanding between East and West, and between the nations and races of his world. And the note that the sufi message is striking at the present time is the note which sounds the divinity of the human soul. If there is any moral principle that the Sufi Movement brings, it is this: that the whole of humanity is like one body, and any organ of that body which is hurt or troubled can indirectly cause damage to the whole body. And as the health of the whole body depends upon the health of each part, so the health of the whole of humanity depends upon the health of every nation. Besides, to those who are awakening and feel that now is the moment to learn more of the deeper side of life, of truth, the Sufi Movement extends a helping hand without asking to what religion, sect, or dogma they belong. The knowledge of the Sufi is helpful to every person, not only in living his life rightly but in regard to his own religion. The Sufi Movement does not call a man away from his belief or chruch: it calls him to live it. In short, it is a movement intended by God to unite humanity in brotherhood and in wisdom."

From *The Sufi Message of Hazrat Inayat Khan,* Volume IX

Those desiring particulars regarding the activities in all countries of the Sufi Movement founded by Hazrat Inayat Khan should apply to the International Headquarters of the Movement as follows:

(for activities in India)	(for activities outside India)
Sufi Movement India,	General Secretariat,
Dargah Hzt. Inayat Khan	Sufi Movement,
129, Basti Hzt. Nizamuddin	Anna Paulownastraat 78
New Delhi 110 013	2518 BJ The Hague
	Holland

Index

The following is an index on generally known names, on some generally known concepts, but firstly on Inayatan concepts.